THEOLOGY FOR THE TWENTY-FIRST CENTURY

CENTER OF THEOLOGICAL INQUIRY

Theology for the Twenty-first Century is a series sponsored by the Center of Theological Inquiry (CTI), an institute, located in Princeton, New Jersey, dedicated to the advanced study of theology. This series is one of its many initiatives and projects.

The goal of the series is to publish inquiries of contemporary scholars into the nature of the Christian faith and its witness and practice in church, society, and culture. The series will include investigations into the uniqueness of the Christian faith. But it will also offer studies that relate the Christian faith to the major cultural, social, and practical issues of our time.

Monographs and symposia will result from research by scholars in residence at the Center of Theological Inquiry or otherwise associated with it. In some cases, publications will come from group research projects sponsored by CTI. It is our intention that the books selected for this series will constitute a major contribution to renewing theology in its service to church and society.

WALLACE M. ALSTON, JR., ROBERT JENSON,
AND DON S. BROWNING
SERIES EDITORS

What Dare We Hope?
by Gerhard Sauter

The End of the World and the Ends of God
edited by John Polkinghorne and Michael Welker

God and Globalization, Volume 1:
Religion and the Powers of the Common Life
edited by Max L. Stackhouse with Peter J. Paris

God and Globalization, Volume 2:
The Spirit and the Modern Authorities
edited by Max L. Stackhouse with Don S. Browning

GOD AND GLOBALIZATION: THEOLOGICAL ETHICS AND THE SPHERES OF LIFE

Max L. Stackhouse, General Editor
with Peter J. Paris, Don S. Browning,
and Diane Obenchain

Sponsored by
The Center of Theological Inquiry
Princeton, N.J.
1999–2001

The world is presently going through a monumental social, political, and economic shift that has implications for faith, ethics, human understanding, and for human well-being. It is clear that the categories of analysis by which most of us have understood the social worlds around us are at least partially obsolete. How are we to understand the new, complex global civilization toward which we are being thrust? What are the ways that religion, theology, and ethics, in close interaction with our social, political, and economic situation can help guide globalization?

The contributors to this set of volumes have sorted the "powers and principalities," "authorities and dominions" that are shaping the multiple spheres of life in our world and have proposed creative new perspectives on a massive range of pertinent issues that lie at the intersection of religion and globalization. The volumes provide insights into ethics, religion, economics, and culture that will interest not only theologians, ethicists, and clergy of many traditions but also academics, social scientists, professionals, and those in business and technology who seek to understand the move toward a global civilization from a social and ethical point of view.

GOD AND GLOBALIZATION:
THEOLOGICAL ETHICS AND THE SPHERES OF LIFE

Vol. 1: *Religion and the Powers of the Common Life*
Edited by Max L. Stackhouse with Peter J. Paris

Vol. 2: *The Spirit and the Modern Authorities*
Edited by Max L. Stackhouse with Don S. Browning

God *and* Globalization

VOLUME 2

THE SPIRIT AND THE MODERN AUTHORITIES

Edited by
Max L. Stackhouse
with Don S. Browning

TRINITY PRESS INTERNATIONAL
Harrisburg, Pennsylvania

Trinity Press International, P.O. Box 1321, Harrisburg, PA 17105
Trinity Press International is a division of the Morehouse Group.

Cover design: Tom Castanzo

The Library of Congress has catalogued the previous volume as follows:

Library of Congress Cataloging-in-Publication Data

God and globalization : religion and the powers of the common life / edited by Max L. Stackhouse with Peter Paris.
p. cm. – (Theology for the twenty-first century)
Includes bibliographical references and index.
ISBN 1-56338-311-X (pbk.)
1. Christian ethics. 2. Globalization – Moral and ethical aspects. 3. Globalization – Religious aspects – Christianity. I. Stackhouse, Max L. II. Paris, Peter J., 1933. III. Series.

BJ1275 .G63 2000
261.8 – dc21

00-020203

Volume 2: The Spirit and the Modern Authorities ISBN 1-56338-330-6

Printed in the United States of America

01 02 03 04 05 06 10 9 8 7 6 5 4 3 2 1

Contents

Contributors

Don S. Browning is the Alexander Campbell Professor of Ethics and the Social Sciences at the Divinity School of the University of Chicago. As director of the Lilly Project on Religion, Culture, and the Family, he is now working on issues pertaining to the future of the postmodern family and has co-authored *From Culture Wars to Common Ground: Religion and the American Family Debate* (1997). An interest in issues and methods in practical theology led to his work *A Fundamental Practical Theology: With Descriptive and Strategic Proposals* (1991).

Ronald Cole-Turner is the H. Parker Sharp Professor of Theology and Ethics at Pittsburgh Theological Seminary, a position that relates theology and ethics to developments in science and technology. He is the author of *The New Genesis: Theology and the Genetic Revolution* (1993), co-author (with Brent Waters) of *Pastoral Genetics: Theology and Care at the Beginning of Life* (1996), editor of *Human Cloning: Religious Responses* (1997), and editor of *Beyond Cloning: Religion and the Remaking of Humanity* (forthcoming 2001).

Jürgen Moltmann is Emeritus Professor of Theology at the University of Tübingen, Germany, and the author of *The Coming of God* (1996), *The Sources of Life* (1997), and *God for a Secular Society: The Public Relevance of Theology* (1999). He delivered a version of the essay that appears in this volume at the University of Beijing, and is also known for his work with the World Alliance of Reformed Churches.

Richard Osmer is the Thomas W. Synnot Professor of Christian Education and Director of the School of Christian Education at Princeton Theological Seminary. He is the author of a number of works on religious education in the American social and political context, and was deeply involved in the development of a new educational program and catechism for the Presbyterian Church (USA).

His *Teachable Spirit: Recovering the Teaching Office in the Church* (1990) is widely used.

PETER J. PARIS is the Elmer G. Homrighausen Professor of Christian Social Ethics at Princeton Theological Seminary, and the seminary's representative to the Princeton University African American Studies Program. A recent past president of the American Academy of Religion, he is also the author of a book widely used in seminaries, *The Social Teaching of the Black Churches* (1985), and *The Spirituality of African Peoples: The Search for a Common Moral Discourse* (1995).

MAX L. STACKHOUSE is the Stephen Colwell Professor of Christian Ethics at Princeton Theological Seminary and Director of the Project on Public Theology. He is the author of several volumes on theology and ethics and their relationship to global social issues, such as *Christian Social Ethics in a Global Era* (1995), and has long studied the comparative patterns of social and religious developments in Asia and Eastern Europe, such as in *Creeds, Societies, and Human Rights* (1986).

ALLEN VERHEY is Professor of Religion at Hope College, Michigan, author of a widely known work on the ethics of the New Testament, *The Great Reversal: Ethics and the New Testament* (1984), and an editor of both *On Moral Medicine* (1992; rev. ed., 1998) and *From Christ to the World* (1996) — texts that have become standard in many universities. He has been an officer of the American Society of Christian Ethics and a regular contributor to a number of scholarly and church-related journals.

JOHN WITTE, JR., is the Jonas Robitscher Professor of Law and Ethics and Director of the Law and Religion Program at Emory University. A specialist in legal history, he has published a dozen books and more than a hundred articles. He has lectured widely in North America, Europe, Israel, and South Africa and edited, with Johann Van der Vyver, *Religious Human Rights in Global Perspective* (2 vols.; 1996), which grew in part from his *Christianity and Democracy in a Global Era* (1993).

Introduction

Max L. Stackhouse

The essays in this volume address the emerging worldwide phenomenon of globalization by identifying and analyzing authoritative "powers" of human practice and thought that have developed in modern, mostly Western, complex societies. These powers, which we identify as the "authorities" or, in some instances, as the "regencies,"[1] stand beyond the "principalities" that can be found in every known society (as treated in volume 1 of this series). Only some religio-cultural traditions have prompted humans to develop certain of their potentialities into specifically transeconomic, transpolitical, transfamilial, transcultural, and transreligious spheres of "authority" that become defining for social life. Yet when these potentialities are cultivated in particular directions, they generate a second set of spheres that not only reshape the principal areas of life and enhance the economic, political, and sometimes the cultural, sexual, and religious power of the society that develops them, they reshape human identity precisely because they establish new institutions and ways of conceiving life that open people to possibilities of thought and action beyond the ordinary contexts of life. We can see this in the example of modern, Western education. Where education is well developed, young people are drawn out of their

1. We here use "regencies" as a translation of the term θρόνοι, which sometimes appears in biblical texts with other terms for the various powers — "principalities," "authorities," and "dominions." Such terms are used for structured prerogatives that not only control spheres of life, but that also claim autonomous legitimacy and capture the loyalty and trust of society. These temporal powers are, however, finally derivative, not self-defining or able to generate life or meaning, as discussed in the introduction to vol. 1. However, they can help preserve or destroy life and meaning, depending on how they are ethically ordered. The terms "authorities" and "regencies" as used here refer specifically to extraordinary social practices or institutions that do not have the power to capture the whole of human loyalties, as can a regime, family, culture, economy, or religion — what we have called the "principalities" — but that exercise nearly sovereign control over certain decisions that become indispensable for the common life in complex civilizations. They are, thus, historic constructs.

communal settings and go "off" to school or "away" to university. They do so as "minds" needing training in "critical" thinking, distinct in principle from familial, political, economic, cultural, and religious attachments. They learn how to analyze their own and other people's natural and social environments. Other examples are law or medicine: when life lacks harmony, people go to court or to the hospital — in either place becoming "a case" for whom questions of property or liberty are addressed, or for whom questions of illness or suffering are treated. Scientific-technological prowess, comprehensive worldviews about the nature of things, and moral leadership that offers new definitions of justice, each stamped by theological perspectives that have spawned and nurtured them and incarnated into social movements, have also become authoritative regencies, generating new spheres of loyalty and practice that are touchstones for modern life.

Under the power of these authorities and regencies, events and conditions are treated in terms that make the powers of the principalities — that is, their familial, political, economic, cultural, or religious dependencies and relationships — irrelevant (in principle). The authorities, in this sense, distance people from and override the duties, purposes, and loyalties of the principalities — often in the name of truth, justice, or health. The more recent regencies do so in terms of the living powers of techné, Gaia, or virtue, each of which may involve a contentiousness against the more established principalities and authorities.

For the contributors to this volume, globalization involves the universalization of the influence of these authorities and regencies as they developed in the West. The process both opens promising possibilities for the improvement of the common life and simultaneously bears acute dangers. Some of the dangers, it will be argued, derive from the fact that aspects of these authorities and regencies have been, in the past, stamped by influences of a moral and spiritual sort. That conferred on them a right to claim relative independence from control by the principalities, much as the church had earlier claimed for itself. However, as the power of these authorities and regencies increased, they developed a spirit of their own, confidence in their own genius and worth, an *esprit de corps* among those engaged in the activities of their sphere, and systemic resistance to the influence of normative principles or purposes derived from external or transcendent sources. Indeed, they became the prototypes of a host of modern developments claiming sovereign authority.

These essays share an underlying conviction that certain strands of Christian theology in the West joined with the intellectual and social possibilities also present either in other religious traditions or more directly connected to philosophical views. These alliances stimulated the development of now-powerful authorities and regencies and nurtured them into a relative autonomy. In modern life, however, they have separated from their spiritual and moral roots and begun to take pride in their own potentialities. They have become bearers of the dynamics now shaping our emerging global civilization, but often lack a basic spiritual guidance system for defining the right and the good. Yet the divorce from overt theological and ethical concerns leaves the authorities vulnerable to spiritual and moral emptiness or superficiality, to manipulation by narrow interests, and thus to potential threats to the human future. To avert the threats and enable the potential promises, theological ethics must reengage the authorities and regencies of modernity and revitalize their inner spirit.

A Revealing Moment

We defer until volume 4 fuller discussion of a kind of institution, recently emerged, that may well become authoritative. I refer to the dozens of global institutions with quasi-governmental regulatory power at the international level. The status of such institutions has been raised throughout the last decade of the twentieth century — in the Vienna Conference on Human Rights, the Kyoto Conference on Ecology and Global Warming, the Cairo Conference on Population, the Beijing Conference on the Rights of Women, the Copenhagen Conference on Poverty, and in the debates about the International Monetary Fund and the World Bank during the East Asian financial crises. The issues became even more dramatic in December 1999, when the World Trade Organization (WTO), which represents some 135 nations, met in Seattle to discuss whether new standards were necessary to govern international commerce. Many of the issues that the WTO considered — human rights, employment opportunities, ecology, and world trade, for example — are by definition global. Yet for months it was clear that the meeting was in trouble. The delegates — scholars, lawyers, doctors, technical experts, ecologists, public leaders, government diplomats — could not even agree on an agenda.

The internal debates were made more intense by demonstrations that led to street riots — the most ideologically driven that the West has seen since Vietnam. Labor, ecology, and advocates of "economic democracy," supported by religious activists, joined as self-appointed representatives of "civil society" to protest the WTO. Some intellectuals supported the dissident agenda, claiming that globalization brings "unimaginable disaster" and "global suicide."[2]

Both the meetings and the demonstrations were failures. It may well be, as C. Fred Alford has said, that "globalization is likely to divide the world into winners and losers,... between those who are able to use the collision and confusion of cultures to foster enlightenment, and those who become merely confused."[3] All parties in Seattle seemed closer to the latter than to the former. The WTO resolved none of the major issues before it, and the opposition coalition neither stopped globalization nor altered its course. For the most part, global dynamics will continue to develop as they have in the twentieth century, under the surface of conflicts. This trend has brought the globalization that some seek to extend and others to block. Few went home from Seattle thinking that they had won a victory for humanity, and no party to the meetings or protests could say with confidence that a common morality had been discovered or advanced. No clarity was attained with regard to the values in operation under globalization, the principles of right and wrong by which the values could be better assessed, or a vision of the good ends that could and should be pursued. It is not unfair to say that the moral contradictions were acute, the intellectual analysis of what is at stake shallow, and the alliances of opposition unstable.

The only clarity is that the current ways of ordering the much expanded common life are neither clear nor compellingly authoritative. Those opposed to the WTO and other such organizations seem to insist simultaneously on more local autonomy and more universal standards; but the universal standards they seek are not shared by all. Those in favor of the new organizations also appear to be driven by interests that not all share and are laden with commitments that not all agree are valid. The issues, however, are sure to

2. See Turning Point Project, "Economic Globalization, #5," *New York Times*, December 13, 1999, A16. This is one of a series of full-page ads sponsored by a coalition of more than sixty nonprofit organizations.

3. C. F. Alford, *Think No Evil: Korean Values in the Age of Globalization* (Ithaca, N.Y.: Cornell University Press, 1999), 166.

continue, as demonstrations early in 2000 against the World Bank and the IMF suggest.

These new international regulatory agencies are organized by multilateral treaty arrangements in which "experts" with specialized knowledge are commissioned to interpret the treaty agreements and to limit conflict among societies. The WTO, for example, was founded (after the collapse of the Soviet Union) in 1994 out of the negotiations for a General Agreement on Tariffs and Trade, as a parallel to the International Monetary Fund and the World Bank, established half a century earlier.[4] The nature and scale of these institutions is heatedly debated today in some circles, because they all tend to foment capitalist institutions and practices and appear to serve the more developed as opposed to the less developed peoples of the world, but they are not structurally different from the World Health Organization (since 1948), the World Meteorological Organization (since 1951), or the United Nations Educational, Scientific, and Cultural Organization (since 1956). All of these institutions are based on modern concepts of how we may most effectively guide behavior in desired directions. All were anticipated by agreements from earlier centuries about international postal service, police cooperation, and codes of the sea. Still, all are derivative institutions; they have no genuinely independent authority and could be changed or abolished by international agreement or by the withdrawal of major powers — although most would have to be quickly reinvented, like traffic conventions. They are a kind of postmodern quasi-authority, based on a "confederation" model that may invite a reconstitution of life, as we shall explore in the fourth volume of this series.[5]

These derivative institutions are quite unlike the spheres of life that form the principalities. Humans are sexual, political, economic, cultural, and religious creatures. Each one of these dimensions of life involves a certain potentiality and needs an institutional matrix to house, guide, and channel its energies. Nor are these spheres of society quite representative of the essays here. Humans are less than wise, vulnerable to injustice, prone to disease, and inclined to use craft and ideology to exploit the riches of the earth and one an-

---

4. The nature of the WTO, its functions, structure, and relationship to other organizations is carefully studied in Anne O. Krueger, ed., *The WTO as an International Organization* (Chicago: University of Chicago Press, 1998).

5. See also Daniel J. Elazar, *Constitutionalizing Globalization* (New York: Rowman and Littlefield, 1999), especially chap. 7.

other for short-term advantage rather than to embrace science and technology, expansive worldviews, and prophetic leadership that enhances benefit but demands sacrifice. For this reason, we need complex institutions to overcome ignorance and seek wisdom, to constrain injustice and encourage fairness, to treat illness and struggle against the causes of disease, to utilize the resources of the earth for long-term improvement, and to celebrate those exemplary humans who lead us to such ends. It is these institutions that may embody the more effective and important authorities of modernity. Moreover, the long-range effectiveness of these new international institutions depends practically on whether they sustain basic norms such as truth, justice, and health, in the context of a responsible regard for others and for the resources of creation. Many of the organized practices and movements that we call "regencies" have already become accepted as international courts of appeal. What they share with the authorities is a presumption that human life is, within limits, malleable for those who master its laws and dynamics, and that those initiated into these laws and dynamics will act in accord with moral and spiritual principles and purposes to serve humanity so that immediate, crass interests do not override the attempt to uphold fair regulations and just ends. The relative embodiment of such moral qualities in excellent practice and collegial discipline historically have legitimated the authorities of modernity and formed them into the classical professions in the West — education, law, medicine, and ministry. Later, another profession emerged — "science." Some aspects of science were of immediate interest to education. Other aspects increasingly augmented the power of technology, as seen in the professionalization of engineering, with massive implications for the environment.[6] All these professions deal with global issues, from global warming to violations of human rights, to the AIDS epidemic, to crises of meaning.

It must quickly be said, however, that whom to include in the list of professionals is now a matter of debate, partly because many occupations seek to become "professions." For those who seek to attain expertise, reliability, and status, the classic professions have set the model in complex societies for purposeful life and work, and rewards. Thus, in our time, the line between the classical professions

6. One can see the influence of science not only in the debates about cloning, but in the formation of new fields. See, e.g., Braden Allenby, *Industrial Ecology: Policy Framework and Implementation* (London: Prentice Hall, 1999).

and business is blurring, as one can see with the professionalization of "business administration," although we shall not treat that here.[7] Those in corporate management or the crafts see themselves as professionals, and many in the professions see what they do as a business. More profoundly, the list is in flux because most of the professions have declared independence from religiously based moral or spiritual values. Professionals may have a personal faith or belong to a religious community, and they may be people of high moral integrity; but the professions themselves have largely severed the intellectual and ethical content of their work from overt theological content, even if some experience in this a grave loss.[8]

We treat the three classical, "secular" professions in the first three chapters of this volume as key examples of acknowledged modern authorities. We note that the severance of professional consciousness and practice from theology has taken place based on the claim that the values professions seek to advance by their professional ethic are universalistic. Those in secular professions tend to see all religions, theologies, and ethics as particularistic, that is, not universal. Ironically, however, in the last several centuries the social authority of the classical professions has become more dependent on the modern nation-state. In the twentieth century, states sometimes became more particularistic than the great religions and less constrained by the principles to which the great religions and theology point. Dependent on the modern, intentionally secular nation-state, many in the professions feel that they are losing contact with their moral and spiritual rootage and authority, and that what they do is becoming "merely business."[9] Further, many clergy have turned

7. We do not take up the issue of "management" as a profession, in part because it has only recently aspired to become a profession in the classical sense, and in part because that is a central issue discussed in *On Moral Business*, ed. Max Stackhouse et al. (Grand Rapids, Mich.: Eerdmans, 1995). Cf. also Shirley Roels et al., *Organization Man; Organization Woman* (Nashville: Abingdon Press, 1997); and David Krueger et al., *The Business Corporation and Productive Justice* (Nashville: Abingdon Press, 1998). These studies informed the design of this globalization project. Some of the key themes, moreover, will be treated in volume 4.

8. For example, see the collected papers from two symposia on the relevance of religion to the lawyer's work, published in the *Fordham Law Review* 66 (March 1998), and the *Fordham Urban Law Journal* 26 (April 1999). The relationship of religion and ethics to education and medicine, and to the work of the teacher and doctor, is also widely discussed.

9. Examples of recent scholarly explorations of the renewed connections can be found in Warren A. Nord, *Religion and American Education* (Chapel Hill: University of North Carolina Press, 1995); James T. Burtchaell, *The Dying of the Light* (Grand Rapids, Mich.: Eerdmans, 1998); Eric Mount, Jr., *Professional Ethics in Context*

the world over to the professionals so long as they are free to concentrate on the unworldly.

The new class of contenders for authority, what we call the regencies, has emerged recently, distinct from the classical professions, less dependent on the state, and more removed from any identifiable theological ethics. These contenders are rooted in scientific-technological developments, and they adopt, often with enthusiasm, the social form of the independent corporation as it developed in the West and is being adopted elsewhere. They, too, claim to work in more universalistic ways than a state or religions would allow. Scientific methods have influenced the classical professions — academia most of all, but law and medicine as well. Aspects of technology were developed to aid education in its quest for knowledge, law in pursuit of forensic proofs, and medicine in its search for accurate diagnoses. Most remarkable about current developments is that technology has grown exponentially in every area of life, in and beyond the professions, and increasingly makes science its servant. Science wants to know how things are; technology wants to change things into something else, to make them better. That capacity to alter things frees humanity from what is. What is natural becomes more artifactual. Particularly when science becomes the servant of technology, the capacity to transform increases, from selecting the genetic makeup of children to communicating around the world instantly to altering the environment and our view of it.

A globalizing influence occurred when space exploration allowed millions to see pictures of the earth from afar and demonstrated the possibility of living in a totally artificial environment — a spaceship. While the term "Spaceship Earth" has a clinical ring, removing human life from involvement in both the earth and in the technology reshaping it, the idea enhanced a sense of transcendence over nature, awareness that the earth itself must become a common concern, and the assertion that a global ethic was needed to transcend conventional cultural, political, and religious divisions. The dynamics of society and the usual loyalties were put in a new perspective. Many sensed that humanity had to take responsibility for planning the total environment. Some accented the "spaceship" side of "Spaceship Earth," and we treat the implications of what the French theologian and professor of law Jacques Ellul called techné

(Philadelphia: Westminster Press, 1990); and Stephen Lammers with Allen Verhey, *On Moral Medicine,* rev. ed. (Grand Rapids, Mich.: Eerdmans, 1998).

in chapter 4. Others accented the "earth" side, invoking Gaia, not as "nature," as we see in chapter 5, but as an affective notion of the earth as an enspirited, organic whole which may claim our loyalty.

Paralleling these developments, but growing out of social developments in the postcolonial era, several moral leaders who exemplified larger if sometimes contradictory visions of ethical inclusiveness rose to international prominence, taking as their base of operations the voluntary associations and nongovernmental organizations that developed out of paraparochial ministries into new prophetic "movements." These moral leaders too became authorities in our time, all reaching toward the actualization of virtues in civil society, often in ways that more traditional ministries did not sustain, as we see in chapter 6.

In brief, the authorities and regencies of our times have become focused less on the powers intrinsic to human nature and present in every society than on a complex set of cultivated powers that transcend the inevitable embeddedness of humanity in certain spheres of the common life. These new authorities and regencies have become voluntaristic, often transcending natural, social, or traditional associations, and increasingly operate outside constraints set by nation, state, culture, historic economy, or religion. They have formed new professional associations, transnational corporations, international bureaucracies, and advocacy groups that exist within, but also beyond, every established institution. They offer a view of possibilities and strategies for remaking the world in a new mold, and for resisting changes that could violate principles of right and bring evil results — if these new authorities link to first principles and allow good ends to guide them.

In one way, this observation brings us back to the issues exposed in Seattle. Journalist Thomas Friedman, who has closely followed the debates on globalization, recently identified one of the key problems that some of these new associations posed and that only some acknowledge: rediscovery of the need for universal rules and laws. He noted the failure of those protesting the WTO meeting to see this critical issue. He asked whether there has been anything more ridiculous in the news than the debacle protesters engendered in Seattle, and suggests that the only thing uniting the crowd was

> their realization that we now live in a world without walls. The Cold War system we just emerged from was built around

> division and walls; the globalization system that we are now in is built around integration and webs. In this new system, jobs, cultures, environmental problems, and labor standards can much more easily flow back and forth. The ridiculous thing...is that they...blame the WTO. The WTO is not the cause of this world without walls, it is the effect. The more countries trade with one another, the more they need an institution to set the basic rules of trade, and that is all the WTO does. "Rules are a substitute for walls—when you don't have walls you need more rules."[10]

In a set of articles on the Seattle events, the *Economist* points out that not only "the rules" are at stake. Also involved are purpose and organizational base. Regarding purpose, the articles point out that the WTO convenes often, but the perennial problem is that "their prospects are clouded by the lack of agreed objectives...."[11] We find everywhere a desire of "more for us," but the "us" is variously defined; a contrary view that "less is more" is well developed among those who live in primal communities and those who have developed a love for nature, as well as a contempt for contemporary social and economic life that disrupts it. These concerns are not, however, integrated by any coherent vision of "the good life," "the common good," or a definition of "the chief end of life." In short, derivative organizations such as the WTO must draw on what the professionals and the dissident groups say about a compelling sense of "the right" to guide the rules, and a shared vision of "the good" to guide the goals of life, but none has a universalistic ethic to guide and integrate such ideas into a cohesive polity or policy. Yet they are making rules and setting goals for the world.

In this connection, the *Economist* also identifies confusions about organizational issues. No person and no theory of the right and the good seems to be in charge of the new bodies such as the WTO or of the protesting organizations. Most of the world is used to someone or some institution running things and being accountable for what happens. But if we want a world governed by just laws, good purposes, and responsible caring, and not simply by the will of powerful persons or interested parties, we need

---

10. The column, "WTO Protesters: Senseless in Seattle," appeared in the *New York Times,* December 2, 1999. At the end of the excerpt, Friedman quotes an unidentified expert from the Council on Foreign Relations.

11. "A Global Disaster," *The Economist,* December 11–17, 1999, 19–20.

moral and spiritual guidelines. No one wants the WTO or other international organization to become the instrument of a world leader, government, coalition of powerful states, or transnational corporations. Some fear that there is already too much of that. Thus, increasingly, the NGOs are gaining influence in the emerging global society. These nongovernmental organizations, as the UN names them, are religious bodies, voluntary associations, professional groups, advocacy organizations, unions, political action committees, industrial alliances, and other institutions of civil society that have no official political status. They are raising the more ultimate issues, even if they do so awkwardly and without a coherent vision.

Such organizations developed a significant record of activism in the last half of the twentieth century and have become the focus of moral involvement for many around the world. They supported the anticolonial movements of Gandhi and others in the 1940s. They marched with Martin Luther King, Jr., in the 1960s. They opposed Vietnam and boycotted Nestle over the sale of powdered formula for babies in the 1970s. They organized protests against apartheid in South Africa, especially in the 1980s. They showed their power in the 1992 "Earth Summit" in Rio de Janeiro. They dominated the World Bank's anniversary meeting in 1994. They targeted Nike for poor labor conditions in the mid-1990s. And they pressed the International Monetary Fund for forgiveness of debts in the "Jubilee Year" of 2000, although the NGOs had originally demanded that the international banks make massive loans to these nations emerging from colonialization in the 1960s and 1970s. The loans were made whether or not the new leaders were accountable, willing and able to limit corruption, or likely to establish the conditions under which developing societies could generate enough economic development to repay those debts.

The number of international NGOs at century's end was said to be more than twenty-six thousand, compared to six thousand a decade before. They dominated the story of Seattle, and faced with these organizations from their homelands and in the international arena "official" delegates to the WTO found it difficult to exercise their own authority, just as the national governments who sent these delegates found that their authority is subject to the moral sentiment generated by the NGOs. In brief, besides the now worldwide professional associations and the research- or profit-oriented corporation-organized centers of technological innovation and ecological concern, we also have a new cluster of activists in contemporary global society.[12]

Seattle, thus, serves as a kind of parable. It stands as a symbolically revealing moment that exposed moral, spiritual, and social issues of globalization that are, at best, unresolved. It is doubtful that we have a ready ethology adequate to define our new social matrix or a deontology or teleology to frame the normative issues of the right and the good that could guide the era's mighty technological and organizational possibilities. What ought we support — or protest? How shall we envision authority in an increasingly complex civilization, so that it will be more just for all and more promising for the future under radically altered social conditions? Seattle showed that the professionals, experts, and leaders of various movements in the contemporary world have formed new powers that are reshaping the common life and that manifest a highly ambiguous moral and spiritual base. Should we take them as our authorities, or as authoritative regencies?

A Review of the "Powers and Principalities"

Before turning to a deeper analysis of the authorities of contemporary life, a brief overview of the conceptual tools these volumes use to discuss globalization might be helpful. In the introduction to volume 1, we spoke of the necessity of a "public theological ethic" that could help discern the values that operate in a sociocultural ethos. These values order the powers necessary to life and that, without ethical guidance, can destroy viable human relationships and community life. These values have both a functional validity and a transfunctional basis, for they are held to be both morally and spiritually valid. We also pointed out that basic theories of "the right" and of "the good" would be necessary to ethical evaluation of these values. A basic view of what ought to be done must be connected to a realistic assessment of what can be done in the context of the several powers and spheres which drive and order every viable social system.

We identified, as indispensable to every society, five primary "powers." Each may become organized, channeling its potentialities into a distinctive institutional sphere of society, and become one

12. See the suggestive article in *The Economist,* "The Non-governmental Order," December 11–17, 1999, 20–21.

of "the principalities" of life. No society is without Eros, which invites us to participate in and, indeed, to worship sexuality, family, kinship, tribe, or ethnicity in ways that distort life, relationship, and intimacy, and lead to the economic, political, cultural, and religious exploitation of others. But Eros can be channeled into patterns of fidelity and fecundity in families, representing a just mutuality that replicates and nurtures, generation after generation, the capacity to trust and be trusted in covenantal relations.[13] Similarly, no society can avoid Mars, although it tempts us to honor the arts of violence and the unforgiving might of military power. Mars can lead to cults of national pride and of violence, but it can also be constrained and empowered to serve the right and the good, if constituted into responsible political regimes.[14] In either case, we have the prospect of principalities — those of gene-pool identities and those of governments.

Moreover, no society is without the gifts of the Muses. They enable communication, the expression of profound feeling, and the delight of entertainment. They are necessary for the arts, and they tend to work within a distinctive culture. Although the masters of the Muses are tempted to create the world in their own image, and thus to deify themselves as they serve up fragments of narrative or image lacking moral or spiritual depth, they can also lead humanity to discover and delight in sustained meaning by invoking creative powers beyond themselves and by evoking social commitments to actuate that meaning. Today, the media have become a primary locus and arbiter of the Muses, a basic Principality.[15] They have been enabled to do so in part because of their adoption of highly complex technology and a corporate model of organization, both of which allow them to declare increased independence from a specific cultural tradition, especially one tied to a distinctive familial (clan, tribal, or ethnic-linguistic) community, and from a particular political government or regime. The new patterns of economic life have themselves become principalities, influencing all the other powers.[16]

---

13. See Mary Stewart Van Leeuwen, "Faith, Feminism, and the Family in an Age of Globalization," in vol. 1.

14. See Donald W. Shriver, Jr., "The Taming of Mars: Can Humans of the Twenty-first Century Contain Their Propensity for Violence?" in vol. 1.

15. See David Tracy, "Public Theology, Hope, and the Mass Media: Can the Muses Still Inspire?" in vol. 1.

16. See William Schweiker, " Responsibility in the World of Mammon: Theology, Justice, and Transnational Corporations," in vol. 1.

Of course, no civilization can survive without a viable economy, one that generates goods, services, and the means for their exchange and distribution. Although this human activity has historically been conducted largely within familial, governmental, and cultural institutions, it has long been known that it has its own logic — called, by its enemies, "greed," *Das Kapital,* or "possessive individualism." By its friends, economic activity has been called "entrepreneurship," *laissez faire,* or "the wisdom of the market." Like all the other principalities, the impulse toward Mammon, the worship of money, possession, and proprietary claim, can become demonic if it is not drawn into an ordered community of cooperative discipline, one that also guides it into the service of the commonwealth. The modern corporation is an attempt to do that, one that has, in substantial measure, escaped the traditional means of control. Thus, while Mammon is not, by any means, the only feature of globalization, many see it as the only or as the driving power of contemporary life. So believed many in Seattle. The construction of regulatory, professional, and advocacy bodies outside ordinary society, in response to the power of Mammon, is partly responsible for a new quest for basic moral authority.[17]

Finally, religion, taking shape in religions, attempts to articulate the transcendent source of meaning and morality to guide the whole of the common life. As often as not, this fundamental feature of what it means to be human is organized into a specific religious tradition, and as such it blesses a particular way of ordering and relating Eros, Mars, the Muses, and Mammon, defining in the process their moral limits. At their best, religions become self-critical and self-consciously ethical as they seek to discern and define what is right, good, and fitting in familial, political, cultural, and economic life — and, above all, in our relationship with God. These characteristics appear particularly in normative statements about how God wants us to live in the world under first principles and for ultimate ends, both of which transcend particular religions and our social and cultural histories. Today, various religions are developing organizations outside traditional communities of worship to reshape familial, political, cultural, and economic life.

It is doubtful that "globalization," as it is developing around the world, can be reduced to any one of these powers, organized as

17. See Yersu Kim, "Philosophy and the Prospects for a Universal Ethics," in vol. 1.

they are into principalities that become sectors of every empirical society. The processes leading to the wider future are rooted in even more complex sectors of the common life than any one of them or all of them together. Those who interpret globalization only as the expansion of corporate interest have seen only part of the picture, although to many the economic side of globalization is most obvious. The prospects for our future, however, are still being discussed by disciplines such as psychology with regard to sexuality and familial relationships, political science with regard to politics and power, cultural analysis with regard to communications and the arts, economics with regard to production and distribution, and religious studies with regard to the conditions of and consequences of faith and belief, especially as these interact in "sociology of religion." The latter points to transnational, transcultural, transethnic, and worldwide dynamics that are redefining every field, including religion.[18]

The "Authorities" of Our Times

Societies guided by particular religious traditions and founded in the principalities have taken a long and tortured route to generating the new authorities that now define much of life. Globalization is proceeding, according to various opinions, on the basis of rediscovered, newly discovered, newly invented, or newly imposed universalistic values borne by a host of new social institutions and practices. Disagreements about these values, as seen in Seattle, are not without tension, resistance, and misunderstandings. Nevertheless, the defining authorities for the future increasingly are those that derive from a long-forgotten marriage of the secular arts and Christian theology as this combination emerged, most graphically, in the modern professions of education, law, and medicine, and that now again are undergoing transformation. Few spheres have the status that these professions possess as they have developed in modern research universities and colleges, in law schools and courts, and in medical schools as well as hospitals and research laboratories around the world. Professors, scholars, and teachers; lawyers, legislators, and judges; doctors, researchers, and nurses over the past two hundred years have become among the most honored authorities of the com-

18. See Roland Robertson, "Globalization and the Future of 'Traditional Religion,' " in vol. 1.

mon life. They have increasingly served as models of cross-cultural, global standards, and were often put in another class than parents, rulers, creative artists, and economic bosses — all of whom may have been just as powerful socially or financially.

It is useful to survey the history of the professions, for they are still driven by values and principles that serve as a moral genetic code. People may not know what values form these professions, but they drive much of what people do. The professions became deeply tied to theology because of the Christian sense of vocation, and because theological ethics guided the definition of first principles and ultimate ends which legitimated what the professions did. Wherever Christians have gone, they have established schools, adjudicating bodies, and institutions to care for the sick; legitimated the fact that people turn their minds over to teachers, their material well-being over to advocates, and their bodies over to caregivers; and demanded that teachers, advocates, and the caregivers exercise their tasks under the watchful eye of God, in the spirit of Christ, and in the service of the Holy Spirit. These professions were parallel ministries to those who preach and lead worship.

Every known society has differentiated roles among those who teach, advocate, and heal. No society is without its educational system — not only parents but wise elders, custodians of the lore, those given charge of initiation and apprentices, mentors and scribes. Further, no society is without those who advocate for others in disputes, not only relatives or friends, but those authorized to speak in councils and courts, those who know the rules of rhetoric and evidence, alert to both code and commentary, decision and precedent. No society is without ways of dealing with sickness and promoting health, not only the medicine men and midwives, but those who guide others in illness-treating ingestion or purges, surgery or poultice, or in health-inducing nutrition or fasting, attitudes or behaviors. Historically no society has been without priests, prophets, and holy leaders who have been called on to interpret events in terms of the ultimate realities of the universe, and to guide the people and the patterns of the common life in view of that ultimate authority. Educational, legal, and medical roles everywhere are played by religious leaders and associated with a spiritual vocation.

Only some societies, however, developed distinctive and self-governing spheres of institutional practice and theory that became relatively independent of external control. To be sure, there are parallels in other traditions. The gurus, pundits, ayurvedic practitioners, and sadhus (holy men) of India; and the scholars, *literati,* shamans, and monks of China, for example (with parallels in other civilizations, as we will see especially in volume 3), developed highly differentiated roles for the "professionals" of those societies, with sophisticated bodies of knowledge and lore. Islam, too, adopted many of the ancient Greek traditions in philosophy and medicine, not only integrating them into their own practices, but mediating them to the West and to the East in ways that surpassed both, and that allowed several societies to flourish.

Other traditions did not, however, form those dynamic spheres that became decisive for the modernization of the professions. They did not do so in part because they subordinated the professions to the traditional authorities of family or regime, which also dominated the economy, or to cultural or religious values that opposed the intentional intervention in and transformation of what was considered "natural" in the bio-physical universe or in society. The societies fostered by these traditions also had little place for an independent corporate body that could cultivate the professions' possibilities — a collegium organized for excellence and service distinct from other organizations, a university, bar, hospital, or professional associations that defined and enforced standards.[19]

In this connection, we must recognize that the areas where such professions and their respective institutions flourished were under the influence of traditions that derive their impulses from certain readings of the biblical tradition. These traditions were decisive for the ways in which the various authorities developed as professions. The connection between the doctrine of vocation and the development of the professions in Western Christianity took a very distinctive direction. Not only were all believers "called" to join the church as an association distinct from, although inevitably linked to and transformative of, the ruling powers of Eros, Mars, the Muses, and Mammon, but some were also called to special offices in leadership for other persons and the society at large. Leadership was not determined by heredity, caste, class, or political power, although these factors were inevitably involved from time to time and place to place.

---

19. See, for example, the compelling interpretation given to the religious, legal, philosophical, and institutional contexts in which science was practiced in several traditions, in Toby E. Huff, *The Rise of Early Modern Science: Islam, China, and the West* (New York: Cambridge University Press, 1993).

The doctrine of vocation points essentially toward a sense of divine call, to be confirmed by the discernments of a community of conviction that certifies spiritual, moral, and intellectual competence to serve God in accord with God's laws, purposes, and mercies. Precisely this sense of serving God and humanity presses all who are called to reach for a frame of reference by which to interpret and guide particular practices. This frame may take several forms but is in principle self-correcting, since it sees every perspective and practice as subject to that which is more comprehensive than any humans could construct. A profession, in this view, is an ethical engagement, intellectual task, and spiritual commitment that one makes in response to a personal sense of vocation and a communal certification. One takes upon oneself the obligation to develop learned expertise in a sphere that is important for the well-being of the common life and to offer that expertise as a fitting service to others in terms sustained by a holy dedication to the right and the good.

This understanding of vocation has undergone several shifts. In early times it applied to all the people in a community of faith called by God to be a light to the nations, but it also applied in a personal way to the prophets, priests, and kings of ancient Israel — as well as to the many judges, prophetesses, scholars, matriarchs, and patriarchs only sometimes named, but remembered, in the texts. These individuals were given special responsibilities within the larger called community for the faithfulness, morality, and well-being of the people. This understanding was later applied by Christians to the disciples, the elders, deacons, deaconesses, preachers, and teachers of the early church and occasionally to occupations which people had in the world to sustain life. Later, it became limited to those who took vows of poverty, chastity, and obedience to clerical authority. It appeared that those with a vocation, and the church itself, would be swallowed into social practices of property, heredity, subservience to political command and territorial culture — which would make individuals chaplains for feudalism. This, indeed, is what happened in other religious traditions, for in a sense it is the natural place for religion among the principalities. Where that happened, however, the professional fields have not found a path to universalistic values.

Some strands of Christian theology, in contrast to these temptations, encouraged scholars to develop extensive competence in the "secular" fields of study — that became these professions whenever the social possibilities opened. On these bases some spheres of civil society became distinct from the authority of family and clan ties and political regimes, and distinct from both exclusive cultural expressions and perennial temptations to turn all intellectual and social advantages into economic ones.

Furthermore, some late-medieval mystics and then the Reformers broadened the idea of vocation to "the priesthood of all believers," to use Luther's famous phrase, a concept that has been broadened more recently to include "the prophethood of all believers" and the political or "public theological responsibilities of all believers."[20] Such ideas have deeply influenced the classic professions.[21] The professionals thus became, in principle, those dedicated to the quest for truth and the formation of institutions for its transmission to the next generation; those dedicated to the quest for justice and the formation of legal institutions and procedures that can render viable constitutions and fair judgments; those dedicated to the quest for health and the formation of institutions and regimens that can reduce suffering and disability; and those dedicated to the quest for faith and the formation of institutions that can evoke trusting and trustworthy living in all the basic relationships of life, including that with God.[22] These professionals have also influenced in less direct ways the "new" professions from architecture and accounting to management and pharmaceutics, family counseling and business consulting. As we will see, through a particular understanding of the vocation of the sciences, this heritage has influenced engineering. These developments have indeed shaped every occupational area and fostered a new set of spheres that operate outside the axial spheres of society.

Education, law, medicine, and engineering (and other occupations) depend on aspects of knowledge independent of a particular

---

20. See James Luther Adams, *The Prophethood of All Believers,* ed. G. K. Beach (Boston: Beacon Press, 1986). See also Roger Stronstad, *The Prophethood of All Believers: A Study in Luke's Charismatic Theology* (Sheffield, England: Academic Press, 1999). I have traced some of these developments further in "If Globalization Is True, What Then Shall We Do?" *Theological Education* 35 (Spring 1999): 155–66.

21. The academic, legal, and medical communities spawned a great number of reform institutions in the twentieth century, from independent research organizations to legal-defense funds to "doctors without borders."

22. On the history of this idea of the professions, see Karl Holl, "Die Geschichte des Worts Beruf," *Aufsätze zur Kirchengeschichte,* vol. 3 (Tübingen, 1928); James Luther Adams, "The Social Import of the Professions," in *Voluntary Associations,* ed. R. Engel (Chicago: Exploration Press, 1986); Eric Mount, *Professional Ethics in Context* (Louisville: Westminster Press, 1990); and Max Stackhouse, *On Moral Business,* especially pp. 14–19, and chapters 4 and 5.

faith. Philosophical traditions and practical wisdom have shaped learning in these areas for centuries, and none is necessarily tied to Christian doctrines of vocation. The role of the philosopher in ancient Greece and Rome, and that of the sage in China and India, have shaped thought enormously, but these traditions are not necessarily theological; nor are ancient legal traditions of Solon and Justinian, or of the Anglo-Saxon and the African tribes. Neither are the ancient "hospices" set up by Egyptian pharaohs and Buddhist kings. The disciplines of education, law, medicine, and engineering have, in other words, something of their own history, something of their own spirit. It is not nonsense to speak of the spirit of learning, the spirit of justice, and the spirit of medical care, and these "spirits" are not limited to those who believe in the Holy Spirit as it appears in the Christian understanding of vocation.

Interesting for our purposes, however, is that strands of the Christian tradition not only gave these professions distinctive institutional homes, but also gave these fields and the spirit behind them a distinctive character. It linked the professions with other developments over the centuries that generated the peculiar modern authorities as relatively autonomous spheres. Thus, peoples from non-Christian religious traditions often see the professions as "Christian" in character and sometimes resent that influence, yet selectively find ways to participate. Others seek to secularize the professions and deny the influence of theological ethics, or paint the Western Christian traditions as inhibiting the free and fully humanistic development of these fields — a development which invites those from other cultures to see the professions as without spiritual content, and thus as only part of "Western" cultural imperialism. Many may seek to adopt and adapt the professions selectively, but some also find the deep presumptions now built into them alien and strange. At the same time, Christian educators, lawyers, and doctors, plus some engineers and activists, find themselves ambivalent that these fields have, in modernity, declared their independence from theological ethics, and developed patterns of action that now appear to be perilous to both meaning and well-being.

The professional authorities today are well established, and they bear values distinguishable from the practices that defined their host societies before the professions were introduced or developed. Their status is seen in the explosion of education in the last few centuries, the growth of international law, the expansion of modern medicine. Such developments have opened the door to universalistic thinking that surpasses many classical and modern philosophers and, even more, the suspicions of their postmodern critics. We are, to say this another way, on the brink of a different kind of postmodernism, a new, highly complex, and differentiated cosmopolitanism, stamped by a theologically influenced history that many of these professions, technologies, and associations now ignore. Yet in every culture that does not wish to be left behind, highly differentiated spheres of authority, sometimes overriding the status of the principalities and no longer only in their service, are opening the doors to a global civilization.

At the same time, it must be said that great ambiguity attends the professions. The sense of vocation is sometimes lost in the values of modern corporate life, and many professors, lawyers, and doctors, as mentioned earlier, lament that what they are doing is "becoming a business." More often, the overtly religious influence is lost, repudiated, or modulated in favor of perspectives more rooted in the heroic celebrations of our capacities to technologically transform nature and history, to bend them to our best ends. In direct opposition to such efforts, the religious influence is sometimes used to deny the arrogance of trying to control everything and to demand that we develop a greater respect for nature and historical movements as they arise.

These tendencies, to control and direct or to allow to develop and to accept, are not quite professions, although they are profound, quasi-religious visions of the world and its meanings, and these too have become a kind of authority, as the earlier WTO example suggests. Indeed, the I.M.F., the World Bank, the United Nations, the coalitions of transnational human rights, ecology, and peace advocacy organizations who meet in grand world conferences have become the new "regencies." They are often the bearers of "moral" frameworks of reference. They do not themselves rule but are being developed to order the new common life.

The Influence of the New Regencies

The "regencies" of our world not only depend on familial stability, governmental order, cultural complexity, and relative economic affluence, they also depend on specific educational opportunities, legal arrangements, health conditions, and scientific access that allow people to think that they can, even must, control the world without reference to God, theology, or religion. They all, ultimately, depend on a technocratic presumption — humans can and must manage the world and its destiny by technical control mechanisms. The present intellectual, financial, and social investment in these developments raises the question whether the drive toward such achievement is opposed to theology and theological ethics. Many ways of reading the faith have seen the results of "technology" as a rebellion against God and the right order of creation. It is held that these fields set up notions of human rationality, freedom from moral authority, and sovereignty of human will that lead quickly to Promethean pretense, ethical arrogance, and a defiance of the God-given. Further, say many religious figures, science and technology cannot save humanity; it is precisely from them that we need to be saved. Others are willing to honor Prometheus, to claim that the pretended authority of "religion" is merely conventional fiction rooted in past need, and to demand that we now take responsibility for the evolutionary process of which we are a part — since, in some measure, it is possible to do so.

Without doubt, intellectual intrigue is one of the major elements behind the development of these regencies. Biological research can illustrate what is at stake, for the complexity of its problems and the subtlety of the technologies are inherently fascinating. Good minds are drawn to interesting puzzles, and there are many in biology, with windows to new ones opening daily. Biology is, indeed, one area that could have vast implications for the global future; there is little doubt that some biological researchers have a surplus of confidence — not only in human rationality, freedom, and sovereignty, but in themselves. Their confidence is often handsomely rewarded. There is fame and fortune in part because people with means want to invest in the prospect that people will want to reverse the processes of death and dying. Hence, biotech firms, although high-risk, form one of the great areas of growth in our globally expanding economy.[23]

The presence of hubris and Mammon, however, does not mean

---

23. One important social-ethical consideration is that this growth is taking place in a global economy. If governmental efforts to constrain research and experimentation are made more stringent, opportunities to do the research elsewhere are available. Bill Clinton, by executive order in 1996, and Congress by legislation, for example, banned some forms of human-embryo research, although the Department of Health and Human Services ruled in 1999 that these actions do not apply to cell research. The forbidden research could, however, be conducted outside the country, where highly skilled technicians could work for less, and the supply of embryos, for a nominal fee, would be unending. Thus, without major changes in international law

that theological issues (beyond the predictable presence of sin) are not behind these developments among regencies. In fact, there is good reason to believe that theological discussion belongs precisely in their midst, for what guides the regencies at the deepest levels is an often implicit, even if explicitly denied, theological orientation about the propriety of humanity intervening in nature—an orientation that, if not understood, is likely to bend further to hubris and Mammon.

A clue to this theological orientation appears in Robert K. Merton's much-debated essay, "Puritanism, Pietism, and Science." Following Weberian analysis, Merton argued that not only economic life, but science, was deeply stamped by Protestant attitudes toward material life. Tracing the motivations, as set forth in the works of the founders and leaders of the Royal Society, he cites Boyle's *Apologia,* which states that "the study of Nature is to the greater glory of God and the Good of Man."[24] Science was also intended to lead to the constraint and guidance of nature, for while nature is stamped by its Creator with an intended order that made science possible, it was also sufficiently disordered; reordering could conduce it to "good in the light of the Doctrine of Salvation by Jesus Christ." But this attitude did not arise only among the Puritans and the Pietists, and Merton concludes with reference to Whitehead's observation that "faith in the possibility of science, generated antecedently to the development of modern scientific story, is an unconscious derivative from medieval theology." Merton then points out that the medieval orientation needed the impetus of both active and ascetic engagement to bring it to fruition.[25]

Merton was not alone in making such claims, which remain very much alive in debates about current biotechnologies. Nancy Pearcey, for example, who lectures and writes often about biotechnology, argues that modern science rests on certain assumptions

---

controlling professional behavior, political constraints are likely to be of limited success.

24. Cited in R. K. Merton, *Social Theory and Social Structure* (New York: Free Press, 1957), 575. Cf. also his *Science, Technology, and Society in Seventeenth-Century England* (New York: Harper, 1970). Merton's theory was, for a time, critiqued by neo-Marxist social historians. However, subsequent historical scholarship suggests that, in fact, Merton was quite accurate. See I. B. Cohen, ed., *Puritanism and the Rise of Modern Science: The Merton Thesis* (New Brunswick, N.J.: Rutgers University Press, 1990), and P. Sztompke, ed., *On Social Structure and Science* (Chicago: University of Chicago Press, 1996).

25. Merton, *Social Theory,* 580, 583.

provided by Christian belief—especially that the world has a rational, intelligible order because it was created by a singular and rational God, and that we can discover that order because we are created in God's image. She argues that three additional principles have been necessary to produce the technology we now have:

1. The universe, while orderly in its deepest grain, is also contingent and can be changed at other levels, a fact that fundamentally challenged the ontocratic assumption that nature—as it is by itself, or as it is created by God; that is, in Aristotelianism or Thomism—is teleological and has inherent purposes. Instead, the expected transformation to a "new heaven and a new earth" indicated that nature is unstable, and less to be contemplated and followed than to be intentionally altered and used for godly and humane purposes.[26]

2. Humans find their primary kinship not with nature but with a transcendent God and with other humans created in that image. This gives permission for humans to have an active role in engaging nature and denies that humans are so embedded in nature that they can only conform to it.[27] She argues, as had Merton, that this view was widespread among the Puritans and notes that the Puritans echo much older motifs.

3. Beyond the fact that the world is malleable and that humans can intervene is the presumption that we humans have a duty to do so, that we are, indeed, commissioned by God to have dominion. To help people overcome health problems, for example, is a moral and spiritual duty. "Both Luther and Calvin applied the Christian ideal of charity and service to the arts and sciences, arguing that they should be used not for personal ambition but to promote the public good,"[28] especially because nature had no inclination to the good without the intervention of transformed persons. Again she notes that this idea has deeper roots.

Pearcey is surely correct. In a new treatment of these roots, David Noble states that

> the dynamic project of Western technology, the defining mark of modernity, is actually medieval in origin and spirit.... [It]

26. N. R. Pearcey, "Technology, History, and Worldview," in *Genetic Ethics: Do the Ends Justify the Genes?* ed. John Kilner (Grand Rapids, Mich.: Wm. Eerdmans, 1997), 41f. See also her *Soul of Science,* written with Charles Thaxton (Wheaton, Ill.: Crossway, 1994).

27. Pearcey, "Technology, History, and Worldview," 43. Cf. Christopher Kaiser, *Creation and the History of Science* (Grand Rapids, Mich.: Eerdmans, 1991).

28. Pearcey, "Technology, History, and Worldview," 43–44.

> was rooted in an ideological innovation which invested the useful arts with a significance beyond mere utility. Technology had come to be identified with transcendence, implicated as never before in the Christian idea of redemption. . . . The other-worldly roots of the religion of technology were distinctly Christian. For Christianity alone blurred the distinction and bridged the divide between the human and the divine.[29]

It is not that technology sprang directly from the Bible as revelation, but rather that deep assumptions in the biblical tradition altered pagan attitudes as they interacted with philosophy and the sciences of the day. Noble shows sympathy for the tradition which some trace to Augustine and other early theologians, that the capacity for technology, properly used for the service of humanity in the fallen state, is a residual manifestation of the *justitia originalis*. Technology may have no ultimate significance for the salvation of our souls, in that we cannot invent our way to heaven or discover eternal life. If we turn to technology to save us, or allow it alone to drive us, it will destroy us.[30]

Moreover, Noble traces what other scholars have documented about how technology came to be seen as a gift for serving God and neighbor. In this view, technology could help save the world against the many threats that are in it. Noble cites Ernst Benz, who writes of "the striking acceleration and intensification of technological development in post-Carolingian Europe," almost all of it emerging from the monasteries.[31] These developments were based on the view that humanity was created good, but is fallen. The fact of goodness means that residual capacities to improve life are present; the fact of fallenness means that improvement is required.

---

29. D. F. Noble, *The Religion of Technology: The Divinity of Man and the Spirit of Invention* (New York: Knopf, 1998), 9. Noble refers also to Lynn White, Jr., "Cultural Climates and Technological Advance in the Middle Ages," *Viator* 2 (1971); and Elspeth Whitney, *Paradise Restored: The Mechanical Arts from Antiquity through the Thirteenth Century* (Philadelphia: American Philosophical Society, 1990).

30. Noble draws attention to Jacques Ellul's "Technique and the Opening Chapters of Genesis," in C. Mitchum et al., eds., *Theology and Technology* (Lanham, Md.: University Press of America, 1984); but the motif is already stated, more ominously, in Jacques Ellul, *The Technological Society* (New York: Knopf, 1964).

31. Noble is dependent on several well-known sources: Lynn White, Jr., *Medieval Technology and Social Change* (New York: Oxford University Press, 1962); and Ernst Benz, *Evolution and Christian Hope* (Garden City, N.Y.: Doubleday, 1975). Closely related is John Staudenmaier, *Technology's Storytellers* (Cambridge, Mass.: MIT Press, 1985), a remarkable review of the first twenty-five years of the journal *Technology and Culture*.

Asceticism focuses on the means whereby residual goodness makes, with God's help, improvement possible.

It is fascinating to note how, from at least the ninth century through the twelfth, the "mechanical arts" became more integral to monastic education and to the formation of the professions. Technological developments were seen as aids to help humans recover primal capacities and, properly cultivated, could help us reclaim the wisdom and virtue that God implanted with the gift of the *imago*, disrupted in the Fall. This view became absorbed into the mainstream of theology and philosophy. In the thirteenth century, moreover, affected by Joachite movements and related apocalyptic speculations, Roger Bacon further revised this tradition. He saw the mechanical arts not only as a way of correcting what had gone wrong in the past, but as a means of anticipating and preparing for the future. To Bacon, the rapid expansion of mechanical arts indicated that God's promised future was at hand. While they might help restore humankind by recovering the knowledge lost in the Fall, these arts would be even more useful for moving humanity, as an ally and servant of God, closer to a new kind of perfection. Humanity, indeed, had a duty to correct old wrongs and to seek progress toward a better end — a view taken up by many and mediated by Thomas More, Francis Bacon, and others in the complex history of the Royal Society, one of the first scientific-technological "regencies."

Most significant is that three enduring attitudes, beyond the assumptions charted by Pearcey, were well developed before our technological revolutions and in substantive measure are surely responsible for them. One assumption is that technology is a practical adjustment to a fallen world, and has no positive significance for salvation, although it could have a negative meaning insofar as we come to love or trust it unduly. Exaggerated confidence in technology could plunge us and the social world into nonbeing. A second assumption is that technology can help us restore the pristine state of creation, to repair what was broken in the Fall — our divinelike qualities and a direct communion with God. The third assumption that influenced the Royal Society is that technology can, indeed must, be an instrument of God to repair a broken world, less to recover Eden than to approximate the New Jerusalem.[32]

---

32. Older, but substantially compatible accounts of these developments appear in R. J. Hooykaas, *Religion and the Rise of Modern Science* (Oxford: Claren-

The conservative preservationist, the romantic restorationist, and the motifs of triumphal progress remain. Only sometimes do these traditions show awareness of their roots in theological ethics, which knows the constraints of sacred limit and the guidance of sanctifying purpose.

The Ascendancy of Nature

These motifs persisted into modernity when the authority of God was transferred to the authority of nature. If there is a God-given divine order, and it can be discerned in nature, why do we need God? If nature, of which we humans are a part, has its own order and logic — without God — there is no way to transform it except perhaps with a very imaginative brain. The theological tradition could speak philosophically and nostalgically of a golden age from which we have, in some sense, departed, thus making necessary a vision of a new golden city that both restores and transforms. A compelling hypothesis of Ernst Troeltsch, set forth nearly a century ago, argued that the ethics of modern naturalism and historicism derive from the deep affinities between the biblical understanding of ethics and aspects of Stoic philosophy. When a God-granted reason or religious *a priori* is lost, all we have is nature and history as is, with no basis for anything beyond.[33] With the enthronement of "non-fallen" Nature in modernity, we see what appears to be a fundamental break with the classic theological heritage, not only with regard to technology, but with the underlying concerns of theological ethics. With this enthronement, sin and Fall are inconceivable. We are no longer under a normative order that we cannot control, although we are part of a natural process that we do not yet fully control; we must either adjust or invent means of control in accord with our natural inclinations.

The ascendancy of nature has put modernity, with its advanced professions and regencies, into an environment where, although it is possible to do almost anything with nature, there is little sense of what we ought to do, except what comes naturally. Yet nature by it-

---

don, 1974); and Eugene Klaaren, *The Religious Origins of Modern Science* (Grand Rapids, Mich.: Eerdmans, 1977).

33. See especially Ernst Troeltsch, "Stoic-Christian Natural Law and Modern Secular Natural Law (1911)," in *Religion in History,* trans. J. L. Adams and W. F. Bense (Minneapolis: Fortress Press, 1991), 273–321; and "Christian Natural Law," in ibid., 159–68.

self is unstable; it changes over time. The idea of nature is constantly reinterpreted by various philosophies and sciences and malleable to the most virtuous interventions, and thus also to the most lethal human intentions. These are the insights of the Gang of Five — Hume, Darwin, Feuerbach, Marx, and Nietzsche — who intellectually, often agonistically, anticipated the drama of godlessness. As R. G. Collingwood pointed out, the idea of the sovereignty of nature leads inexorably to human attempts to assert the sovereignty of history, that is, to humanity constructing itself according to the constantly fluctuating inclinations of will. This idea is the source of what Reinhold Niebuhr recognized as "the easy conscience of modern man," held by Francis Fukuyama to be the root of the terrors of the twentieth century.[34] This focus on nature, and on the human capacity to manipulate it, brought a shift which led directly to the eugenic terrors of the Nazi era and Communism's attempt to construct a "new man" — developments anticipated by Troeltsch, fought by Collingwood and Niebuhr, and declared complete by Fukuyama. These dangers are still with us.

This cluster of arguments represents an enormously complex appreciation and simultaneous critique of "modernity," and points to the necessity of taking historical developments and contingencies into account. These developments demand self-reflective and contextual assessments of how ideas work in social life — a point denied in principle by some forms of "universalistic naturalism" and epistemological foundationalism. Historical realities also demand critique of the context in which nature gained ascendancy, and thus implicit dependence on moral principles that challenge radical historicism, which threatens science, theology, and morality. Since nature is being altered by the new biotechnology, we cannot rely on it. Nor can we rely on history, for history has no normative order to guide what we ought to do when it is possible to do what we want. Nature is historicized and history is naturalized, and both cater to unencumbered will. In a sense, we are "free at last," but we cannot rely on freedom if it is nothing more than naturalistic urges

34. See R. G. Collingwood, *The Idea of Nature* (New York: Oxford University Press, 1945); and idem, *The Idea of History* (New York: Galaxy Books, 1946). See also R. Niebuhr, *Nature and Destiny*, 2 vols. (New York: Charles Scribner's Sons, 1939–41), vol. 1, chap. 1. This tendency to exalt nature, which leads from Hegel to Marx on the one hand and to Nietzsche on the other, is resisted by Francis Fukuyama in *The End of History and the Last Man* (New York: Basic Books, 1991), and in A. J. Dyck, "Eugenics in Historical and Ethical Perspective," in *Genetic Ethics*, ed. Kilner, 25–50.

and historicist constructions. If that is true, Nietzsche was right—the global future is nihilistic chaos.

The basic argument of this volume can now be stated. The authorities of modernity depend on spiritual themes and insights, which made the professions and the newer regencies possible. Where those presumptions were not in place, the professions and regencies did not develop in the dynamic and promising forms in which they are now being adopted around the globe, shaping a worldwide civilization. The fruits of these developments should, and do, augment human freedom, at least of those who master the ways of these authorities. But the authorities lack a conscious moral rudder because, not only are they largely ignorant of their roots, they have often repudiated them, leaving these fields morally and spiritually vacuous and sometimes frightening, as the twentieth century revealed.[35] But this is not the whole story, for there are resources that can reengage these authorities and regencies and offer them guidance. These resources are theological and ethical in nature, Christian in root, public in character, and universal in implication.

It could be argued that the repudiation of theological and ethical concerns is understandable. Some strands of the theological tradition have at times been irrelevant to, overcontrolling of, or even abusive toward promising allies in the professions and regencies. Some contemporary schools of theology have renounced claims about moral standards or guidelines that should inform life outside the community of faith. Thus, some Christians have repudiated their capacity to shape the ethical issues the professions and the newer technologies raise. It is not clear, however, that we can leave connections between theology and the professions behind, even if we want to. The clutter of pre-modern obscurantism, modernist secularization, and postmodern deconstruction cannot erase the continuing pertinence of theology to these fields.

If theology reengages these issues, it must do so confidently, not

---

35. The complicity of the modern educational, legal, and medical professions, as well as some religious groups and many in technology—both of the right and left—in the terrors of the twentieth century is well documented. Now, in the context of a religiously and culturally pluralistic, capitalistic, increasingly democratic, and technologically driven world, we note the explosion of fields dealing with "education and morality," "law and religion," "medical ethics," and "business ethics," as well as a turn by many religious groups toward more rigid ethical systems. This development suggests awareness of the absence of, and need for, a clear frame of reference to guide widespread technical excellence.

condescendingly. It has to assure that the partner in dialogue is also a contributor to theological and ethical analysis. The partner's contribution is most important in ethological analysis, in which theology and ethics depend on those with professional expertise. Such experts know certain areas of research better than theologians or ethicists; further, they often exemplify the values that have been built into their field, even if theological, philosophical, and critical reflection on the roots and character of these values is not systematically developed or overtly expressed.

Still, the fact is that the purpose of much science and contemporary biotechnology is to transform results so they better accord with human needs and wants, which links the discoveries and inventions to commerce and market values. The issue arises of what those needs and wants are and whether they comport with God's intent in creation, so far as we can know. Insights from the theological tradition commend themselves at this point. The transformations that humans can make in the destiny of the soul are limited, although the capacity to change external conditions becomes ever more expansive. At the same time, human efforts to alter either the moral law or the purposes of God in creation and history could destroy the fragile value systems by which human societies exist, and lead to the emptiness of nonbeing. Such human attempts would neither repair what is broken nor improve what promises to get better.

What Can Guide the Authorities?

The essays in this volume are bound not only by their efforts to deal with some of the great authorities of modernity — the professions of education, law, and medicine, plus the regencies of technology, nature, and charismatic personality — but also by a conviction that Christian theology and theological ethics have the spiritual power and moral insight to comprehend, modulate, and guide these powers. Each essay recognizes that these efforts occur under changed global conditions, and that they attempt a wider reach than has often been the case with dogmatic and confessional theological traditions.

In chapter 1, Richard Osmer addresses factors of globalization that affect the nature, structure, and ends of *education*. Drawing from social-scientific literature, he reviews motifs that appeared in the first volume, particularly their implications for contemporary public and Christian education. He argues that Christian education, dedicated to catechesis, edification, and discernment, is well equipped to grasp, to interpret, to guide, and, where necessary, to confront the challenges of the global context. Christian education will help the next generations face an altered economy and polity and the need to reconcile homogenized culture and multicultural awareness, issues also faced in public education. In and for this context, Osmer calls for the theological community to offer itself boldly and, at the same time, to learn from what the world offers the teaching ministry, especially through reflexivity — in the church, in the public schools, and at the highest levels of research and learning.

The second profession discussed is *law.* John Witte, Jr., focuses on one area that has been most globalized — the emphasis on human rights. Witte is aware that debates about the definition and character of human rights continue, and that violations of these rights are widespread. Yet in continuity with his earlier writings, Witte argues both that definitions might be clearer and violations less frequent if it were acknowledged that international human rights are, at root, religious in derivation and implications. Certain legal arrangements are necessary to protect and cultivate the possible contributions of religion to the common life. The reciprocal relationship of theology and jurisprudence is critical.

One can see aspects of this argument in the history of Judaism, Islam, and Orthodox Christianity, as well as in major strands of other religions. But religion's influence was more clearly developed in older Catholic theory on the spirit of the law, and more fully actualized in themes advanced by Protestantism. These are the roots of what is often called "modern" human rights theory, as if it grew only out of the Enlightenment's repudiation of religion. That, Witte knows, is an academic lie with damaging consequences. He presents a "hermeneutic" of human rights that suggests, as does this introduction with regard to the professions and "new regencies," that a failure to recognize the theological roots of our globalizing impulses may distort our understanding of the more profound aspects of humanity. Such failure may inhibit the positive, even redemptive, contributions of universalistic principles such as human rights to our common future.

The cause of human rights today is widely accepted in revised forms by all of the great religions and often taken as religious leaders' message to the wider world. The future of human rights is indebted to its past, one with universalistic implications. If the great themes of this past are not revised and recast in the present, the results are likely to be tragic. The theological perspectives that gave birth to these universalist principles will be seen as only the parochial concerns of some, and the universalist principles will be seen as particularist impositions.

Allen Verhey takes us into the heart of key issues in *medicine*. He shows how "modern medicine," rooted in the hospital and the vocation to heal, was approved by Christianity, expanded by churches that founded hospitals all over the West, then spread to much of the world by the missionary movement. Yet the heirs of this legacy have often repudiated that which nurtured it. It is proper to honor the ways in which modern medicine "resists death and those forerunners of death, sickness and suffering," Verhey writes, but the resistance is often "presumptuous, sometimes desperate, and finally powerless"—especially when it is disconnected from a theology of death and of meaning beyond death.

His argument, in certain respects, parallels others in this volume. He holds that a larger theological vision is necessary to face life and death, health and suffering, healing and sickness, and that since these are universal in human experience, they must be dealt with in universalistic terms. But this does not mean the denial of religion or theology; it means drawing on their resources. Verhey notes that as globalization shrinks the world, medical techniques encounter and borrow from each other. In this process the church has often been both pioneer and advocate for societies that do not have access to health care in its most simple forms. The church is also a prophetic community that calls on those with resources to share material possibilities and to cure illnesses that debilitate prematurely.

In these roles, the church repudiates magical practices, with which both medicine and religion have mixed in the past. Still, medicine must see its own limits and acknowledge the psychosomatic aspects of illness. If medicine is not to alienate us from our own bodies, relationships, and destiny, it must acknowledge meaning deeper than itself, one informed by the Spirit of God, which alone can comprehend the issues confronted.

Verhey's argument differs in certain respects from others in this volume. He sees the church in some ways as part of society and clearly as a community of moral discourse with theological resources to guide the common life. But Verhey argues more forcefully than others that the church is an alternative community of healing, one that faces death, suffering, and sickness differently than medicine, particularly "Western, modern medicine." This alternative community speaks of being with and ministering to the sick in ways that are closer to a caring paraprofessional than a doctor. Even more, the church speaks of the resurrection hope, of meaning and the promise of life beyond death, and the final impoverishment of us all. That, were it the end, would void all justice and purpose in and beyond life. But, Verhey argues, the church knows that, theologically, the end is not the end. This knowledge, that "we live by the Spirit," is the most profound offering we have to medicine and to life.

The essay that follows, by Ronald Cole-Turner, concerns contemporary *science and technology*. It takes us outside the professions into the "regencies," to focus on issues raised by cloning, genetic engineering, and direct computer communication with the human brain. Cole-Turner writes that many believers and scientists are convinced that, as science makes more extensive incursions into nature and human nature, theology must retreat. Yet he poses what is, in certain respects, the question of this volume: Should theology become an ally of ethically oriented professional standards in modern science?

At the center of his essay are the ways in which science is opening new vistas — particularly as it seems to come closer, in contrast to classical ideas of "soul," to the "animating" force of human nature, but even more as it invites the prospect that we can change human nature. Bioengineering, digital communication, and pharmacological management of emotional states are converging. What they can do together is likely to be subject to control, although whether the "person" redesigned by these developments or external agent is in control remains an open question.

We cannot charge that these developments are the modern version of a lonely madman who likes to "play God." Several on the cutting edges of these excursions speak openly about the divinization of human capacity in these efforts. In short, as distant as some of these motifs seem from ordinary belief, profound theological issues are at stake. Cole-Turner fears that "it is altogether too likely that the church will marginalize itself in the role of chaplain, picking up the pieces, caring for the bruised, mopping up the damage, but never engaging the engines of transformation themselves, steering, persuading, and transforming the transformers." He knows that if the church engages these issues, it is uncertain how it can do so creatively, effectively, and faithfully.

It is not only our internal natures that face possible reconstruction—the external universe does also. The newer technologies that may alter personhood are paralleled by technologies transforming the earth as an *ecological system*. In an essay on threats to the environment, Jürgen Moltmann extends arguments that modern industrial society in the West, and now industrializing societies around the world, are creating the conditions for ecological death.

It is curious that, as a vast set of authorities and regencies gains mastery over nature, a redefinition of nature has emerged. Moltmann notes the changing reputation of "nature." Distinct from earlier ideas, Moltmann brings the idea of "Gaia" into his theological perspective. In doing so, he acknowledges the divine desire that humans respect God's creation as an organic gift, which bears residual marks of God's Spirit, groaning toward fulfillment.

With several of the contributors, Moltmann is suspicious of post-socialist interpretations of society that others are inclined to accept. He is more sympathetic than others to some arguments advanced by protesters at the WTO meeting in Seattle, discussed above. But Moltmann is not interested in a neonaturalism that displaces theology. By weaving biblical, doctrinal, mystical, and contemporary evidence into a fresh synthesis, he demands that we think through the doctrine of creation in relation to the doctrines of Fall, sin, redemption, and eschatological hope. He invites us to reflect again on the locus of the Spirit of God. God is not only "other than nature"; the traces of God's character are in the fabric of creation, and the Spirit of God is preparing the earth to be the dwelling place for God's presence. The resources of the earth are not simply the supply room for human wants, but a sacred space to be treated as a divine gift.

Moltmann's contribution, like others, suggests linkages to the wider project of these volumes. In his view, nature has a kind of regulative function, ordering the principalities treated in volume 1. In offering versions of his essay in several conferences in Asia, Moltmann may have found ways of relating key Christian insights to other traditions—what this series calls "the dominions," discussed in volume 3. He ends his essay with a call to revive biblical insights into God's covenantal relationship *with all of creation*—a theme that will be central to volume 4. Such themes may help us connect the parts of this complex study. For the present volume we need only note that ecological concerns have become increasingly central to education, law, and medicine, interlock with science and technology, and are increasingly important to the leadership of nongovernmental organizations.

We end these first two volumes with an essay by Peter Paris on global virtue. Drawing on his "Christian Aristotelian" approach to character and moral leadership in a pluralistic world, he discusses several internationally known figures. These individuals have become authorities among the regencies — in the sense of this series — not only because of their charismatic qualities, but because of their abilities to articulate ethical issues, to set moral agendas, and to exemplify the virtues they advocate. Their views have reshaped social, political, economic, and cultural life throughout the world.

Disputing trends in ethics that have grown since publication of Alasdair MacIntyre's *After Virtue* (1981) and *Whose Reason? Whose Rationality?* (1988), Paris argues that virtue and character in community have public moral meaning. Such meaning is not "incommensurable" among peoples, practices, or traditions, any more than it is incompatible with human rights, universal reason, and common justice. Known for his books and articles on racism, particularly in African and African American contexts, Paris turns his attention to Martin Luther King, Jr., and Desmond Tutu as major Christian voices speaking for and with the oppressed. Recognized worldwide as prophetic voices able to mobilize movements for rights, justice, peace, and tolerance, King and Tutu created speeches and writings filled with references that entwine with these volumes.

Paris also discusses other Nobel Peace Prize recipients, Daw Aung San Suu Kyi, heroine of the democratic movement in Burma, and Nelson Mandela. Suu Kyi is representative of cosmopolitan Buddhist thinking, while Mandela is heir of Gandhi and King. Mandela also draws from the revolutionary socialism of Frantz Fanon, arguably the most important leader of liberation movements in the postcolonial period. Both Suu Kyi and Mandela come from families that boast generations of leadership. A religious perspective is not dominant in their public discourse, although it apparently is critical to their private convictions and motivations. Publicly they have become emblems of democratic thought as expressed in the UN Declaration of Human Rights and the Covenants of Rights, and as unexpressed in others' aspirations.

King, Tutu, Suu Kyi, and Mandela spent much time in confinement for their views and for their abilities to evoke hope, confidence, and ethically driven social action among disenfranchised peoples. Yet all have seen themselves as instruments of the right and good in making a just peace in their own societies and for humanity. In short, they meet the criteria Paris sets for exemplars of moral excellence. They have become international icons of ethical authority, acknowledged across national, ethnic, and religious boundaries. This final essay points toward the interaction of theological ethics in a global society — the topic of volume 3 — and toward biblical-theological shaping of global civilization — the topic of volume 4.

In summary, this volume makes the following contribution to the whole. Beyond those powers which for every society are indispensable — families, economies, politics, cultures, and religions — another influential set of institutions has emerged. We called these "the principalities." However, as the chaos in Seattle over the WTO exemplifies, we are on the brink of new power structures that we do not know how to evaluate. The professions of education, law, and medicine, what we have called "the authorities," have largely defined modernity and are leading us to the new postmodernity. The authors in this volume seek to put the genius of these powers into a larger moral and spiritual context, one shaped by consciousness of the Holy Spirit. Thus, a theological understanding of wisdom and truth is the proper, necessary, universal context for teaching and learning; a theological understanding of justice and rights is the proper, necessary, and universal context for making and enforcing law; and a theological understanding of suffering and death is the proper, necessary, and universal context for guiding medical care.

But emerging out of the social and intellectual conditions that shaped education, law, and medicine, we find three newer authorities, which we have called the new regencies: techné, Gaia, and exemplars of a new transethnic, transcultural, transnational, transreligious moral Hero. All these newer authorities are powerful, all seem driven by spiritualities neither integrated into traditional religious conceptions of morality nor grasped by the secular theories of modernity, yet all have features potentially pertinent to sin and salvation. These authors see, with due caution and recognition of ambiguities, possibilities of the Holy Spirit. As we will see in the next volume, the presence of God in such authorities and regencies will have to be discussed in an interreligious context. The encounter will be with those of primal religions, with those from the academic study of religion, with followers of Krishna, Confucius, Buddha, and the Prophet, Mohammed. Our question will be whether Christ is, can be, and should become Lord over all the powers, principalities, authorities, and regencies in a global civilization.

– *Chapter 1* –

The Teaching Ministry in a Multicultural World

Richard Osmer

As we saw in the first volume of this series, there is a consensus among thoughtful scholars of history and society that the world is undergoing changes of major proportions.[1] It is not merely that we have recently passed the end of the twentieth century or even entered a new millennium, although the changes these scholars have in mind are probably best seen if the longer lens of centuries and eras is used. For the purposes of this essay, these changes will be described as aspects of globalization: the emergence of interconnected systems of communication, transportation, and economic exchange knitting the world together into a transnational, heterogeneous global community. Certain trends in education reinforce these developments, and the dynamics of the present situation are, in turn, having a major impact on education in general and on religious education in particular.

Globalization: The Emerging Context of Education

While the term "global" is more than four hundred years old, the widespread use of closely related terms like "globalization" and "globalizing" only became common in the 1960s.[2] Indeed, it was not until the mid-1980s that they became academically significant in sociology, political science, economics, and communication studies.[3] From that point forward, however, globalization has become

1. *Religion and the Powers of the Common Life,* God and Globalization 1, ed. Max Stackhouse with Peter Paris (Harrisburg, Pa.: Trinity Press International, 2000).

2. Malcolm Waters, *Globalization* (New York: Routledge, 1995), 2.

3. Roland Robertson, *Globalization: Social Theory and Global Culture* (Thousand Oaks, Calif.: Sage, 1992), 8.

increasingly important conceptually, leading to a fundamental rethinking of inherited academic frameworks in many fields.[4] Writing on this topic has proliferated, making it exceedingly difficult to summarize in short order the range of theoretical paradigms that are currently part of the globalization discussion.

To locate the perspective employed in this essay in relation to other models of globalization, two comments of a general nature are in order. First, globalization theories differ in their accounts of the relationship between modernization and globalization. Some authors like Giddens make the latter largely a function of the former. In their view, the acceleration of the forces of modernization leads to globalization.[5] In contrast, others like Robertson, Huntington, and Waters view globalization as standing in a close but distinguishable relationship to modernization.[6] Globalization is viewed as a long historical process that predates modernity and which both builds on and reconfigures modernizing trends like secularization, individualization, and nationalism, trends particularly prominent in the West.

A second issue of debate in globalization theory is the extent to which civilizational and cultural factors enter into an analysis of globalization. Certain authors like Wallerstein portray globalization almost exclusively in terms of the emergence of a global economic system, placing cultural factors in a secondary position.[7] In contrast, others like Appadurai, Robertson, and Huntington view cultural and civilizational responses to such trends as an intrinsic dimension of globalization.[8] The emergence of what I will call *global reflexivity* — a heightened awareness of cultural others and diverse images of the global whole — is portrayed as a key dimension of

---

4. See ibid., chap. 2; Waters, *Globalization,* chap. 7; and M. Albrow, "Globalization, Knowledge, and Society," in *Globalization, Knowledge, and Society,* ed. M. Albrow and E. King (Thousand Oaks, Calif.: Sage, 1990).

5. Anthony Giddens, *Modernity and Self-Identity: Self and Society in the Late Modern Age* (Stanford, Calif.: Stanford University Press, 1991), and idem, "Living in a Post-traditional Society," in U. Beck, A. Giddens, and S. Lash, *Reflexive Modernization* (Stanford, Calif.: Stanford University Press, 1994).

6. Robertson and Waters are cited above. Samuel Huntington, *The Clash of Civilizations and the Remaking of World Order* (New York: Simon & Schuster, 1996).

7. Immanuel Wallerstein, *The Modern World-System* (New York: Academic Press, 1974) and *The Modern World-System II* (New York: Academic Press, 1980).

8. Robertson and Huntington are cited above. Arjun Appadurai, *Modernity at Large: Cultural Dimensions of Globalization* (Minneapolis: University of Minnesota Press, 1996).

globalization, giving rise to a wide range of responses to the global economic trends to which Wallerstein points.

The perspective adopted here comes down squarely with those who distinguish modernization and globalization and make global reflexivity a key dimension of the latter. Robertson's definition of globalization will provide the organizational principle:

> Globalization as a concept refers both to the compression of the world and the intensification of consciousness of the world as a whole. . . . its main empirical focus is in line with the increasing acceleration in both concrete global interdependence and consciousness of the global whole in the twentieth century.[9]

Accordingly, this discussion will focus on both the emergence of systems which have compressed the world into "a single place," as Robertson aptly puts it, and the widely divergent consciousness of and responses to this global interconnectedness found in different cultural groups.[10]

The compression of the world into "a single place" is largely the result of the emergence of advanced systems of electronic communication and transportation. The former makes communication across great distances instantaneous, creating information flows linking virtually every part of the world. Advanced systems of transportation, likewise, link the world more closely, making worldwide tourism and global marketing possible. Harvey aptly describes the effect of this interconnection as the "annihilation of space by time" and "time-space compression."[11] Space is removed as a barrier to communication, allowing relationships to be formed and monitored across great distances. The effects of these communication and transportation revolutions can be traced briefly in three areas: economics, polity, and culture.

The Global Economy

Key features of a world economy were largely in place by the middle of the twentieth century. Transportation and communication systems, the rapid growth of international trade, and the flow of capital

---

9. Robertson, *Globalization,* 8.
10. Ibid., 6.
11. David Harvey, *The Postmodern Condition* (Oxford: Basil Blackwell, 1989), 241.

around the world were already beginning to occur.[12] Technological advances in electronic communications, especially the computer, and air transportation accelerated each of these trends, bringing into being a truly global economy for the first time. As Waters notes, the spread of capitalism has played a key role in the emergence of a global economy, "because its particular institutions — financial markets, commodities, contractualized labour, alienable property — facilitate economic exchanges over great distances."[13]

Of particular importance has been the emergence of multinational corporations as key actors in the global economy. These entities have evolved through several phases: corporations oriented toward mass production in national economies, national corporations oriented toward global markets, and multinational corporations oriented toward the dispersal of production, management, finance, and research around the world. Some argue that multinational corporations are currently entering a new phase characterized by hyperdifferentiation of tasks and greater flexibility. The recent spate of partial mergers, joint licensing, cooperative ventures, and subcontracting is seen as a sign of new forms of multinational organization in which transnational business alliances and hyperdifferentiation of functions allow greater flexibility in product development, production, and dispersal.

The impact of multinational corporations on the global economy is enormous. Dunning estimates that in 1988 they accounted for 25–30 percent of the GNP of all market economies, 75 percent of international commodity trade, and 80 percent of all international exchanges of technology.[14] Their practices reflect in a particularly powerful way the global economy's shift from a high-volume to a high-value orientation.[15] Financial gain no longer accrues primarily to corporations that can produce commodities in high volume, that is, through the use of standard assembly-line or automation techniques of production. The manufacturing phase of production in the global economy largely is located in those parts of the world where it can be carried out most inexpensively, greatly reducing the margin

---

12. See Waters's discussion in *Globalization,* chap. 4.
13. Ibid., 66.
14. James Dunning, *Multinational Enterprises in a Global Economy* (Workingham, England: Addison-Wesley, 1993), 14–15. See also Waters, *Globalization,* 76–80.
15. Charles Reich, *The Work of Nations* (New York: Vintage Books, 1991), chap. 7.

of profit. Rather, financial gain accrues to high-value, that is, the creation of goods or services that meet the special needs of consumers or businesses and cannot be duplicated by other competitors.[16]

The overall effect of these trends is hotly debated. On the one hand, it is clear that some parts of the world have benefited enormously from the emergence of a global economy. In spite of their recent financial difficulties, Japan, South Korea, Taiwan, and other parts of Asia have become major players in the global marketplace. Further, the three population giants of Asia — China, India, and Indonesia — for all their problems are generating new middle classes at astounding rates. This means that parts of these population masses will participate more actively in the global reflexivity which is so fateful for contemporary education. On the other hand, there is much evidence that an international division of labor has become a relatively stable part of the global economic system. Core societies engage in capital-intensive, high-value production of goods and services on the leading edge of technological innovation. Peripheral societies engage in labor-intensive, low-value-adding production.[17] Complicating this characterization of the global economy's division of labor in nation-states is the economic stratification within societies. In both newly developing nations and those with advanced economies, an increasingly wide gap has begun to emerge between those groups with the education and skills needed to participate in the global economy and those stuck in low-paying, menial jobs on its periphery.

When coupled with population demographics, this trend is truly frightening. Kennedy estimates that between the 1990s and 2025, 95 percent of all population growth will take place in developing countries.[18] The erosion of traditional village life based on agriculture is driving more of the population of these countries to cities. In the near future, Kennedy notes, there will be twenty megacities of eleven million or more, and seventeen of these will be located in developing countries.[19] It is not difficult to recognize the social unrest and political instability this situation portends. As research has doc-

16. Ibid., 83.

17. For a more nuanced discussion of the stratification of societies, see Richard Barnet and John Cavanagh, *Global Dreams: Imperial Corporations and the New World Order* (New York: Touchstone Books, 1994), pt. 3, chap. 2.

18. Paul Kennedy, *Preparing for the Twenty-first Century* (New York: Random House, 1993), 21–25.

19. Ibid., 26.

umented repeatedly, increasingly large numbers of young people, leaving their villages to live in overcrowded cities which offer them limited prospects of meaningful participation in the global economy, are prime candidates for fundamentalistic religion and revolutionary ideology.[20] This makes them less likely to participate creatively in global reflexivity.

The Global Polity

The emergence of multinational corporations as key actors in the global economy opens directly to the second topic of polity. The discussion will be relatively brief and point to the obvious: the changing role of the nation-state. Two trends are apparent: (1) the declining power of nation-states, and (2) the growth of international organizations and intergovernmental forms of cooperation to handle matters pertaining to trade, ecology, human rights, and other issues of a transnational nature.

The rise of the nation-state was an important aspect of modernization. It involved four basic features: (1) territoriality — sovereignty in a bounded geographical area; (2) control of the means of violence — monopoly of law enforcement and the military within this territory; (3) an impersonal structure — a legally circumscribed structure of power with jurisdiction over a territory; and (4) legitimacy — procurement of allegiance through the perception that government reflects the people's interests.[21] That legitimacy was assured in large measure by a governmentally controlled educational system that often privatized or subordinated religious loyalties and theological-ethical perspectives on life.[22] The consolidation of these four features during the nineteenth and twentieth centuries went hand-in-hand with the creation of an interstate system that simultaneously asserted the sovereignty of particular states — sometimes forging relationships between states, sometimes leading to war.

Accelerated globalization during the last third of the twentieth century has altered the role of nation-states considerably, calling

---

20. For an excellent discussion of this trend on a worldwide basis, see William McNeill, "Fundamentalism and the World of the 1990s," in *Fundamentalisms and Society: Reclaiming the Sciences, the Family, and Education,* ed. M. Marty and S. Appleby (Chicago: University of Chicago Press, 1995).

21. David Held, *Democracy and the Global Order: From the Modern State to Cosmopolitan Governance* (Stanford, Calif.: Stanford University Press, 1995), 48–49.

22. See, for example, Warren Nord, *Religion in American Education* (Chapel Hill: University of North Carolina Press, 1995).

into question each of the four features noted above. The emergence of a global economy characterized by a high degree of fluidity across national boundaries in the flows of information, technology, marketing, and investment have made the idea of a national economy anachronistic. States cannot control financial markets, capital investment, and other key factors that affect the economic well-being of their citizens. Questions of legitimacy follow. In Niklas Luhmann's terms, the global economic system constitutes the encompassing environment to which state systems must adapt.[23] The principles of sovereignty and territoriality, upon which the modern state was based, become questionable in an economy without borders.

The most important debate among globalization theorists about this process is the role nation-states will continue to play in the emerging global order. Some like Held forecast a continuing decline of their power and the possibility of new transnational forms of political community.[24] He points to Hedley Bull's image of a "new medievalism" as a seminal way of conceptualizing the emerging political order: one not characterized by a single global state but by a wide diversity of power centers at various levels of social life. It is an order in which states will continue to play a role but will no longer serve as the primary center of the polity. International law, metropolitan government, and regional associations will be equally important.

Waters, in contrast, sees nation-states continuing a key role in the emerging global polity.[25] While acknowledging the increased role of international organizations and forums, on the one hand, and decentralized forms of political life, on the other, he rightly points out that the state remains one of the few centers of power strong enough to counterbalance the influence of the global marketplace. Nation-states have been the primary carriers of democratic institutions and rights. National polity represents an alternative to the logic of the marketplace, focusing on the rights of citizens *qua* citizens, as members of a political community. Do citizens, for example, have the right to a minimal level of health care, not dictated exclusively by their ability to pay? Similar questions can be asked about education, air and water standards, and the safety of foods, as well as funda-

23. A helpful discussion of Luhmann's contribution to globalization is found in Peter Beyer, *Religion and Globalization* (Thousand Oaks, Calif.: Sage, 1994).

24. Held, *Democracy and the Global Order.*

25. Waters, *Globalization,* chap. 5.

mental political rights like the free flow of communication and the right to form voluntary associations. More than ever, Water argues, nation-states must play an active role in mediating the influences of the global marketplace to local and national communities. An enhancement of national identities in the face of cosmopolitanism may well be in order.[26] Education would necessarily be a primary means.

Cultural Homogenization

One final area begins the transition to the discussion of global reflexivity. This is the realm of culture. For the present, I will confine the discussion solely to the homogenization of culture that appears to be taking place under globalization. Three aspects of this trend are pertinent: (1) the emergence of a global consumer culture based on appeals to lifestyle, taste, and individual preference; (2) the spread of rationalization in conjunction with the increased administrative needs of modern states and multinational economic organizations; and (3) the communication of idealized, Western lifestyles through the global media, including television, movies, and music.

Benjamin Barber refers to the first of these aspects as "McWorld."[27] The term symbolizes far more than the ability to purchase standardized fast foods in Turkey, Ghana, or Brazil. It represents the emergence of a common consumer culture characterized by appeals to lifestyle variations and individual taste fostered by marketing in the global economy. Slight variations in similar products (e.g., the style of basketball sneakers or hiking boots) can have enormous influence on consumer demand. The aggressive advertising and the "just-in-time" principle of inventory control used by Japanese companies like Toyota (commonly known as Toyotism) build on and intensify patterns long associated with modern market economies.[28] Those who capture and influence consumption patterns are those who will be most successful.

Closely related is the spread of what Max Weber called rationalization: the kind of means-ends instrumental reasoning that

---

26. See Reich's argument in this regard in parts 3 and 4 of *The Work of Nations.*

27. Benjamin Barber, *Jihad vs. McWorld: How Globalism and Tribalism are Reshaping the World* (New York: Ballantine Books, 1995). But see J. L. Watson, *Golden Arches East* (Stanford, Calif.: Stanford University Press, 1999).

28. K. Dohse, U. Jürgens, and T. Malsch, "From 'Fordism' to 'Toyotism'? The Social Organization of the Japanese Automobile Industry," *Politics and Society* 14, no. 2: 115–46. The just-in-time principle is the principle by which inventories are kept low and adjusted "just in time" to meet market needs.

accompanies modern industrialization and bureaucratic administration.[29] Advocates of convergence theory have long argued that as national economies modernized they would foster similar rationalized attitudes toward the world.[30] An increasingly interconnected global economy in which production, research, finance, and marketing are dispersed around the world lends credence to this theory. While Japanese management practices may differ somewhat from those employed in the United States, for example, both must adopt the rationalized orientation of modern economic life. The hyperdifferentiation of the global economy and its reliance on advanced forms of electronic communication are likely to make instrumental reason more pervasive than ever.

Finally, the "videology of McWorld," as Barber calls it, represents a third trend toward the homogenization of culture.[31] Long ago, Marshall McLuhan coined the phrase "the medium is the message," calling attention to the shift in consciousness that would accompany the communication of culture through radio, television, and computers.[32] It lies beyond the scope of this essay to discuss in detail what is involved in moving from a literate to an electronic age. Suffice it to say that the swiftly moving images of film and television shape a very different form of consciousness from that formed through the print media or oral communication. Their images "wash" over us at a subliminal level rather than evoking sustained and focused attention. They foster cognitive passivity and accentuate elementary cognitive scripts rather than higher-order thinking.[33]

An important dimension of globalization is the spread of this form of consciousness along with the spread of electronic media around the world. Not only is the form of consciousness influenced but the contents are as well. The bulk of popular television and film around the world originates in the United States. In Europe, for

---

29. Max Weber, *From Max Weber: Essays in Sociology,* ed. H. Gerth and C. W. Mills (New York: Oxford University Press, 1946), and idem, *Economy and Society: An Outline of Interpretive Sociology* (Berkeley: University of California Press, 1978).

30. C. Kerr et al., *Industrialism and Industrial Man* (Harmondsworth, England: Penguin Books, 1973).

31. Ibid., *Jihad vs. McWorld,* chap. 6.

32. M. McLuhan and Q. Fiore, *The Medium Is the Message* (London: Allen Lane, 1967).

33. One of the most helpful discussions of these processes in relation to contemporary political advertisements is Kathleen Hall Jamieson's *Dirty Politics: Deception, Distraction, and Democracy* (New York: Oxford University Press, 1992).

example, American films account for 85 percent of all box-office receipts.[34] Pay TV and satellite broadcasting, likewise, are dominated by the American entertainment industry, even as American TV is influenced by European trends (e.g., talks shows and game shows). Idealized Western lifestyles are beamed throughout the globe, placing local cultures under pressure by crippling their ability to socialize children and youth who spend large amounts of time watching TV and movies or listening to American popular music.

Global Reflexivity

On the surface, the creation of a common consumer culture, the spread of rationalization, and the dissemination of American popular culture seem to indicate that an inexorable process of cultural homogenization accompanies globalization. In fact, the opposite may prove to be the case. While the various shifts in economics, polity, and culture described above have created a world that is more closely linked, it does not necessarily follow that this leads to a world that is more fully integrated. It can lead to a reaffirmation of ethnic, religious, national, and civilizational identities that take their shape explicitly in response to cultural homogenization.

This lies at the heart of global reflexivity: a heightened awareness of cultural others and the construction of diverse images of the global whole. Recall Robertson's definition. Globalization, he argues, includes not only the interlocking systems that bring the world closer together, but also consciousness of the global whole. This consciousness is shaped in two directions simultaneously. It involves the relativization of local traditions, on the one hand, and a renewed interest in these traditions as repositories of cultural resources by which to understand and respond to the forces of globalization, on the other. It is a mistake, Robertson goes on to argue, to view the Western image of globalization — the inexorable movement of humankind toward a secularized, capitalistic, rationalized, and democratic end-state — as the only form global reflexivity can take. It is far more likely that we will see the emergence of a wide range of cultural and civilizational responses.

It is not difficult to point to examples. The Japanese have been quite successful in combining traditional Japanese values with corporate business practices to compete successfully in the global

34. Barber, *Jihad vs. McWorld,* 93.

economy. A key part of Japanese elementary schools are *han* groups, small teams that work closely in all academic subjects. This is a precursor to the close-knit groups of executives and subordinates that are such an important part of Japanese corporate life.[35] Neo-Confucian familial obligations, likewise, continue to exert a powerful influence throughout Asia. It is not uncommon for Asian commentators on globalization to point to these kinds of cultural and civilizational factors as mediating this region's response to globalization. Asia has been successful, they argue, not because it has become more like the West, but because it has resisted certain Western trends like the decline of the family and individualistic careerism. It is precisely this heightened self-consciousness of cultural identities that stands at the heart of global reflexivity.

Especially important for our purpose is the role religion is playing in this process. Two closely related trends are apparent. The first is what Casanova aptly calls the "deprivatization" of religion: religion's refusal to accept confinement to the private sphere and its success in crossing over public/private boundaries to influence matters of political and social import.[36] A second trend is the rise of religious fundamentalism as a form of global reflexivity. In virtually all of the major religions of the world, this trend is evident and, as such, is best construed as a response to globalization. Indeed, it is not uncommon for fundamentalism to cast its reassertion of tradition explicitly over against certain features of global culture: the materialism of consumer culture, the injustice of the international division of labor, or the hedonism of McWorld's videology. For example, Islamic fundamentalism's call for a Muslim state and a transnational Islamic order is finding a hearing, not only among urban youth newly arrived from the countryside, but also among the urban middle class.[37]

Is religious fundamentalism the only form religion can take under the impress of global reflexivity? This is an especially important question for countries that seek to maintain or establish democratic polities in the emerging global order. Religious intolerance, when linked to ethnic or racial strife, has become an exceptionally vir-

---

35. Gail Benjamin, *Japanese Lessons* (New York: New York University Press, 1997), chap. 4.

36. Jose Casanova, *Public Religions in the Modern World* (Chicago: University of Chicago Press, 1994).

37. McNeill, "Fundamentalism," 562–64. Huntington, *Clash of Civilizations,* 72–78.

ulent force in the emerging global community. Is this the wave of the future? Does religion necessarily exacerbate racial and ethnic strife, making it difficult to maintain pluralistic, national societies and multicultural international communities? Fortunately, social commentators also can point to non-fundamentalistic religious responses to globalization. One of the most promising discussions of these alternatives frames the role of religion in terms of its contribution to civil societies at both national and international levels.

The idea of civil society first gained prominence in the eighteenth century in attempts to describe the relationship of a circumscribed democratic polity to sectors of society relatively independent of the state: the economy, the family, and private and public associations of various sorts.[38] It was an important way of describing in social terms the location of rights like free assembly and speech, religious toleration, and the pursuit of economic gain. Recent discussions of civil society span a wide range of positions, from neoconservatives, positing a minimalist role for the state in liberal democracies, to communitarians, seeking a revival of moral notions and practices of the common good, to critical social theorists, advocating a Habermasian model of deliberative or discourse democracy.[39] Some authors recently have extended the ideal of civil society to emerging forms of global community.[40]

Especially noteworthy in this discussion is the recognition that religion potentially plays an important, positive role in national and global civil societies, mediating virtues and practices important to democratic polity and the pre-political society on which it rests.[41] Its

---

38. Adam Seligman, *The Idea of Civil Society* (Princeton: Princeton University Press, 1992), chaps. 1–3. Daniel Bell, " 'American Exceptionalism' Revisited: The Role of Civil Society," *Public Interest* 95 (Spring 1989): 38–56. Edward Shils, "The Virtue of Civil Society," *Government and Opposition* 26, no. 1: 3–20.

39. Francis Fukuyama seems to represent a minimalist-state position in *Trust: The Social Virtues and the Creation of Prosperity* (New York: Free Press, 1995). A communitarian discussion is found in Michael Walzer, "The Idea of Civil Society," *Dissent* (Spring 1991): 293–304, and Charles Taylor, "Modes of Civil Society," *Public Culture* 3 (Fall 1990): 95–131. The most extended Habermasian treatment of civil society is found in Jean Cohen and Andrew Arato, *Civil Society and Political Theory* (Cambridge, Mass.: MIT Press, 1992). See also Seyla Benhabib, ed., *Democracy and Difference* (Princeton: Princeton University Press, 1996), and John Dryzek, *Discursive Democracy* (Cambridge: Cambridge University Press, 1990).

40. Held, *Democracy and the Global Order,* cited in n. 21 above. See also Max Stackhouse et al., *Christian Social Ethics in a Global Era* (Nashville: Abingdon Press, 1995).

41. Robert Wuthnow, *Christianity and Civil Society: The Contemporary Debate*

role in generating social movements, in teaching the language and practice of democratic argumentation, and in fostering virtues like hospitality, fidelity, civility, and tolerance has received considerable attention.[42] As I argue below, globalization represents a challenge, not only to the extant systems of general, state-supported education, but also to education in religious communities.

Challenges to Modern Public Education

Virtually all interpreters of globalization point to the need for new forms of education that can equip coming generations to respond to the challenges which globalization poses to the human community. In the nomenclature informing this book, education is one of the important *authorities* of social life that will need to be reshaped if nations are to equip their members to participate effectively in the multicultural world that globalization is bringing into being. The authority of education is inherent in its selectivity and normativity. What knowledge, skills, values, and dispositions are deemed worthy of the systematic and intentional efforts of a society's educational system? Should these focus primarily on equipping people for gainful employment? Should they cultivate the *humanitas* of students, grounding them in a broad array of fields that cultivate the varied intelligences with which the human species is endowed? Should different types of education be offered to the various groups within a particular society? Should the nation-state continue to serve as the frame of reference for education or should it focus on teaching those moral and cognitive excellences that are appropriate to the emerging global community?

Education inevitably asks and gives answer to questions of this sort, selectively emphasizing some subjects and virtues while neglecting others. Herein lies its *authority,* which it may use wisely

(Valley Forge, Pa.: Trinity Press International, 1996). Robert Bellah, "How to Understand the Church in an Individualistic Society," in *Christianity and Civil Society: Theological Education for Public Life,* ed. R. Petersen (Maryknoll, N.Y.: Orbis Books, 1995), 1–14. For an excellent discussion of theologians in dialogue with Habermas, see D. Browning and F. Fiorenza, eds., *Habermas, Modernity, and Public Theology* (New York: Crossroad, 1992).

42. Stephen Carter, *Civility: Manners, Morals, and the Etiquette of Democracy* (New York: Basic Books, 1998); James Fowler, *Faithful Change: The Personal and Public Challenges of Postmodern Life* (Nashville: Abingdon Press, 1996); Shils, "Virtue of Civil Society." See also Bellah, "How to Understand the Church"; Walzer, "Idea of Civil Society"; Bell, " 'American Exceptionalism' "; and Wuthnow, *Christianity and Civil Society.*

or poorly. It must conserve what has proved valuable in a community across many generations. At the same time, it must equip each new generation to respond to the particular challenges of its own time and place. This balancing act becomes particularly difficult in times of national or civilizational transition. Such transitions take place relatively infrequently. When they do occur, however, the success of a community in shaping new forms of life that are both just and efficacious in the long-run often rests on its ability to create a new vision and practice for the education of its children and youth. Long-established patterns of education lose their authority as new ones rise to take their place. Hence the scholastic education of the medieval universities gave way to the humanistic curriculums of the Reformation universities, marking a revival of preaching and civic culture more generally. So, too, this same classical education gave way to the modern research university, marking the rise of modern science and specialized forms of academic inquiry.

Globalization represents just this sort of challenge to contemporary systems of education around the world. Modern education in the West, for example, took shape with the advent of the Industrial Revolution, giving rise to state-sponsored systems designed to support mass literacy and to create national identities. In the face of globalization, this system is increasingly antiquated in light of the trends described in the previous section: (1) the emergence of a global economy uncoupled from national communities; (2) the alteration of the place of the nation-state in the face of new legal and political systems at local, regional, and international levels; and (3) the reconfiguration of cultural identities in ways that are responsive to the emergence of global culture, on the one hand, and recovery of particularized identities of culture, religion, ethnicity, and race, on the other. The challenges these trends pose to modern patterns of education can be noted briefly.

Challenge One: Education in the Face of a Global Economy

The advent of a global economy has made education a more important resource than ever in a country's economic well-being. The creation of a class of professionals and skilled workers has become a key to participation in the global economy. Both depend on a nation's ability to sponsor high levels of literacy throughout the population and to provide affordable pathways through secondary and higher education. The relationship between education and productivity, of course, poses the proverbial dilemma of the chicken and the egg. Which comes first: development of educational resources or the elements of an industrial base? Countries overwhelmed by population growth and limited resources find it difficult to create pathways to higher education. In the late 1980s, for example, China had 128 million students in primary schools but only 54 million in secondary schools and 2 million in universities. During this same period, the United States, Japan, and Western Europe spent approximately 6 percent of their GNPs on education, while China and India spent approximately 3 percent of their considerably smaller GNPs.

Increasingly, moreover, education in the traditional literacies of reading, writing, and arithmetic is not sufficient to create a work force of professionals and skilled workers who can participate in the cutting edge of research and development or the highest echelons of international trade and corporate management. Charles Reich points to the kind of education this requires in his apt phrase, the education of the "symbolic analyst."[43] It is the ability to think abstractly, experimentally, collaboratively, and systemically that enables people to identify, resolve, and broker emergent problems in a highly dynamic economic system. These abilities are not fostered by a few years of traditional education. Nor can they be closely identified with the tasks of a stable work role. As technological innovation creates new jobs, it destroys old ones, making reeducation over the course of adult life more important than ever.

The emergence of a global economy, however, challenges modern patterns of education in an even more fundamental way. In dramatic fashion, it symbolizes the complexity, multiplicity, and interdependence of emerging global systems and the pressing need for education in cross-disciplinary models of cooperation and thinking. This, of course, is an insight that stretches far beyond globalization theory. It is apparent across many fields, from the human genome to the evolution of the universe. The cutting edge of human inquiry is based on the recognition that the perspective of a single field or discipline does not comprehend dynamic systems in their complexity.[44] Rather, the research and perspectives of a number of disciplines must be brought together in an interdisciplinary and

---

43. Reich, *Work of Nations*, chaps. 18–19.

44. For a discussion of these issues as they pertain to theology, see Nancey Murphy and George Ellis, *On the Moral Nature of the Universe: Theology, Cosmology, and Ethics* (Minneapolis: Fortress Press, 1996), and Richard Osmer, "A New Clue for a New Millennium: Cross-Disciplinary Thinking in the Quest for Integrity and

multidisciplinary fashion.[45] Indeed, the use of a single disciplinary frame can be misleading. Can economic behavior, for example, be reduced to rational-choice theory, bracketing out the perspectives of religion, culture, and ethics?

Yet it is precisely this sort of narrow disciplinary orientation that stands at the heart of modern higher education, focusing almost exclusively on the specialized language and practices of disciplines in relative isolation from one another. Indeed, the further people advance in higher education, the more specialized their education becomes. Development of an alternative to this pattern — one that focuses on education toward cross-disciplinary competence — represents one of the most important challenges facing contemporary education, especially with the acceleration of globalization. Scientific research and technological innovation are proceeding at an ever more rapid pace, fueling virtually all of the systems globalization is bringing into being. But what institutions will develop the frameworks of meaning and morality that can guide these systems? If education is to have *authority* in the future, it must do more than prepare students for gainful employment in the global economy. It must teach them how to think about these kinds of global systems in a cross-disciplinary fashion, raising the larger and more difficult questions of meaning and morality across all fields of study.

Challenge Two: Cosmopolitanism and National Identities

The scope of the challenge to inherited patterns of education is equally apparent when we turn our attention to a second dimension of globalization: the alteration of the place of the nation-state in the face of new legal and political systems at local, regional, and international levels. Across the modern period, public education has been closely identified with the nation-state, playing a key role in the formation of common cultural identities among the members of national political communities. At its best, public education has cultivated the virtues of citizenship requisite to active participation in public life. In the Western democracies, particularly, state-supported, public education has been viewed as playing

---

Intelligibility," in *Toward a New Religious Education* (Birmingham, Ala.: Religious Education Press, 2000).

45. For a discussion of these issues, see Stephen Jay Kline, *Conceptual Foundations for Multidisciplinary Thinking* (Stanford, Calif.: Stanford University Press, 1995).

a crucial role in the education of the public, teaching the intellectual virtues of open inquiry and moral virtues like tolerance, respect, and sacrifice. Since the Enlightenment, it frequently has been argued that while the religions may cultivate a distinctive sense of goodness among their members, public education alone can foster a sense of the common good among all members of a national community, moderating the tendencies of individuals and groups to seek their own well-being alone.

There is no question that this thrust of modern education is being challenged by globalization along two lines. First, the uncoupling of the global economy from national political communities creates a tension in modern education. On the one hand, education that equips people for participation in a global economy has a tendency to foster a cosmopolitan orientation.[46] Corporate success and career advancement are now tied to economic institutions that stretch far beyond any single national community. Studying English and acquiring problem-solving skills consistent with scientific research and management, for example, are commonplace in education around the world. On the other hand, many contemporary educational systems remain closely tied to the cultivation of a strong sense of national identity through public education, noted above. How the public education of different nations handles the tension between cosmopolitanism and national loyalty will undoubtedly be a key factor differentiating them in the future. The emphasis placed on group identity in Japanese education, for example, stands in stark contrast to the individualistic orientation of most American education.

The tension between cosmopolitan commitments and loyalty to traditional identities makes the emergence of legal and political publics that transcend national communities more complex. The European Union and international courts of law adjudicating human rights violations are two notable examples. Moreover, the global nature of problems like pollution, nuclear proliferation, the warming of the atmosphere, and terrorism make it clear that we can no longer think of public life exclusively in terms of national communities. Are not the ocean, which we fish and pollute, and the air that we breathe and through which we travel now a part of the global commons? Should not education begin to cultivate understandings of public life and the common good that transcend

46. Reich, *Work of Nations,* 310–11.

national communities, understandings more consistent with the new institutions of the emerging global community? Giving answers to these questions represents a major challenge to inherited patterns of education.

Challenge Three: Multiculturalism and the Quest for Truth, Goodness, and Beauty

This brings us to a third challenge to inherited patterns of modern education: the widely varied responses to globalized forms of popular culture. As we have seen, the emergence of a global popular culture has the twofold effect of eroding local identities and, simultaneously, of eliciting a reassertion of particularized identities over against this erosion. The reach of global popular culture is such that the children and youth of the privileged classes around the world listen to the same music, wear the same clothes, and watch the same TV programs and videos. A kind of "collaging" of the local and global in identity formation often results, aptly described by Robertson as the "glocal."[47] Traditional standards of truth, goodness, and beauty fall by the wayside, only to be taken up and reasserted with vehemence by fundamentalist groups. Here, too, education faces a challenge of great complexity: How can it foster openness to a multicultural world without abandoning a community's long-standing ways of pursuing truth, goodness, and beauty?

One of the most important educational responses to this challenge in the West has been the emergence of the multicultural education-reform movement. This movement contains a wide range of perspectives.[48] Uniting them all, however, is a commitment to the reconstruction of both the canon and practices of modern education in ways that include the histories, present needs, and learning styles of different cultural groups, both within a single society and across civilizational lines. While there is much to commend this movement, its most important proponents do not deal adequately with the hardest issues facing the emerging multicultural world: Can questions of truth, goodness, and beauty be addressed within the highly relativistic frameworks of culture and language? Are there commonalties across the human species that are missed by simple

47. Robertson, *Globalization,* 173–74.

48. See the comments of James Banks in "The Need for a Broad Definition of Multicultural Education," *Multicultural Leader* (Edmonds, Wash.: Educational Materials and Services) 4 (Winter–Spring 1991).

affirmations of cultural difference? Does social constructivism have the resources to guide us beyond the centrifugal forces of cultural fragmentation, toward new forms of cultural identity supportive of public life in the emerging global commons? While there is no question that modern education must be reformed in ways that are sensitive to the reaffirmation of particularized identities of culture, ethnicity, and race in the face of a global popular culture, it is not obvious to me that the current proponents of multicultural education point to the right path. At present, the challenge of education for a multicultural world remains an open question, awaiting the arrival of a new Comenius or Dewey who can more adequately address the questions this world faces.

A New Role for Religious Communities in the Education of the Public?

The three challenges of globalization to modern education, described above, indicate the complexity of the task before education in communities around the world. It has left to one side a question that must now be taken up: Is state-supported, public education the only (or even the primary) institution that must forge new forms of education responsive to the challenges of globalization? As we have seen, one of the most important assumptions of modern educational theory has been the close identification of public education with the education of the public. Is this assumption adequate in the face of globalization? Was it ever adequate, even in the modern period?

Increasingly, many scholars are giving negative answers to both of these questions. Perhaps the most important perspectives on this issue have emerged out of the recent discussion of civil society, noted in the first part of this essay. From this perspective, it is a mistake to identify public, state-supported education too closely with the education of the public. To do so is to overlook the all-important contribution of families, businesses, unions, professional societies, media, and religious associations located in civil society.

By themselves, for example, public schools find it very difficult to teach virtues like tolerance, respect for others, and courtesy that are best learned initially in the home. Indeed, in many of the Western democracies, questions of moral goodness are difficult to raise in the context of state-supported education. The pluralistic nature of these societies puts pressure on public education to avoid teaching substantive notions of the good, much less cultivating virtues in a manner vigorous enough to resist the seductive power of the global consumer culture. Many scholars have come to realize that other institutions, particularly religious communities, play an important role in moral education. Drawing on substantive notions of the good and offering a clear set of social practices, these communities have the potential of fostering a vision of the common good and teaching virtues like sharing, humility, truth-telling, and the importance of speaking and acting courageously in the face of evil.

As the civil-society discussion has broadened to include forms of life that stretch beyond the nation-state, the crucial role of education by communities outside the modern parameters of state education has increasingly come into focus. In the remainder of this essay, I explore the challenges of globalization to the education offered by one religious community, the Christian community. In the third volume of this set, the responses of other religious communities to globalization will be taken up.[49] My focus on Christian education proceeds in two steps. It begins by providing a relatively brief introduction to the perennial tasks of the church's teaching ministry, arguing that in a time of rapid social change like globalization the church would do well to set its sights squarely on those aspects of its educational ministry that are essential to its being as the people of God. It will then take up the challenge of globalization to these perennials, indicating new directions in which they can develop and would respond to the dangers and possibilities of the emerging global context.

The Perennial Tasks of Christian Education

As a young child, I was "recruited" by my mother to help her tend her flower gardens. My job mainly involved weeding. Every spring, she would give me the same cautionary lecture: "Don't pull up the perennials. The annuals we have to replace every year, but the perennials will keep coming back if you don't pull them up along with the weeds!" The warning was taken to heart, although more than once some emergency "replanting" of perennials was necessary under my mother's watchful eye.

In an era of rapid and large-scale social change, the church would do well to remind itself of the perennial tasks of its teaching min-

49. *Christ and the Dominions of Civilization*, God and Globalization 3, ed. Max Stackhouse (Harrisburg, Pa.: Trinity Press International, forthcoming).

istry. These are tasks that it must carry out in every age if its members are to make a faithful and effective witness in their own time and place. It is tempting to neglect these tasks in times of major transition, latching on to forms of education that seem more up-to-date or socially relevant. This may lead to a situation in which emergency "replanting" is in order.

The perennial tasks of the teaching ministry are three: (1) catechesis, (2) edification, and (3) discernment. While the church in all its ministries is charged with these three, the teaching ministry stands in a special relation to these tasks, ensuring that the members of the church acquire the requisite knowledge, dispositions, and skills associated with each. A brief overview of these perennials will allow us to see how the emerging multicultural world poses a particularly demanding set of challenges to the church's teaching ministry.

Catechesis

By "catechesis" is meant the task of handing on the core beliefs and practices of the Christian tradition to every new generation and to Christian converts. While the term "catechesis" comes from the early church and not the New Testament, the task to which it points is given ample expression in Paul's use of the Greek term *paradidomi,* typically translated "to hand on." We find it in 1 Corinthians 15:3, where Paul writes, "I *handed on* to you as of first importance what I in turn had received: that Christ died for our sins in accordance with the scriptures, and that he was buried, and that he was raised on the third day in accordance with the scriptures. . . . " Paul uses this term several times in a similar fashion earlier in this letter (1 Cor. 11:2; 11:23) and at other points in his correspondence to Christian communities. In 2 Thessalonians 2:15, for example, he writes: "So then, brothers and sisters, stand firm and hold fast to the traditions that you were *taught* [*paradidomi*] by us, either by word of mouth or by our letter."

The early church uses the term "catechesis" to refer to this task. Literally, the term means "to echo" or "answer back." Initially, it referred to the creed's use in baptism. Having studied the creed during the catechumenate immediately preceding baptism, the convert would "answer back" in response to the creedal questions asked during the water-washing. Gradually, "catechesis" was expanded to refer to all of the teaching that was a part of initiation. Converts were given instruction in the moral standards of the Christian community, and they were expected to "answer back" in the way they lived their lives. They were taught core practices like prayer, almsgiving, and the spiritual reading of scripture, and they were expected to "echo" these practices in the pattern of their everyday lives.

"Catechesis," thus, means to hand on the core beliefs and practices of the Christian tradition. The church in every age must engage in catechesis if its young and new members are to receive the biblical and ecclesial inheritance that is rightfully theirs. At its best, however, catechesis has never been satisfied with merely inculcating the tradition. Its more important goal has been an invitation to and a deepening of faith: personal belief and trust in the God disclosed in Jesus Christ. In catechesis, the church teaches for faith, something that remains outside of its control and squarely in the hands of God.

Edification

The second perennial task of the teaching ministry is edification. The New Testament term commonly translated "edification" is *oikodomeo,* which also is translated to "build up," "improve," and "encourage." Perhaps the programmatic statement of this task is found in Ephesians 4:12, where Christ is described as giving gifts to the church "to equip the saints for the work of ministry, for *building up* [*oikodomeo*] the body of Christ." A key to Paul's use of the term is found in 1 Corinthians 3, where he portrays the church as "God's building." He uses this image to describe the role of church leaders as similar to specialized workers in the construction of a building. Each has something unique and important to contribute to the edification or upbuilding of the church, ruling out the sort of factionalism that had emerged in the Corinthian community. At a later point in 1 Corinthians, especially chapters 12 and 14, Paul extends this understanding of edification to the entire Christian community. Here he develops his famous analogy of the body. In its diversity of spiritual gifts and ministries, the church is like a body in which every part plays an important role. All gifts and ministries are given for the "common good," for building up the body of Christ (12:7; 14:3, 12).[50]

Edification, thus, is the goal of every ministry of the church. The teaching ministry, however, plays a special role in the identification and cultivation of the spiritual gifts by which ministry through all

---

50. In 1 Corinthians 8:1 and 14:3, Paul contrasts the proper and improper use of spiritual gifts, portraying edification as the test of proper use. He uses the word in a similar fashion in his discussion of what is lawful and what builds up the community. See 10:23–24.

parts of the body is possible. Paul's letter is itself instruction to the community, prompted by the abuse of spiritual gifts by "super-Christians" in the Corinthian church (most likely, people placing an exaggerated emphasis on the gift of tongues, the "angelic" language mentioned in 13:1).[51] Precisely because these gifts are more than natural endowments, bestowed by the Holy Spirit for the common good of the community, they can only be acquired and cultivated in concert with other Christians. The community plays a crucial role in recognizing the gifts given by the Spirit and in nurturing their use in ministry.

In our consideration of this perennial task of the teaching ministry, it is once more important to realize that edification is not an end in itself. Just as the goal of catechesis is faith and not merely inculcation of the Christian tradition, so, too, the goal of edification is not merely building a stronger church. It is no accident that Paul places an extended discussion of love in 1 Corinthians 13 between his treatment of gifts and ministries in chapters 12 and 14. In edification, the church teaches for love. It identifies and cultivates spiritual gifts for ministries of Christ-like love. The apparent inwardness of building the body gives way to the outwardness of loving and serving the world, for it is the world which Christ came to save (John 3:16).

Discernment

The third perennial task of the teaching ministry is discernment. Here, too, I point to something that stands at the heart of the Christian life and that is not the concern of the teaching ministry alone. The teaching ministry, however, stands in a special relationship to discernment, helping the members of the Christian community acquire the knowledge, dispositions, and skills which discernment demands and providing settings in which it can be practiced. The New Testament uses two terms that are closely associated with discernment, *diakrino* and *dokimazo*. They have a cluster of closely related meanings: to judge, separate, test, distinguish, and interpret. Paul uses these terms in both narrow and broad senses. In 1 Corinthians 14:29, he uses *diakrino* in a restricted sense to refer to the spiritual gift of interpreting tongues. More broadly, he uses it to describe a Christian leader's ability to judge disputes in the

51. Gordon Fee, *God's Empowering Presence: The Holy Spirit in the Letters of Paul* (Peabody, Mass.: Hendrickson, 1994), 146–51.

community (1 Cor. 6:5). Its background is the legal sphere, pointing to the activity by which judges test and weigh evidence before rendering a verdict. In both the New Testament and later Christian usage, the kernel of this legal background is retained. Discernment is the activity by which Christians attempt to determine the will of God in the face of a confusing or complex set of circumstances. It involves making judgments, examining the particularities of the situation at hand, and listening closely for the guidance of the Spirit in the context of Christian community. In both New Testament and contemporary understandings of discernment, however, the legal background is given a distinctive, eschatological twist. Christians are to judge the particular circumstances of their lives in light of God's future transformation of the world.

The *locus classicus* of this eschatological understanding of discernment is found in Matthew 16:2–3 and Romans 12:2. In Matthew 16:2–3, Jesus is being tested by the Pharisees and the Sadducees, and he responds: "When it is evening you say, 'It will be fair weather, for the sky is red.' And in the morning, 'It will be stormy today, for the sky is red and threatening.' You know how to *interpret* [*diakrino*] the appearance of the sky, but you cannot interpret the signs of the times." The religious leaders know how to interpret the coming weather, but they cannot discern the signs that God is in their midst in the person of Jesus. In Jesus' acts of healing, words of forgiveness, and proclamation of the good news, God's future kingdom has broken into the present already. As Jesus put it at an earlier point in Matthew, "If it is by the Spirit of God that I cast out demons, then the kingdom of God has come to you" (12:28).

In Romans 12:2, Paul exhorts the Christian community to live as members of the coming age, not the present world: "Do not be conformed to this world, but be transformed by the renewing of your minds, so that you may *discern* [*dokimazo*] what is the will of God — what is good and acceptable and perfect." As members of the new creation, community members' discernment is not governed by the world's standards. They have the capacity to see the hidden possibilities of transformation, the points at which the future kingdom is breaking into the world in the present.

Discernment in this broad, eschatological sense stands at the heart of the Christian life. In all of its ministries, the church invites its members to engage in this activity. The teaching ministry, however, has the special task of preparing the members of the Christian community to engage in the discernment which other forms of ministry evoke. Across the ages, the church has taught practices like prayer and the spiritual reading of scripture that stand at the heart of discernment. It has offered moral education that teaches the ethical principles, patterns of reasoning, and dispositions with which Christians can think and act in situations of moral import. It has invited members of the Christian community to join with others in close-knit groups in which moral accountability, confession, prayer, and personal sharing play important roles. In these and many other ways, the church has made preparation for and the practice of discernment one of its perennial tasks.

Just as catechesis has as its goal teaching for faith and edification, teaching for love, education for discernment focuses on one of the central dimensions of the Christian life: hope. Discernment quickly becomes warped if it is not animated by a lively hope in God's coming transformation of the world, a hope that allows it to see hidden possibilities of transformation in the present that anticipate a fuller realization. Without this kind of hope, moral reasoning and acting quickly degenerate into legalism; prayer becomes little more than adjustment to life as it is; and the fellowship of small groups lapses into self-serving sharing. Hope is the animating force of discernment and the larger goal of the practices by which discernment is taught.

In short, there are three perennial tasks of the teaching ministry: catechesis, edification, and discernment. Catechesis is the task of handing on the Christian tradition with an eye to inviting people to faith or helping them deepen the faith they already have. Edification is the task of identifying and nurturing the spiritual gifts that equip people to carry out ministries of Christ-like love. Discernment involves teaching the members of the Christian community how to judge the circumstances of their lives in hope, seeing the hidden possibilities of transformation in the present that serve as anticipations of God's complete transformation of the world in the future. Paul once wrote: "Now faith, hope, and love abide, these three" (1 Cor. 13:13). In an era of rapid change, the church would do well to remind itself of its perennial teaching tasks, even as it rethinks these tasks in the face of globalization. Hans Küng captures well the tension between continuity and change when he argues paradoxically that for the church to remain the same it must change, but for the church to change, it must remain the same.[52] This is the challenge before the church in the face of globalization.

---

52. Hans Küng, *The Church* (New York: Sheed and Ward, 1967), 14.

The Challenges of Globalization to the Perennial Tasks

The issues raised in this final section are not treated in a comprehensive fashion. Rather I seek to demonstrate the kind of thinking that needs to take place if the teaching ministry is to carry out its perennial tasks in a manner that recognizes the multicultural world which globalization is bringing into being. The items pointed to in the discussion of each task are meant to be suggestive, an invitation for others to continue this sort of reflection.

Catechesis and Globalization

Catechesis, we recall, is the task of handing on the core beliefs and practices of the Christian tradition. Its larger goal is to invite people to faith and to deepen the faith they already have. Catechesis in the emerging multicultural world should be particularly sensitive to the contents it hands on and the processes by which it educates the members of the Christian community toward maturity of faith. These issues can be framed in the form of a question: What in the Christian tradition warrants special attention in the face of globalization and how can it be taught in ways that invite people to achieve a postconventional Christian faith?

By postconventional Christian faith, I mean a cognitive stance in which the Christian tradition is simultaneously relativized and affirmed. Core beliefs and practices of the faith are affirmed as true and salvific but are not absolutized. This stance represents a clear alternative to a Christian fundamentalism that reasserts some version of the Christian tradition as the only way to God. It also is an alternative to a simplistic relativism that affirms every way to God as equally good and true.

The most helpful treatment of postconventional religious and moral identities is found in the work of James Fowler, Thomas Lickona, Robert Kegan, and Sharon Parks.[53] They draw on the structural-developmental tradition of psychology to describe stages

53. James Fowler, *Stages of Faith: The Psychology of Human Development and the Quest for Meaning* (San Francisco: Harper & Row, 1981). Thomas Lickona, *Raising Good Children: Helping Your Child through the Stages of Moral Development* (New York: Bantam Books, 1983). Robert Kegan, *In Over Our Heads: The Mental Demands of Modern Life* (Cambridge: Harvard University Press, 1994). Sharon Parks, *The Critical Years: The Young Adult Search for a Faith to Live By* (San Francisco: Harper & Row, 1986).

of human growth that are consistent with pluralistic and differentiated social contexts. Renewed interest in their work is warranted in light of Jürgen Habermas's recent discussion of the importance of postconventional moral identities in pluralistic societies.[54] Fowler's work, in particular, provides a way of describing faith stances that not only achieves a critical perspective on the beliefs and practices of one's own tradition, but also a postcritical "second naïveté" in which they are reaffirmed as penultimate expressions of truth and goodness.

Of importance for our purposes are the implications of these theories for catechesis in a multicultural world. In my own work, I have pointed to the kinds of educational processes that can challenge people to move toward postconventional faith.[55] These involve educational processes that inculcate the core beliefs and practices of the Christian tradition during childhood and support the personal appropriation of the conventional norms of the faith community during adolescence. The pluralism of a multicultural world, however, points to the importance of additional forms of catechesis during adulthood.

Ideally, these include educational processes and practices supporting the critical appropriation of the Christian tradition during late adolescence and young adulthood. This sort of education would afford people the opportunity to assess the conventions into which they were socialized during childhood and early adolescence and to construct an explicit, self-chosen set of beliefs by which to articulate their faith. Beyond this, catechesis for adults also should include processes that cultivate a principled openness. This is a faith stance in which beliefs formed during earlier stages of life are brought into dialogue with other perspectives, both within and outside the Christian community, that challenge them. This involves the risk of encountering others who may expand and even correct one's understanding of God.

Clearly, catechesis as described here goes beyond handing on the faith during childhood and adolescence. The cognitive demands of life in a multicultural world warrant an equally rich educational program of catechesis for adults as well. A second general area of importance in contemporary catechesis has to do with the contents

54. Jürgen Habermas, *Moral Consciousness and Communicative Action,* trans. C. Lenhardt and S. Weber Nicholsen (Cambridge, Mass.: MIT Press, 1990).

55. Richard Osmer, *A Teachable Spirit: Recovering the Teaching Office in the Church* (Louisville: Westminster/John Knox Press, 1990), chap. 10.

of the Christian tradition that are handed down. Education is necessarily selective, and Christian education is no different. What in the Christian tradition is especially relevant to life in a multicultural world? Three doctrinal emphases come to mind: the Trinity, reconciliation, and covenant. Each is the object of renewed interest in contemporary theology in ways that make them particularly important resources for a church seeking to come to terms with globalization.

The *doctrine of the Trinity,* perhaps, has received the greatest attention in contemporary theology, leading one author to write of a "renaissance" of trinitarian theology.[56] The salient issue for our purposes is the sustained attention given to the unity-in-differentiation that trinitarian thinking ascribes to the Christian God. How this is conceptualized ranges all the way from Moltmann's social doctrine of the Trinity to Barth's doctrine of active trinitarian relations. In each case, the grammar of the Christian doctrine of God is portrayed as balancing differentiation and unity, God's threeness and oneness. This has been developed in the direction of anthropology and ethics. Humans, created in God's image, are portrayed as inherently social beings. Moreover, the model of their sociality is in the perichoretic love of the Godhead, love in which the other does not negate the self but is necessary for its fulfillment. It is not difficult to see the implications for teaching that seeks to prepare Christians for life in a multicultural world. Otherness and difference need not be viewed as threatening, but rather are a necessary dimension of the human condition. Belief in the triune God, as such, opens out to human associations that find unity in and through differentiation, not in eradicating cultural differences.

Clearly the gulf between this kind of abstract reflection on the Trinity and teaching appropriate to children and youth is great. The Trinity is one of the most complex doctrines to teach young people. Nonetheless, it is not difficult to think of creative and developmentally appropriate ways the basic ideas expressed in this doctrinal theme can be taught. Even young children understand the importance of relationships and can be taught how the loving relationships of the "divine family" serve as a model for their relationships with others who are culturally different.

Similar teaching potential is present in the doctrine of *reconcili-*

---

56. David Cunningham, *These Three Are One: The Practice of Trinitarian Theology* (Malden, Mass.: Basil Blackwell, 1998), ix.

ation. If this doctrine is viewed along the lines of an incarnational soteriology and does not focus exclusively on Jesus' death, then Jesus' many acts of reconciliation over the course of his earthly ministry can serve as potent resources. What could be more important in a world that increasingly is torn apart by acts of violence and intolerance originating in cultural and racial differences? As Hannah Arendt once pointed out, forgiveness alone has the capacity to break the cycles of mutual hatred that violence and intolerance breed.[57] Christians should be the first to practice forgiveness, not the last. This is not something that comes easily or naturally — hence the need to give it explicit, sustained attention in the teaching ministry.[58]

The biblical theme of *covenant* also warrants special treatment in contemporary catechesis. In the Reformed tradition, this theme has been lifted up for doctrinal treatment in ways that have relevance to the challenges of multiculturalism in both national and global communities.[59] Human associations of various types, both religious and secular, are viewed as covenants, relationships of trust and acceptance involving consent and mutual obligation. Covenants, not contracts, are seen as the standard by which social relationships should be construed. Stackhouse, Allen, and H. R. Niebuhr have developed this theme in the direction of a social ethic that can guide Christians in the family, community, marketplace, and politics.[60] The standard in these arenas is not self-interest or self-fulfillment but an appropriate actualization of covenant love.

Edification and Globalization

Edification, we recall, has to do with the identification and nurture of spiritual gifts that equip Christians for ministries of Christ-like love. It is the task of building the body of Christ, not as an end in itself, but as a means of preparing the church for its mission

57. Hannah Arendt, *The Human Condition* (Chicago: University of Chicago Press, 1958).

58. The best resource for this purpose, combining theological depth and practical guidance, is L. Gregory Jones, *Embodying Forgiveness: A Theological Analysis* (Grand Rapids, Mich.: Eerdmans, 1995).

59. The best contemporary treatment of the covenant-theology tradition is Max Stackhouse, *Covenant and Commitments: Faith, Family, and Economic Life* (Louisville: Westminster/John Knox Press, 1997).

60. Joseph Allen, *Love and Conflict: A Covenantal Model of Christian Ethics* (Nashville: Abingdon Press, 1984). H. Richard Niebuhr, *The Responsible Self* (New York: Harper & Row, 1963), and idem, *Radical Monotheism and Western Culture* (New York: Harper & Brothers, 1960).

in the world. In an era of rapid social change, it is by no means self-apparent what this entails. Over the course of the twentieth century, the church has found it difficult to create links between the life of faith and life in other social spheres. Now it must help people relate their faith to areas of life that are swiftly changing under the impact of globalization.

In the brief space this essay affords, I focus on only one aspect of edification: moral education. Indeed, I will consider only one aspect of moral education: the nurture of reciprocity in perspective-taking and of the universalization of moral regard, items explained more fully below. Teaching Christians how to engage in ministries of love, obviously, involves much more than this. It entails a theory of the religious affections, a discussion of spiritual gifts, and attention to the practices by which Christians are exposed to models of love in action. Attention here is paid to the cognitive dimensions of love: the capacity to construct and sympathetically enter the perspectives of other people and groups and the willingness to view these others as having moral worth.

The importance of these cognitive dimensions of moral discourse has been articulated most forcefully in contemporary philosophical ethics by Jürgen Habermas and Seyla Benhabib and in practical theology by Don Browning.[61] As they point out, the pluralism of national societies and the multiculturalism of the global whole represent a major challenge to moral communities like the church, which make strong moral claims on the basis of their particular beliefs and ethical principles. How in the face of competing claims by other moral communities can churches enter a moral conversation in which the needs and interests of all are given their due? These writers point to two key conditions of moral conversation in the face of this kind of pluralism: the capacity to engage in general, reciprocal perspective-taking and the willingness to regard all conversation partners as having equal moral worth.

The first of these conditions points to a long developmental process in which people gradually learn how to construct the point of view of others. Young children are egocentric in their perspective-taking abilities with little capacity to decenter from their own point of view. Over time, most people in modern societies pass through

61. Habermas, *Moral Consciousness,* cited in n. 54 above. Seyla Benhabib, *Situating the Self: Gender, Community, and Postmodernism in Contemporary Ethics* (New York: Routledge, 1992). Don Browning, *A Fundamental Practical Theology: Descriptive and Strategic Proposals* (Minneapolis: Fortress Press, 1991).

the stages of simple perspective-taking and mutual interpersonal perspective-taking until they gain the capacity to construct the point of view of the "generalized other," that is, the conventionalized social perspectives of their primary reference groups. Moral conversation in pluralistic social contexts, however, requires two further steps toward postconventional perspective-taking. The first step is the ability to reflect on the conventions into which one has been socialized, assessing them critically from the point of view of higher-order theories of knowledge. The second is the ability to set aside one's own point of view temporarily and to enter sympathetically, but critically, into those of other people and groups. Together, these steps allow reciprocity in perspective-taking: the ability to articulate one's own point of view as one among others and to enter into those of people and groups whose perspective is different from one's own.

The second condition of moral conversation among pluralistic partners is the universalization of moral regard. It refers to an attitude in which all participants in the conversation are viewed as having moral worth. They are granted equality in the conversation. Their needs and interests are taken seriously, as is their right to influence the course of the conversation. No one person or group has undue power to control the issues raised or the outcomes achieved. How to justify this second condition has been a matter of considerable debate in contemporary philosophical ethics, and its importance cannot be minimized. The achievement of general, reciprocal perspective-taking by itself does not constitute "the moral point of view." It can be used for purposes of manipulation and control in which the perspectives of others are taken into account solely for the achievement of strategic ends. Habermas's attempt to ground this universalization in obligations inherent in communication that is oriented toward understanding has been criticized even by sympathetic interpreters of his work like Benhabib, Held, and McCarthy.[62] Their alternatives, however, seem equally arbitrary, resting as they do on a positive valorization of the democratic traditions of the modern West. In a multicultural world, why should

62. Benhabib, introduction to *Situating the Self;* Held, *Democracy and the Global Order,* chap. 8; Thomas McCarthy, "Rationality and Relativism: Habermas's 'Overcoming' of Hermeneutics," in *Habermas: Critical Debates,* ed. J. Thompson and D. Held (Cambridge, Mass.: MIT Press, 1982). See also S. Benhabib and F. Dallmayr, eds., *The Communicative Ethics Controversy* (Cambridge, Mass.: MIT Press, 1991).

this justification of the universalization of moral regard be viewed as more convincing than other possibilities?

Michael Walzer's insights in *Thick and Thin* are telling in this regard.[63] Moral regard for others of the sort Habermas articulates represents a "thinned-out" version of notions that are part of a "thick" tradition of moral practices, beliefs, and principles. Indeed, not every moral or religious community possesses the resources to shape its members toward recognition of the moral worth of others. Even within a particular community, there may be arguments about how its traditions construe the moral status of those who are not a part of the community. One need only look as far as contemporary American Protestantism to find examples of this sort of intracommunal debate.

The position adopted here argues that Christian love, properly understood, opens to the universalization of moral regard. Joseph Allen's treatment of covenant love represents an especially powerful argument along these lines.[64] God's covenant love as found in scripture, he argues, can be characterized along six lines: (1) It fashions us as social beings and binds us in a covenant community; (2) it creates and affirms the moral worth of each covenant member; (3) it is inclusive, reaching out universally to embrace all of creation; (4) it seeks to meet the needs of the members of the covenant community; (5) it is steadfast, offering care over time; and (6) it is reconciling, extending forgiveness to and seeking reunion with enemies.

Allen goes on to argue that these same characteristics form the standard of Christian covenant love. Christians, too, are called to affirm the moral worth of the members of the various covenants in which they participate, not merely intracommunal covenants of home and hearth, but also those forged in the marketplace, the political arena, civil society, and emerging forms of global community. To be sure, further development of this point is needed for a genuinely "thick" description of Christian beliefs and moral notions that justifies this claim. But enough has been said to allow us to return to the theme of edification.

I can now give greater specificity to what is at stake in edification as moral education. Christian moral education should support development toward general, reciprocal perspective-taking and the

---

63. Michael Walzer, *Thick and Thin* (Notre Dame, Ind.: University of Notre Dame Press, 1994).

64. Allen, *Love and Conflict*, chap. 2.

universalization of moral regard. Three concrete examples will flesh out the implications this might have for edification. The first example has to do with Christian parenting. In contrast to widely influential programs that encourage parents to break the will of the child early in life and to maintain traditional patterns of female and child subordination to the authority of the father, the kind of parenting consistent with the position outlined above would encourage perspective-taking opportunities in the home and conceptualize all members of the family as having equal moral worth.

In his book *Raising Good Children,* Thomas Lickona points to some of the practices this entails.[65] Rather than demanding blind obedience by the child, parents are encouraged both to give respect to their children and to expect respect in return. They will give reasons for the rules of family life; they will constantly encourage their children to enter the perspectives of others at home and at school; they will invite children to participate in the making of family rules in order to inculcate an orientation toward fairness; and they will model in their own interactions a relationship of equal moral regard. Children receiving this kind of parenting will develop the kinds of attitudes and cognitive skills that can be expanded, when they are ready developmentally, to other spheres of life.

This is only likely to occur, however, if the congregation joins the family in encouraging this same kind of reciprocity and moral regard in its various ministries. Two further examples illustrate this point. Mission projects oriented to those beyond the church can foster paternalism and even reinforce prejudice unless explicit attention is given to perspective-taking and moral regard in the education accompanying such projects. Anyone who has worked with a white, middle-class youth group refurbishing houses in Appalachia or the inner city knows how common it is for young people to raise questions like these: "Why do the people we're trying to help seem to waste so much of their money on frivolous items for their children, when this is going to leave them broke at the end of the month? I don't see why they can't get a job when there seem to be so many available?" These kinds of questions represent important opportunities for young people to grow in their ability to enter into the perspectives of those to whom they are ministering and to gain a richer understanding of the nature of covenant love.

---

65. Cited in n. 53 above.

The same kinds of issues are evident in other forms of edification. One illustration will suffice: preparation of lay people to carry out congregational care. Many churches sponsor Stephen Ministries or devise their own programs of congregational care. These represent wonderful opportunities for members of the church to learn how to enter the perspective of those who often feel alienated from the church: people recently divorced, people angry at God for a tragedy that has befallen them, and people addicted to alcohol or drugs. Edification that encourages caregivers to view such people as having moral worth and genuinely to walk in their shoes is teaching precisely the kind of moral skills necessary to practice love in pluralistic communities. The focus in such care may be on those inside the Christian community, but the body is being built up in ways that equip Christians to reach out to people outside the community as well.

Discernment and Globalization

Discernment, as described above, focuses on teaching members of the Christian community how to judge the circumstances of their life and world in light of the coming kingdom. It is both animated by and oriented toward Christian hope: the ability to see the hidden possibilities of change in the present that anticipate the complete transformation of the world God will bring fully in the future. In the limited space available, I focus on only one key aspect of discernment: the church as a utopian community of prayer.

Prayer, as the seeking of God's will amid the complex circumstances of human life, lies at the heart of discernment. To be sure, discernment involves more than prayer. It involves hard-headed analysis of the contemporary world and moral reflection on how the church ought to respond to the issues this analysis raises. As a community of prayer, however, the church is reminded that its relationship with God is a living relationship and that God's commands come anew in the particularities of the church's own time and place.

The contemporary discussion of spirituality rightly has reminded the church that prayer includes more than supplication. It also involves adoration, confession, and thanksgiving.[66] Contemporary spirituality also has reminded the church that prayer can be more

---

66. Two of the best introductions are Marjorie Thompson, *Soul Feast: An Invitation to the Christian Spiritual Life* (Louisville: Westminster/John Knox Press, 1995), and Richard Foster, *Prayer: Finding the Heart's True Home* (San Francisco: Harper & Row, 1992).

than explicit acts of communication with God, taking place at special times and places. Recalling Paul's injunction to pray without ceasing, it has helped the church remember that prayer is a posture of receptivity to God that can pervade every aspect of life. What often is missing from contemporary spirituality, however, is the eschatological orientation of Christian prayer. Jesus taught his disciples to pray: "Thy kingdom come, thy will be done on earth as it is in heaven." When this orientation is missing, spirituality runs the risk of cutting the Christian community off from the broader reach of its hope. Prayer for the coming of God's kingdom is cosmic in scope. It includes the transformation of all forms of life, from the most far-reaching political, economic, and ecological systems to the smaller circles of concern so typically the object of prayer.

More than any contemporary theologian, Jürgen Moltmann has drawn attention to the utopian potential of this eschatological orientation.[67] His dialogue with Ernst Bloch in his early writings led him to describe the church as a community that lives out of God's inbreaking future, placing it in a permanent, creative tension with the world as it is. The church's stance, Moltmann argues, is not one of simple negation. It is genuinely utopian, projecting imaginative alternatives that animate concrete engagement in the present. The utopian nature of Christian hope, thus, is neither escapist nor otherworldly. It is an orientation toward God's future for creation that enlivens the imagination and evokes engagement of the pressing issues of the day. When the church as a community of prayer is animated by this sort of hope, its circle of concern and its yearning for change are broadened considerably. That which it seeks to discern is God's will for the present viewed through the lens of God's promised future.

There is, perhaps, no more important task before the church today than to live as a community of prayer animated by its hope in God's future. The forces of globalization are so complex and overwhelming that many are driven to attitudes of cynicism, despair, and apathy. The hyperdifferentiated global economy leaves many feeling powerless to shape their economic destinies. The sheer enormity of planetary issues like global warming and the spread of weapons of mass destruction leads many to throw up their hands in resignation. A community of hope that prays for and works toward God's prom-

67. Jürgen Moltmann, *Theology of Hope: On the Ground and the Implications of a Christian Eschatology* (New York: Harper & Row, 1967).

ised future represents an alternative. It discerns hidden possibilities of change in the present that can only be seen through eyes of faith.

How can the teaching ministry nurture discernment that is rooted in a utopian community of prayer? Three courses of education can be noted briefly. The first and most obvious is that the church should teach its members to pray. Without question, the liturgy of public worship is the most important teacher of prayer.[68] Its movement through praise, thanksgiving, supplication, and adoration teaches a grammar of prayer that is internalized over time by participants. When the teaching ministry invites members of the community to appropriate this liturgy self-consciously, its role is like that of an English teacher who instructs her students in the grammatical rules of a language they have already acquired naturally.

The importance of public worship in teaching the community to pray places a special responsibility on the leaders of worship to consistently bring the concerns of the world before God on behalf of God's people. In so doing, they model an attitude of expectation in which God's promised future guides the range of concerns that rightfully are brought before God in prayer. When this occurs, the task of the teaching ministry is to educate the members of the community in practices and disciplines by which they can reiterate in their personal devotional life the same attitude of hopeful concern for the world they consistently find in public worship. As a starting point, teachers can make prayer a regular part of their classes. They would do well to pray, not merely *for* their students, but *with* them. As Christians mature, it is appropriate to teach them devotional practices long a part of the tradition, like the spiritual reading of scripture, contemplative prayer, and the examen.

When taught as means of discernment grounded in Christian hope, such practices invite the members of the Christian community to view their relationship with God as a living relationship, creating an expectation that God can and will transform the circumstances of their lives and their world. Prayer, as such, is the practice of hope par excellence and lies at the heart of discernment. Why, then, must we describe two further dimensions of teaching for discernment? First, prayer without action is like faith without works. It is dead. Discernment of the will of God, informed by prayer, opens to performance of God's will. Second, the utopian dimensions of Christian hope warrant explicit attention to the nurture of the imagination by

---

68. Don Saliers, *Worship and Spirituality* (Philadelphia: Westminster Press, 1984).

the teaching ministry. Prayer is both limited and illumined by the images on which it draws. Both of these concerns point to additional tasks in teaching for discernment. I begin with the imagination.

One of the most underdeveloped aspects of the contemporary teaching ministry is its use of the arts. This is surprising, for it is commonly acknowledged that music, architecture, stained-glass windows, dance, and literature have been powerful modes of teaching across the Christian tradition. Signs of a new appreciation of the arts in Christian education have begun to appear only very recently. Howard Gardner's theory of multiple intelligences, in particular, has spawned greater interest in the role of the arts in general education.[69] Gardner argues that education too frequently has limited its attention to linguistic and logical-mathematical forms of intelligence. Marshaling recent research on the brain and cognition, he argues that at least five additional intelligences can be identified: bodily-kinesthetic, musical, spatial, intrapersonal, and interpersonal. Each has its own locus in the brain and its own developmental history. Education in the arts, Gardner goes on to argue, plays an especially important role in nurturing forms of intelligence left untapped by the traditional three Rs.

The implications of Gardner's theory are manifold. For our purposes, I am especially interested in the perspective it affords on the nurture of hope. Recall the utopian interpretation of Christian hope developed above on the basis of Moltmann's early work. Utopianism was described, not as escapism or otherworldliness, but as the imaginative projection of alternatives to life as it is. Gardner's theory of multiple intelligences provides important clues about the potential role of the arts in the nurture of this utopian sensibility. Education toward a new way of seeing may well best proceed, not by a direct assault on the logical and verbal constructions of modern, scientific worldviews, but through exposure to and participation in artistic performances appealing to other forms of intelligence. The spirituals of African American Christians, for example, have long given expression to the sighs of the oppressed articulating hope in God's future. Even relatively mundane popular music like "We Are the World" has invited young people around the globe to sing their

---

69. Howard Gardner, *Frames of Mind: The Theory of Multiple Intelligences* (New York: Basic Books, 1985); idem, *Art, Mind, and Brain* (New York: Basic Books, 1982); and idem, "Artistic Intelligences," in *Art Education* 36, no. 2: 47–49; and with David Perkins, "Art, Mind, and Education," *Journal of Aesthetic Education* 22, no. 1 (1982).

way into a new way of seeing the problem of famine in Africa. Picasso's *Guernica* evoked a similar response to the Spanish Civil War and the destruction of war generally.

Art has the capacity of inviting us to see our world anew. It should play an increasingly important role in teaching for discernment. Such teaching may well bypass the language and logic of our everyday lives by appealing to the musical, visual, verbal, and bodily-kinesthetic forms of intelligence which great art employs. If discernment is to involve the projection of alternatives to the present course of globalization, one of the teaching ministry's most important tasks may well be uncovering those forms of art that can best help the members of the Christian community see what these alternatives might be.

This brings us to a final dimension of teaching for discernment: explicit study of globalization oriented toward action that seeks to influence globalization's course toward the purposes of God. As noted above, prayer without action is empty. One may pray to forgive one's enemies, for example, but if this does not issue in concrete attempts at reconciliation, then something less than genuine prayer has taken place. The study of globalization and related topics is important for a number of reasons. First, global reflexivity is so pervasive that many church members are ready to gain a better understanding of the larger forces of globalization restructuring their lives. Whether they work for a multinational corporation or simply watch CNN regularly, people are aware that changes of major proportions are taking place around the world. What they often lack is a higher-order perspective on these changes, something they are eager to gain. Second, lay people frequently are best prepared to explicate what is at stake in globalization and are better equipped than clergy to discern ways globalization might be guided toward the purposes of God. Finally, the new social movements that globalization has spawned — for example, the ecological movement, the human rights movement, the multicultural-education reform movement — frequently are misunderstood in the church. When studied as part of a comprehensive examination of globalization, their importance often becomes more evident.

In teaching for discernment, the study of globalization is best linked to action-reflection models of education. These models invite people to press beyond study alone to effect concrete responses to the issue on which they are focusing. Action informs reflection, and reflection guides action. Discernment thus becomes more than an idle intellectual exercise. It becomes a way of shaping one's life and world in response to new understanding of God's purposes. Such action frequently is the seedbed of hope, for it breaks the cycle of passivity and resignation that large-scale institutional forces often engender. Action-reflection education, moreover, commonly has the effect of pressing people back to prayer, as it becomes evident that working for change in the face of global forces can be overwhelming and costly. Perhaps it is here that prayer for the coming of God's promised future becomes most needed and most desired.

Conclusion

This essay has developed a comprehensive framework for the teaching ministry for tomorrow's world. Each of three perennial tasks of this ministry, catechesis, edification, and discernment, has been conceptualized in relation to the emerging global context. The framework offers guidelines for committed educators to assess their own programs, helping them determine areas of strength and weakness. As we begin a new millennium communities of faith would do well to reflect on the kind of teaching and learning their members will need if they are to make a faithful and effective witness in a rapidly globalizing world. This reflection will best take place in the perennial tasks of the teaching ministry. For it to make a contribution to this change, it must in many ways remain the same.

– Chapter 2 –

The Spirit of the Laws, the Laws of the Spirit

RELIGION AND HUMAN RIGHTS IN A NEW GLOBAL ERA

John Witte, Jr.

In its most basic sense, globalization is the process of compressing cultural time and space, of bringing the persons and peoples of the world into increasingly regular interaction.[1] While globalization in this sense has been a perennial feature of cultural expansion, the process has accelerated rapidly in the twentieth century — for better and for worse. On the one hand, globalization has featured stunning advances in worldwide science, medicine, and technology, an emerging global literature, language, and electronic media, and the welcome growth of global movements for social justice, public health, and natural conservation.[2] On the other hand, globalization has brought to this century two devastating world wars,

---

This essay builds in part on my " 'A Dickensian Era' of Religious Rights," in *The Sacred, the Sword, and Global Security*, ed. Scott Appleby (Notre Dame, Ind.: University of Notre Dame Press, forthcoming); *Religion and the American Constitutional Experiment* (Boulder, Colo.: Westview Press, 2000), chaps. 1, 10; and "Law, Religion, and Human Rights," *Columbia Human Rights Law Review* 28 (1996): 1–31.

1. See sources and discussion in Roland Robertson, "Globalization and the Future of Traditional Religion," in *Religions and the Powers of the Common Life,* God and Globalization 1, ed. Max L. Stackhouse with Peter J. Paris (Harrisburg, Pa.: Trinity Press International, 2000), 53–68.

2. See sources and discussion in Mary Stewart van Leeuwen, "Faith, Feminism, and the Family in the Age of Globalization," in ibid., 184–230; Ronald Cole-Turner, "Science, Technology, and the Mission of Theology in a New Century," in *The Spirit and the Modern Authorities* God and Globalization 2, ed. Max L. Stackhouse with Don Browning (Harrisburg, Pa., Trinity Press International, 2000), 139–165; Allen Verhey, "The Spirit of God and the Spirit of Medicine: The Church, Globalization, and a Mission of Health Care," in ibid., 107–138.

unprecedented political machination, environmental degradation, and commercial exploitation, and the increasingly acute threat of a global nuclear or biological holocaust.[3]

Law — as one of the "authorities" alongside education, science, and medicine — has always been an integral part of this process of globalization. Law has provided rules, procedures, and institutions designed both to deter the vices and to facilitate the virtues of globalization. The classical Roman jurists called this the "law of nations" (*ius gentium*), a term which persisted in the West for more than a millennium. It came to describe not only the law governing diplomatic relations among empires, nations, and tribes, but also a host of maritime, mercantile, military, and moral customs. In 1789, the English jurist Jeremy Bentham coined the term "international law." He used it to distinguish the law governing "mutual interactions between [national] sovereigns as such" from maritime, mercantile, military, and moral customs. These latter customs, in Bentham's view, were not truly international laws; in some instances, he argued, they were not even laws at all. By 1900, Bentham's phrase "international law" had largely replaced the traditional phrase "law of nations" — but not in the narrow legal sense that Bentham had urged. Jurists spoke of "public" international law (the law governing "national sovereigns as such") and "private" international law (the various maritime, mercantile, military, and moral norms, which Bentham wanted to exclude).[4] Today, this language of public and private international law remains conventional — although the phrases "transnational law," "world law," and "global law" are also used.[5] The sundry institutions involved in the definition and implementation of this global law range from such large units as the United Nations, World Bank, World Trade Organization, and World Health Organization to the thousands of non-governmental and inter-governmental organizations spread throughout the globe.

---

3. See sources and discussion in Donald W. Shriver, Jr., "The Taming of Mars: Can Humans of the Twenty-First Century Contain Their Propensity for Violence?" in *Religions and the Powers of the Common Life,* God and Globalization 1, ed. Stackhouse with Paris, 140–83; William Schweiker, "Responsibility in the World of Mammon: Theology, Justice, and Transnational Corporations," in ibid., 105–39.

4. See sources and discussion in Mark W. Janis, "Jeremy Bentham and the Fashioning of 'International Law'," *American Journal of International Law* 78 (1984): 405.

5. See Harold J. Berman, "World Law," *Fordham International Law Journal* 18 (1995): 1617. See also, e.g., Phillip C. Jessup, *Transnational Law* (New Haven: Yale University Press, 1956); Henry Steiner, Detlev F. Vagts, and Harold H. Koh, *Transnational Legal Problems,* 4th ed. (Mineola, N.Y.: Foundation Press, 1994).

The language of rights has long been common coinage in the currency of global law — with roots deep into classical Roman law and medieval canon law. In the last half of the twentieth century, however, rights talk has become an increasingly prominent mode of defining and defending the contents and contours of global law. The Universal Declaration of Human Rights (1948) not only distilled earlier rights formulations but also catalyzed a veritable "human rights revolution" around the globe.[6] More than one hundred major international human rights instruments have been issued since 1948, together with thousands of domestic constitutions, statutes, regulations, and cases respecting human rights.

This chapter is addressed to the "spirit" of the modern global law of human rights — to its religious sources and dimensions, especially in the Western tradition. In particular, it seeks to discern the past and potential contributions of Western Christianity to the cultivation and the reformation of the modern law of human rights.

Three texts in Baron de Montesquieu's famous *Spirit of the Laws* (1748) have inspired this exercise:

> It is a principle that every religion which is persecuted becomes itself persecuting; for as soon as by some accidental turn it arises from persecution, it attacks the religion which persecuted it.
>
> The threatenings of religion are so terrible, and its promises so great, that when they actuate the mind, whatever efforts the magistrate may use to oblige us to renounce it, seem to leave us nothing when he deprives us of the exercise of our religion, and to bereave us of nothing when we are allowed to profess it.
>
> The Christian religion, which ordains that men should love each other, would, without doubt, have every nation blest with the best civil, the best political laws; because, these next to this religion, are the greatest good that men can give and receive. . . . The principles of Christianity, deeply engraved on the heart, would be infinitely more powerful than the false honor of monarchies, than the human virtues of republics, or the servile fear of despotic states.[7]

---

6. R. J. Vincent, *Human Rights and International Relations* (Cambridge, Mass.: Harvard University Press, 1986), 93.

7. Baron de Montesquieu, *The Spirit of the Laws*, trans. Thomas Nugent (1748; New York: Hafner Press, 1949), 25.9, 25.12, 24.1.

Building on the first text of Baron Montesquieu, the first section argues that the modern human rights revolution has brought not only new freedom, but also new belligerence to many long-trammeled religious communities, launching something of a new war for souls throughout large parts of the world. Building on the second text, part two argues that religion is, nonetheless, a natural and necessary ally in the global struggle for human rights. Building on the third text, part three argues that Christianity, among other faiths, has unique and vital resources that have been, and can be, brought to bear on the global human rights movement. Accordingly, after outlining the general rubrics of a "hermeneutic of human rights," I use it to analyze the past and potential rights contribution of the church to the spirit of the laws and the laws of the spirit.

A Dickensian Era of Religious Rights

The world has entered something of a "Dickensian era"[8] in the past two decades. We have seen the best of human rights protections inscribed on the books, but some of the worst of human rights violations inflicted on the ground. We have celebrated the creation of more than thirty new constitutional democracies since 1980, but lamented the eruption of more than thirty new civil wars. We have witnessed the wisest of democratic statecraft and the most foolish of autocratic belligerence. For every South African spring of hope, there has been a Yugoslavian winter of despair.

These Dickensian paradoxes of the modern human rights revolution are particularly striking when viewed in their religious dimensions. On the one hand, the modern human rights revolution has helped to catalyze a great awakening of religion around the globe. In regions newly committed to democracy and human rights, ancient faiths once driven underground by autocratic oppressors have sprung forth with new vigor. In the former Soviet bloc, for example, numerous Buddhist, Christian, Hindu, Jewish, Muslim, and other faiths have been awakened, alongside a host of exotic goddess, naturalist, and personality cults.[9] In postcolonial

---

8. The phrase is from Irwin Cotler, "Jewish NGOs and Religious Human Rights: A Case Study," in *Human Rights in Judaism: Cultural, Religious, and Political Perspectives,* ed. Michael J. Broyde and John Witte, Jr. (Northvale, N.J., and Jerusalem: Jason Aronson, 1998), 165–272, at 165.

9. See John Witte, Jr., and Michael Bourdeaux, eds., *Proselytism and Orthodoxy in Russia: The New War for Souls* (Maryknoll, N.Y.: Orbis Books, 1999).

and postrevolutionary Africa, these same mainline religious groups have come to flourish in numerous conventional and inculturated forms, alongside a bewildering array of traditional groups.[10] Many parts of the world have seen the prodigious rise of a host of new or newly minted faiths — Adventists, Ahmadis, Bahā'īs, Hare Krishnas, Jehovah's Witnesses, Mormons, Scientologists, among many others. Religion, in both traditional and new forms, has become the latest "transnational variable" of globalization.[11]

One cause and consequence of this great awakening of religion around the globe is that the ambit of religious rights has been substantially expanded. In the past two decades, more than 150 major new statutes and constitutional provisions on religious rights have been promulgated — guaranteeing liberty of conscience, religious pluralism and equality, free exercise of religion, nondiscrimination on religious grounds, autonomy for religious groups, among other norms. These national guarantees have been matched with a growing body of regional and international norms, notably the 1981 UN Declaration on Intolerance and Discrimination Based upon Religion and Belief and the long catalog of religious-group rights set out in the 1989 Vienna Concluding Document and its progeny.[12]

On the other hand, this very same human rights revolution has helped catalyze new forms of religious and ethnic conflict, oppression, and belligerence of tragic proportions. In some communities, such as the former Yugoslavia, local religious and ethnic rivals, previously kept at bay by a common oppressor, have converted their new liberties into licenses to renew ancient hostilities, with catastrophic results. In other communities, such as the Sudan and Rwanda, ethnic nationalism and religious extremism have conspired to bring violent dislocation and death to hundreds of rival religious believers each year, and persecution, false imprisonment, forced

---

10. See Abdullahi Ahmed An-Na'im, ed., *Proselytization and Communal Self-Determination in Africa* (Maryknoll, N.Y.: Orbis Books, 1999).

11. See Susanne Hoeber Rudolph and James Piscatori, eds., *Transnational Religion and Fading States* (Boulder, Colo.: Westview Press, 1997).

12. For a good sampling, see Tad Stahnke and J. Paul Martin, eds., *Religion and Human Rights: Basic Documents* (New York: Columbia Center for the Study of Human Rights, 1998). For analysis, see Kevin Boyle and Juliet Sheen, *Freedom of Religion and Belief: A World Report* (London and New York: Routledge, 1997); Malcolm D. Evans, *Religious Liberty and International Law in Europe* (Cambridge: Cambridge University Press, 1997); John Witte, Jr., and Johan D. van der Vyver, eds., *Religious Human Rights in Global Perspective*, vol. 1: *Religious Perspectives;* vol. 2: *Legal Perspectives* (The Hague and Boston: Martinus Nijhoff, 1996). Cited hereafter as *Religious Human Rights I* and *II.*

starvation, and savage abuses of thousands of others. In other communities, most notably in North America and Western Europe, political secularism and nationalism have combined to threaten a sort of civil denial and death to a number of believers, particularly "sects" and "cults" of high religious temperature or of low cultural conformity.[13] In still other communities, from Asia to the Middle East, Christians have faced sharply increased restrictions and repression, sometimes even martyrdom.

In Russia and parts of Eastern Europe, Africa, and Latin America, this human rights revolution has brought on something of a new war for souls between indigenous and foreign religious groups. This is the most recent, and the most ironic, chapter in the Dickensian drama. With the political transformations of these regions in the past decade, foreign religious groups have been granted rights to enter these regions for the first time in decades. In the early 1990s, they came in increasing numbers to preach their gospels, to offer their services, to convert new souls. Initially, local religious groups welcomed these foreigners. Today they have come to resent these foreign religions, particularly those from North America and Western Europe who assume a democratic human rights ethic. Local religious groups resent the participation in the marketplace of religious ideas that democracy assumes. They resent the toxic waves of materialism and individualism that democracy inflicts. They resent the massive expansion of religious pluralism that democracy encourages. They resent the extravagant forms of religious speech, press, and assembly that democracy protects.

A new war for souls has thus broken out in these regions — a war to reclaim the traditional cultural and moral souls of these new societies and a war to retain adherence and adherents to the indigenous faiths. In part, this is a theological war, as rival religious communities have begun actively to demonize and defame each other and to gather themselves into ever more dogmatic and fundamentalist stands. The ecumenical spirit of the previous decades is giving way to sharp new forms of religious balkanization. In part, this is a legal war, as local religious groups have begun to conspire with their political leaders to adopt statutes and regulations restricting the constitutional rights of their foreign religious rivals. Beneath a shiny constitutional veneer

---

13. See, e.g., "Endbericht der Enquete-Kommission 'Sogennante Sekten und Psychogruppen,'" (Final report of the Enquete Commission: So-called sects and psychological groups") *Deutscher Bundestag 13.* Wahlperiode Drucksche 13/10950 (June 6, 1998).

of religious rights and freedom for all, a number of countries have come to develop a legal culture of overt favoritism of some faiths and overt oppression of others. Indeed, a good deal of the world seems to be at the dawn of a new era of religious establishments.

Such Dickensian paradoxes have exposed the limitations of a secular human rights paradigm standing alone. They have inspired the earnest search for additional resources to deter violence, resolve disputes, cultivate peace, ensure security — in dialogue, liturgical healing, ceremonies of reconciliation, and more.[14] Human rights are as much the problem as they are the solution in a number of current religious and cultural conflicts. In the current war for souls in Russia, for example, two absolute principles of human rights have come into direct conflict: the foreign religion's free-exercise right to share and expand its faith versus the indigenous religion's liberty-of-conscience right to be left alone on its own territory. Or, put in Christian theological terms, it is one group's rights to abide by the Great Commission ("Go therefore and make disciples of all nations") versus another group's right to insist on the Golden Rule ("Whatever you wish that men would do to you, do so to them").[15] Further rights talk alone cannot resolve this dispute. Likewise, many of the nations given to belligerent religious nationalism have ratified more of the international human rights instruments than the United States has and have crafted more elaborate bills of rights than what appears in the U.S. Constitution.[16] Here, too, further rights talk alone is insufficient.

These paradoxes of the modern human rights revolution underscore an elementary, but essential, point — that human rights norms need a human rights culture to be effective. "Declarations are not deeds," John Noonan reminds us. "[A] form of words by itself secures nothing; words pregnant with meaning in one culture may be entirely barren in another."[17] Human rights norms have little

14. See Donald W. Shriver, "Religion and Violence Prevention," in *Cases and Strategies for Prevention Action,* ed. Barnett R. Rubin (New York: Century Foundation Press, 1998), 169; Wolfgang Huber and Hans-Richard Reuter, *Friedensethik* (Stuttgart: W. Kohlhammer, 1990); Douglas Johnston and Cynthia Sampson, eds., *Religion: The Missing Dimension of Statecraft* (New York: Oxford University Press, 1994).

15. Matthew 7:12; 28:19–20; Mark 16:15–18; Acts 1:8 (RSV).

16. See Johan D. van der Vyver, "Universality and Relativism of Human Rights: American Relativism," *Buffalo Human Rights Law Review* 4 (1998): 43–78.

17. John T. Noonan, Jr., "The Tensions and the Ideals," in *Religious Human Rights II,* 594.

salience in societies that lack constitutional processes to give them meaning and measure. They have little value for parties who lack basic rights to security, succor, and sanctuary, or who are deprived of basic freedoms of speech, press, or association. They have little pertinence for victims who lack standing in courts and other basic procedural rights to pursue apt remedies. They have little cogency in communities that lack the ethos and ethic to render human rights violations a source of shame and regret, restraint and respect, confession and responsibility, reconciliation and restitution. As we have moved from the first generation of human rights declarations following World War II to the current generation of human rights implementation, this need for a human rights culture has become all the more pressing.[18]

These paradoxes, when viewed in their religious dimensions, suggest further that religion and human rights need to be brought into a closer symbiosis. On the one hand, human rights norms need religious narratives to ground them. There is, of course, some value in simply declaring human rights norms of "liberty, equality, and fraternity" or "life, liberty, and property"—if for no other reason than to pose an ideal against which a person or community might measure itself, to preserve a normative totem for later generations to make real. But ultimately these abstract human rights ideals of the good life and the good society depend on the visions and values of human communities and institutions to give them content and coherence, to provide what Jacques Maritain once called "the scale of values governing the[ir] exercise and concrete manifestation."[19] It is here that religion must play a vital role. Religion is an ineradicable condition of human lives and human communities. Religions invariably provide many of the sources and "scales of values" by which many persons and communities govern themselves. Religions inevitably help to define the meanings and measures of shame and regret, restraint and respect, responsibility and restitution that a human rights regime presupposes. Religions must thus be seen as indispensable allies in the modern struggle for human rights. To exclude them from the struggle is impossible, indeed catastrophic. To include them—to enlist their unique resources and to protect their

18. See Jerome J. Shestack, "Globalization of Human Rights Law," *Fordham International Law Journal* 21 (1997): 558.

19. Jacques Maritain, introduction to UNESCO, *Human Rights: Comments and Interpretations* (New York: United Nations, 1949), 15–16.

unique rights — is vital to enhancing the regime of human rights and to blunting some of the worst paradoxes that currently beset it.

On the other hand, religious narratives need human rights norms both to protect them and to challenge them. There is, of course, some value in religions simply accepting the current protections of a human rights regime — the guarantees of liberty of conscience, free exercise, religious-group autonomy, and the like. But passive acquiescence in a secular scheme of human rights ultimately will not do. Religious communities must reclaim their own voices within the secular human rights dialogue, and reclaim the human rights voices within their own internal religious dialogues. Contrary to conventional wisdom, the theory and law of human rights are neither new nor secular in origin. Human rights are, in substantial part, the modern political fruits of ancient religious beliefs and practices — ancient Jewish constructions of covenant and *mitzvot,* original Qur'anic texts on peace and the common good, medieval Catholic concepts of *ius* and *libertas,* classic Protestant ideals of freedom and law. Religious communities must be open to a new "human rights hermeneutic" — fresh methods of interpreting their sacred texts and traditions that will allow them to reclaim their essential roots and roles in the cultivation of human rights. Religious traditions cannot allow secular human rights norms to be imposed on them from without; they must rediscover them from within. It is only then that religious traditions can bring their full doctrinal rigor, liturgical healing, and moral suasion to bear on the problems and paradoxes of the modern human rights regime.

Religion and Human Rights

My first response to our modern Dickensian paradoxes is that religion, in all of its denominational multiplicity, must play a more active role in the modern human rights revolution. Many would consider this thesis to be fundamentally misguided. For even the great religions of the Book do not speak unequivocally about human rights, and none has amassed an exemplary human rights record over the centuries. Their sacred texts and canons say much more about commandments and obligations than about liberties and rights. Their theologians and jurists have resisted the importation of human rights as much as they have helped in their cultivation. Their internal policies and external advocacy have helped to perpetuate bigotry, chauvinism, and violence as much as they have served to propagate equality, liberty, and fraternity. The blood of thousands is at the doors of our churches, temples, and mosques. The bludgeons of pogroms, crusades, jihads, inquisitions, and ostracisms have been used to devastating effect within and among these faiths.

Moreover, the modern cultivation of human rights in the West began in earnest in the 1940s when both Christianity and the Enlightenment seemed incapable of delivering on their promises. In the middle of the twentieth century, there was no second coming of Christ promised by Christians, no heavenly city of reason promised by enlightened libertarians, no withering away of the state promised by enlightened socialists. Instead, there was world war, gulags, and the Holocaust — a vile and evil fascism and irrationalism to which Christianity and the Enlightenment seemed to have no cogent response or effective deterrent.

The modern human rights movement was thus born out of desperation in the aftermath of World War II. It was an attempt to find a world faith to fill a spiritual void. It was an attempt to harvest from the traditions of Christianity and the Enlightenment the rudimentary elements of a new faith and a new law that would unite a badly broken world order. The claims of Article I of the 1948 Universal Declaration of Human Rights — "That all men are born free and equal in rights and dignity [and] are endowed with reason and conscience" — expounded the primitive truths of Christianity and the Enlightenment with little basis in postwar world reality. Freedom and equality were hard to find anywhere. Reason and conscience had just blatantly betrayed themselves in the death camps, battlefields, and gulags.

Though desperate in origin, the human rights movement grew precociously in the decades following World War II. Indeed, after the 1950s a veritable "human rights revolution" erupted. In America and Europe, this rights revolution yielded a powerful grassroots civil rights movement and a welter of landmark cases and statutes. In Africa and Latin America, it produced agitation, and eventually revolt, against colonial and autocratic rule. At the international level, the Universal Declaration of 1948 inspired new declarations, covenants, and conventions on more discrete rights, most notably the 1966 Covenants. Within a generation, human rights had become the "new civic faith" of the postwar world order.[20]

---

20. Jacques Maritain, *Man and the State* (Chicago: University of Chicago Press, 1951), 110–11.

Christianity and other religions participated actively as midwives in the birth of this modern rights revolution, and special religious rights protections were at first actively pursued. Individual religious groups issued bold confessional statements and manifestoes on human rights shortly after World War II. Several denominations and budding ecumenical bodies joined Jewish NGOs in the cultivation of human rights at the international level. The Free Church tradition played a critical role in the civil rights movement in America and beyond, as did the social gospel and Christian democratic movements in Europe and Latin America.

After expressing some initial interest, however, leaders of the rights revolution consigned religious groups and their particular religious rights a low priority. Freedom of speech and press, parity of race and gender, provision of work and welfare captured most of the energy and emoluments of the rights revolution. After the early 1960s, academic inquiries and activist interventions into religious rights and their abuses became increasingly intermittent and isolated, inspired as much by parochial self-interest as by universal golden rules. The rights revolution seemed to be passing religion by.

This deprecation of the special role and rights of religions from the early 1960s onward has introduced several distortions into current human rights theory and law.

First, without religion, many rights are cut from their roots. The right to religion, Georg Jellinek wrote more than a century ago, is "the mother of many other rights."[21] For the religious individual, the right to believe leads ineluctably to the rights to assemble, speak, worship, evangelize, educate, parent, travel, or to abstain from the same on the basis of one's beliefs. For the religious association, the right to exist invariably involves rights to corporate property, collective worship, organized charity, parochial education, freedom of press, and autonomy of governance. To ignore religious rights is to overlook the conceptual, and historical, source of many other individual and associational rights.

Second, without religion, the regime of human rights becomes infinitely expandable. The classic faiths of the Book adopt and advocate human rights in order to protect religious duties. A religious individual or association has rights to exist and act not in the abstract but in order to discharge discrete duties of the faith. Religious

---

21. Georg Jellinek, *Die Erklärung der Menschen- und Bürgerrechte: Ein Beitrag zur modernen Verfassungsgeschichte* (Leipzig, 1895), 42.

theories of rights provide a vital rationale for the organic linkage between rights and duties. Without them, rights become abstract, with no obvious limit on their exercise or their expansion.

Third, without religion, human rights becomes too captive to Western libertarian ideals. Many religious traditions — whether of Buddhist, Confucian, Hindu, Islamic, Orthodox, Reformed, Taoist, or traditional stock — cannot conceive of, or accept, a system of rights that excludes religion. Religion is for these traditions inextricably integrated into every facet of life. Religious rights are, for them, an inherent part of rights of speech, press, assembly, and other individual rights as well as ethnic, cultural, linguistic, and similar associational rights. No system of rights that ignores or deprecates this cardinal place of religion can be respected or adopted.

Fourth, without religion, the state is given an exaggerated role as the guarantor of human rights. The simple state-versus-individual dialectic of many modern human rights theories leaves it to the state to protect and provide rights of all sorts. In reality, the state is not, and cannot be, so omni-competent. Numerous "mediating structures" stand between the state and the individual, religious institutions prominently among them. Religious institutions, among others, play a vital role in the cultivation and realization of rights. They can create the conditions (sometimes the prototypes) for the realization of first-generation civil and political rights. They can provide a critical (sometimes the principal) means to meet second-generation rights of education, work, health care, child care, artistic opportunities, among others. They can offer some of the deepest insights into norms of creation, stewardship, and servanthood that lie at the heart of third-generation rights.

The challenge of the twenty-first century will be to transform religious communities from midwives to mothers of human rights — from agents that assist in the birth of rights norms conceived elsewhere to associations that give birth and nurture to their own unique contributions to human rights norms and practices.

Human Rights and Religion

This leads to my second response to the Dickensian paradoxes of our modern human rights revolution: Human rights must have a more prominent place in the theological discourse of modern religions. Many would consider this second thesis to be as misguided as the first. It is one thing for religious bodies to accept the freedom and autonomy that a human rights regime allows. This at least gives them unencumbered space to pursue their divine callings. It is quite another thing for religious bodies to import human rights within their own polities and theologies. This exposes them to all manner of unseemly challenges.

Human rights norms, religious skeptics argue, challenge the structure of religious bodies. While human rights norms teach liberty and equality, most religious bodies teach authority and hierarchy. While human rights norms encourage pluralism and diversity, many religious bodies require orthodoxy and uniformity. While human rights norms teach freedoms of speech and petition, several religions teach duties of silence and submission. To draw human rights norms into the structures of religion would only seem to embolden members to demand greater access to religious governance, greater freedom from religious discipline, greater latitude in the definition of religious doctrine and liturgy. So why import them?

Moreover, human rights norms challenge the spirit of religious bodies. Human rights norms, religious skeptics argue, are the creed of a secular faith born of the Enlightenment. Human rights advocates regularly describe these norms as our new "civic faith," "our new world religion," "our new global moral language."[22] The French jurist Karel Vasak has pressed these sentiments into a full and famous confession of the secular spirit of the modern human rights movement:

> The Universal Declaration of Human Rights [of 1948], like the French Declaration of the Rights of Man and Citizen in 1789, has had an immense impact throughout the world. It has been called a modern edition of the New Testament, and the Magna Carta of humanity, and has become a constant source of inspiration for governments, for judges, and for national and international legislators.... By recognizing the Universal Declaration as a living document...one can proclaim one's faith in the future of mankind.[23]

In demonstration of this new faith, Vasak converted the "old trinity" of "liberté, égalité, et fraternité" taught by the French Revolution into a "new trinity" of "three generations of rights" for all

22. Robert Traer, *Faith in Human Rights* (Washington, D.C.: Ethics and Public Policy Center, 1991), 10–11.

23. Karel Vasak, "A Thirty-Year Struggle," *UNESCO Courier* (November 1977): 31–32.

humanity. The first generation of civil and political rights elaborates the meaning of *liberté*. The second generation of social, cultural, and economic rights elaborates the meaning of *égalité*. The third generation of solidarity rights to development, peace, health, the environment, and open communication elaborates the meaning of *fraternité*.[24] Such language has become not only the lingua franca but also something of the lingua sacra of the modern human rights movement.[25] Given such an overt secular confession, religious skeptics conclude, a religious body would do well to resist the ideas and institutions of human rights.

Both these skeptical arguments, however, presuppose that human rights norms constitute a static belief system born of Enlightenment liberalism. But the human rights regime is not static. It is fluid, elastic, open to challenge and change. The human rights regime is not a fundamental belief system. It is a relative system of ideas and ideals that presupposes the existence of fundamental beliefs and values that will constantly reshape it. The human rights regime is not the child of Enlightenment liberalism, nor a ward under its exclusive guardianship. It is the *jus gentium* of our times, the common law of nations, which a variety of Hebrew, Greek, Roman, Christian, and Enlightenment movements have historically nurtured in the West and which today still needs the constant nurture of multiple communities. It is beyond doubt that current formulations of human rights are suffused with fundamental libertarian beliefs and values, some of which run counter to the cardinal beliefs of various religious traditions. But libertarianism does not have a monopoly on the nurture of human rights; indeed, a human rights regime cannot long survive under its exclusive patronage.

I use the antique term *jus gentium* advisedly — to signal the place of human rights as "middle axioms" in our moral and political discourse.[26] Historically, Hebrew, Greek, Roman, and Christian writers

---

24. Karel Vasak, "Pour une troisème génération des droits de l'homme," in *Études et essais sur le droit international humanitaire et sur les principes de la Croix-Rouge en l'honneur de Jean Pictet,* ed. Christophe Swinarksi (Geneva and the Hague: Martinus Nijhoff, 1984), 837–45.

25. See, e.g., Burns H. Weston, "Human Rights," *Human Rights Quarterly* 6 (1984): 257; Joy Gordon, "The Concept of Human Rights: The History and Meaning of Its Politicization," *Brooklyn Journal of International Law* 23 (1998): 689.

26. See comparable comments, from a Catholic perspective, by Maritain, *Man and the State,* 97–101, and by Robert P. George, "Response," in Michael Cromartie, ed., *A Preserving Grace: Protestants, Catholics, and Natural Law* (Washington, D.C.: Ethics and Public Policy Center, 1997), 157–72.

alike spoke of a hierarchy of laws — from natural law (*ius naturale*), to common law (*jus gentium*), to positive law (*ius civile*). The natural law was the set of immutable principles of reason and conscience, which are supreme in authority and divinity and must always prevail in instances of dispute. The positive law was the set of enacted laws and procedures of local political communities, reflecting their immediate policies and procedures. Between these two sets of norms was the *jus gentium,* the set of principles and customs common to several communities and often the basis for treaties and other diplomatic conventions. The contents of the *jus gentium* did gradually change over time and across cultures as new interpretations of the natural law were offered, and as new formulations of the positive law became increasingly conventional. But the *jus gentium* was a relatively consistent body of principles governing a person and a people.

This antique typology helps us understand the intermediate place of human rights in our hierarchy of legal norms today. Human rights law is the *jus gentium* of our time, the middle axiom of our discourse. It is derived from and dependent on the transcendent principles that religious traditions (more than other groups) continue to cultivate. And it informs, and is informed by, shifts in the customs and conventions of sundry state law systems. This human rights law does gradually change over time: just compare the international human rights instruments of 1948 with those of today. But human rights norms are a relatively stable set of ideals by which a person and community might be guided and judged.

This antique typology also helps us understand the place of human rights within religion. My argument that human rights must have a more prominent place within religions today is not an attempt to import libertarian ideals into their theologies and polities. It is not an attempt to herd Trojan horses into churches, synagogues, mosques, and temples in order to assail their spirit and structure in secret. My argument is, rather, that religious bodies must again assume their traditional patronage and protection of human rights, bringing to this regime their full doctrinal vigor, liturgical healing, and moral suasion. Using our antique typology, religious bodies must again nurture and challenge the middle axioms of the *jus gentium* with the transcendent principles of the *ius naturale*. This must not be an effort to monopolize the discourse, nor to establish by positive law a particular religious construction of human rights.[27]

27. For comparable arguments regarding prophetic and pluralistic religious wit-

Such an effort must be part of a collective discourse of competing understandings of the *ius naturale* — of competing theological views of the divine and the human, of sin and salvation, of individuality and community — that will serve constantly to inform and reform, to develop and deepen, the human rights ideals now in place.[28]

A Human Rights Hermeneutic within Religion

Several religious traditions, of late, have begun this process of reengaging the regime of human rights, of returning to their traditional roots and routes of nurturing and challenging the human rights regime. This process has been clumsy, casuistic, controversial, at times even fatal for its proponents. But the process of religious engagement of human rights is under way — in Christian, Islamic, Judaic, Buddhist, Hindu, and traditional communities alike. Something of a new "human rights hermeneutic" is slowly beginning to emerge among modern religions.[29]

This is, in part, a hermeneutic of confession. Given their checkered human rights records over the centuries, religious bodies have begun to acknowledge their departures from the cardinal teachings of peace and love that are the heart of their sacred texts and traditions. Christian churches have taken the lead in this process — from the Second Vatican Council's confession of prior complicity

---

ness in politics, see Duncan B. Forrester, *Christian Justice and Public Policy* (Cambridge: Cambridge University Press, 1997); Glenn Tinder, *The Political Meaning of Christianity: The Prophetic Stance* (San Francisco: HarperSanFrancisco, 1991); and idem, *The Fabric of Hope: An Essay* (Atlanta: Scholars Press, 1999).

28. See Wolfgang Huber, "Human Rights and Biblical Legal Thought," in *Religious Human Rights I,* 47–64, at 59ff., and idem, *Gerechtigkeit und Recht: Grundlinien christlicher Rechtsethik* (Gütersloh: Chr. Kaiser, 1996), 252ff., 366ff., 446ff.; Jerome J. Shestack, "The Jurisprudence of Human Rights," in *Human Rights in International Law: Legal and Policy Issues,* ed. Theodor Meron (Oxford: Clarendon Press, 1984), 69–113, at 75ff.

29. See, e.g., Abdullahi Ahmed An-Na'im, *Toward an Islamic Reformation: Civil Liberties, Human Rights, and International Law* (Syracuse: Syracuse University Press, 1990); David Novak, *Covenantal Rights* (Princeton: Princeton University Press, 2000); Max Stackhouse, *Creeds, Society, and Human Rights* (Grand Rapids, Mich.: Eerdmans, 1984), esp. 51–139; Huber, *Gerechtigkeit und Recht,* esp. 158–83, 222–321, 362–419. On emerging rights talk within various Asian and African religions, see Joanne R. Bauer and Daniel A. Bell, *The East Asian Challenge for Human Rights* (Cambridge: Cambridge University Press, 1999); Wm. Theodore de Bary and Tu Weiming, eds., *Confucianism and Human Rights* (New York: Columbia University Press, 1998); Irene Bloom, J. Paul Martin, and Wayne L. Proudfoot, eds., *Religious Diversity and Human Rights* (New York: Columbia University Press, 1996).

in authoritarianism to the contemporary church's repeated confessions of prior support for apartheid, communism, racism, sexism, fascism, and anti-Semitism.[30] Other communities have also begun this process — from recent Muslim academics' condemnations of the politicization of "jihad" to the Dalai Lama's recent lamentations over the "sometimes sorry human rights record" of his own tradition, as well as rival traditions.[31]

This is, in part, a "hermeneutic of suspicion" (in Paul Ricoeur's phrase). Given the pronounced libertarian tone of many recent human rights formulations, a number of religious writers urge that we not idolize or idealize these formulations. We must not be bound by current taxonomies of "three generations of rights" rooted in liberty, equality, and fraternity, several writers argue. Common-law formulations of "life, liberty, or property," canon-law formulations of "natural, ecclesiastical, and civil rights," or Protestant formulations of "civil, theological, and pedagogical uses of rights" might well be more apt classification schemes. We must not accept the seemingly infinite expansion of human rights discourse and demands. Rights bounded by moral duties, by natural capacities, or by covenantal relationships might well provide better boundaries to the legitimate expression and extension of rights. And we must not be bound only to a centralized, legal methodology of articulating and enforcing rights. We might also consider a more pluralistic model of interpretation that respects "the right of the [local] community to be the living frame of interpretation for their own religion and its normative regime."[32]

This is, in part, a hermeneutic of history. While acknowledging the fundamental contributions of Enlightenment liberalism to the modern rights regime, a number of religious writers have also pressed us to see the deeper genesis and genius of many modern rights norms in religious texts and traditions that antedate the Enlightenment by centuries, sometimes millennia. They have urged a return to these religious sources. In part, this is a return to an-

---

30. See, e.g., Luke Timothy Johnson, "Religious Rights and Christian Texts," in *Religious Human Rights I*, 65, 70–73; Charles Villa-Vicencio, *A Theology of Reconstruction: Nation Building and Human Rights* (Cambridge: Cambridge University Press, 1992).

31. Commencement address of the Dalai Lama at Emory University, May 11, 1998.

32. Abdullahi Ahmed An-Na'im, "Towards an Islamic Hermeneutics for Human Rights," in A. An-Na'im et al., eds., *Religion and Human Rights Values: An Uneasy Relationship* (Grand Rapids, Mich.: Eerdmans, 1995), 229–42, at 235.

cient sacred texts freed from the casuistic accretions of generations of jurists and from the cultural trappings of the communities in which these traditions were born. In part, this is a return to slender streams of theological jurisprudence that have not been part of the mainstream of the religious traditions, or that have become diluted by too great a commingling with it. In part, this is a return to prophetic voices of dissent, long purged from traditional religious canons, but, in retrospect, prescient of some of the roles in human rights that the tradition might play today.

Permit me to illustrate this budding new human rights hermeneutic using my own tradition of Christianity. There are various ways to tell the Christian part of this story. One can analyze the rights contributions of seminal figures from Christ and the early church fathers onward. One can sift through the complex patterns of rights talk of various regional and national Christian groups. One can dig into the daily rights narratives of discrete communities of the faithful in different social and political contexts. Ultimately, these and other genres of analysis will need to be pursued and combined to come to full terms with the Christian church's past and potential contribution to human rights.

To outline the main story here, I shall analyze briefly the rights contributions of the Catholic and Protestant traditions. These two traditions have built on the same biblical and patristic precedents, but each has offered a distinctive human rights perspective and practice.[33]

Human Rights and Catholicism

The Roman Catholic Church is, paradoxically, the first and the last tradition within Christianity to embrace the doctrine of human rights. At the opening of the second millennium of the common era, the Catholic Church led the first great "human rights movement" of the West in the name of "freedom of the church" (*libertas ecclesiae*). During the papal revolution of Pope Gregory VII (1073–85) and his successors, the Catholic clergy threw off their royal and civil oppressors and established the church as an autonomous le-

---

33. For discussion of the Eastern Orthodox contribution, see Witte and Bordeaux, *Proselytism and Orthodoxy in Russia,* and Witte, " 'Dickensian Era' of Human Rights."

gal and political corporation within Western Christendom.[34] For the first time, the church successfully claimed jurisdiction over such persons as clerics, pilgrims, students, Jews, and Muslims and over such subjects as doctrine and liturgy; ecclesiastical property, polity, and patronage; marriage and family relations; education, charity, and inheritance; oral promises, oaths, and various contracts; and all manner of moral and ideological crimes. The church predicated these jurisdictional claims in part on Christ's famous delegation of the keys to Peter (Matt. 16:18) — a key of knowledge to discern God's word and will, and a key of power to implement and enforce that word and will by law. The church also predicated these new claims on its traditional authority over the form and function of the Christian sacraments. By the fifteenth century, the church had gathered around the seven sacraments systems of canon-law rules that prevailed throughout the West.[35]

The medieval canon law was based, in part, on the concept of individual and corporate rights (*iura,* the plural of *ius*). The canon law defined the rights of the clergy to their liturgical offices and ecclesiastical benefices, their exemptions from civil taxes and duties, their immunities from civil prosecution and compulsory testimony. It defined the rights of ecclesiastical organizations like parishes, monasteries, charities, and guilds to form and dissolve, to accept and reject members, to establish order and discipline, to acquire, use, and alienate property. It defined the rights of church councils and synods to participate in the election and discipline of bishops, abbots, and other clergy. It defined the rights of the laity to worship, evangelize, maintain religious symbols, participate in the sacraments, travel on religious pilgrimages, and educate their children. It defined the rights of the poor, widows, and needy to seek solace, succor, and sanctuary within the church. A good deal of the rich latticework of medieval canon law was cast, substantively and procedurally, in the form and language of rights.[36]

---

34. See Harold J. Berman, *Law and Revolution: The Formation of the Western Legal Tradition* (Cambridge: Harvard University Press, 1983).

35. Udo Wolter, "Amt und Officium in mittelalterlichen Quellen von 13. bis 15. Jahrhunderts," *Zeitschrift der Savigny-Stiftung* (Kanonische Abteilung) 105 (1988): 246; R. H. Helmholz, *The Spirit of Classical Canon Law* (Athens: University of Georgia, 1996).

36. See sources and discussion in Brian Tierney, *The Idea of Natural Rights: Studies on Natural Rights, Natural Law, and Church Law, 1150–1625* (Atlanta: Scholars Press, 1997); idem, *Rights, Law, and Infallibility in Medieval Thought* (Aldershot, England: Variorum, 1997); Charles J. Reid, Jr., "Thirteenth-Century Canon Law

To be sure, such rights were not unguided by duties. Nor were they available to all parties. Only the Catholic faithful—and notoriously not Jews, Muslims, or heretics—had full rights protection, and their rights were to be exercised with appropriate ecclesiastical and sacramental constraints. But the basic medieval rights formulations of exemptions, immunities, privileges, and benefits, and the free exercise of religious worship, travel, speech, and education have persisted, with ever greater inclusivity, to this day. Many of the common formulations of individual and collective rights and liberties in vogue today were first forged not by a John Locke or a James Madison, but by twelfth- and thirteenth-century canonists and theologians.

It was, in part, the perceived excesses of the sixteenth-century Protestant Reformation that closed the door to the Catholic Church's own secular elaboration of this refined rights regime. The Council of Trent (1545–63) confirmed, with some modifications, the internal rights structure of the canon law, and these formulations were elaborated in the writings of Spanish and Portuguese neoscholastics.[37] But the church left it largely to nonchurch bodies and non-Catholic believers to draw out the secular implications of the medieval human rights tradition. The Catholic Church largely tolerated Protestant and humanist rights efforts in the later sixteenth century and beyond, which built on biblical and canon law foundations. The church grew increasingly intolerant, however, of the rights theories of the Enlightenment, which built on secular theories of individualism and rationalism. Enlightenment teachings on liberties, rights, and separation of church and state conflicted directly with Catholic teachings on natural law, the common good, and subsidiarity. The church's intolerance of such formulations gave way to outright hostility after the French Revolution, most notably in the blistering *Syllabus of Errors* of 1864. Notwithstanding the social teachings of subsequent instruments such as *Rerum Novarum* (1891) and *Quadragesimo Anno* (1934), the Catholic Church had little patience with the human rights reforms and democratic regimes of the later nineteenth and early twentieth centuries. It acquiesced more readily in the authoritative regimes and policies that governed the European, Latin American, and African nations where Catholicism was strong.[38]

---

and Rights: The Word *ius* and Its Range of Subjective Meanings," *Studia Canonica* 30 (1996): 295.

37. See Tierney, *Idea of Natural Rights*, 255–315.

38. For documents, see Sidney Z. Ehler and John B. Morrall, eds., *Church and*

The Second Vatican Council (1962–65) and its progeny transformed the Catholic Church's theological attitude toward human rights and democracy. In a series of sweeping new doctrinal statements — from *Mater et Magistra* (1961) onward — the church came to endorse many of the very same human rights and democratic principles that it had spurned a century before. First, the church endorsed human rights and liberties — not only in the internal, canon-law context but also now in a global, secular-law context. Every person, the church taught, is created by God with "dignity, intelligence and free will... and has rights flowing directly and simultaneously from his very nature."[39] Such rights include the right to life and adequate standards of living, to moral and cultural values, to religious activities, to assembly and association, to marriage and family life, and to various social, political, and economic benefits and opportunities. The church emphasized the religious rights of conscience, worship, assembly, and education, calling them the "first rights" of any civic order. The church also stressed the need to balance individual and associational rights, particularly those involving the church, family, and school. Governments everywhere were encouraged to create conditions conducive to the realization and protection of these "inviolable rights" and to root out every type of discrimination, whether social or cultural, whether based on sex, race, color, social distinction, language, or religion. Second, as a corollary, the church advocated limited constitutional government, disestablishment of religion, and the separation of church and state. The vast pluralism of religions and cultures, and the inherent dangers in state endorsement of any religion, in the church's view, rendered mandatory such democratic forms of government.[40]

Vatican II and its progeny transformed not only the theological attitude but also the social actions of the Catholic Church respecting human rights and democracy. After Vatican II, the church was less centralized and more socially active. Local bishops and clergy

---

State through the Centuries (Westminster, Md.: Newman, 1954). For discussion, see Mary Elsbernd, "Papal Statements on Rights: A Historical-Contextual Study of Encyclical Teachings from Pius VI–Pius XI (1791–1939)" (Ph.D. diss., Catholic University of Louvain, 1985).

39. *Pacem in Terris* (1963), paragraph 9.

40. See esp. *Dignitatis Humanae* (On religious freedom) (1965). See commentary in David Hollenbach, *Claims in Conflict: Retrieving and Renewing the Catholic Human Rights Tradition* (New York: Paulist Press, 1979); George Weigel and Robert Royal, eds., *A Century of Catholic Social Thought: Essays on "Rerum Novarum" and Nine Other Key Documents* (Washington, D.C.: Ethics and Public Policy Center, 1991).

were given greater autonomy and incentive to participate in local and national affairs, to bring the church's new doctrines to bear on matters political and cultural. Particularly in North America and Europe, bishops and bishops' conferences became active in cultivating and advocating a variety of political and legal reforms. Likewise, in Latin America, the rise of liberation theologies and base communities helped to translate many of the enduring and evolving rights perspectives of the church into intensely active social and political programs. The Catholic Church was thereby transformed from a passive accomplice in authoritarian regimes to a powerful advocate of democratic and human rights reform.

The Catholic church has been a critical force in the new wave of political democratization that has been breaking over the world since the early 1970s — both through the announcements and interventions of the papal see, and through the efforts of its local clergy. New democratic and human rights movements in Brazil, Chile, Central America, the Philippines, South Korea, Poland, Hungary, the Czech Republic, Ukraine, and elsewhere owe much of their inspiration to the teaching and activity of the Catholic Church.[41]

The Catholic Church has thus come full circle. The church led the first human rights movement of the West at the opening of the second millennium. It stands ready to lead the church's next human rights movement at the opening of the third millennium — equipped with a refined theology and law of human rights and some one billion members worldwide. The Catholic Church offers a unique combination of local and global, confessional and universal human rights strategies for the twenty-first century. Within the internal forum and the canon law, the church has a distinctly Catholic human rights framework that protects especially the second-generation rights of education, charity, and health care within a sacramental and sacerdotal context. Within the external forum of the world and its secular law, however, the church has a decidedly universal human rights framework that advocates especially first-generation civil and political rights for all. Critics view this two-pronged human rights ministry as a self-serving attempt to advocate equality and liberty outside the church, but to perpetuate patriarchy and elitism

41. See J. Bryan Hehir, "Religious Activism for Human Rights," in *Religious Human Rights I,* 107–19; George Weigel, *The Final Revolution: The Resistance Church and the Collapse of Communism* (New York: Oxford University Press, 1992).

within.[42] But this criticism has had little apparent effect. The Catholic Church's human rights ministry, if pursued with the zealotry shown by the current episcopacy, promises to have a monumental effect on law, religion, and human rights in the twenty-first century.

Human Rights and Protestantism

One of the ironies of the contemporary human rights movement is the relative silence of the Protestant churches. Historically, Protestant churches produced the most refined theories and laws of human rights. Today, many Protestant churches have been content simply to confirm human rights norms and to condemn human rights abuses without deep corporate theological reflection. To be sure, some leading Protestant lights have taken up the subject in their writings.[43] A number of Protestant groups within the church, particularly new liberationist and feminist groups, have developed important new themes. The American civil rights movement found some of its strongest support among Baptist, Methodist, and other Free Churches. But, to date, no comprehensive and systematic human rights theory or program has taken the Protestant field: twentieth-century Protestantism has produced no John Courtney Murray and no Vatican II.

The irony is that the Protestant Reformation was, in effect, the second great human rights movement of the West. Prior to the sixteenth century, there was one universal Catholic faith and church, one universal system of canon law and sacramental life, one universal hierarchy of courts and administrators centered in Rome that ruled throughout much of the West. Martin Luther, John Calvin, Thomas Cranmer, Menno Simons, and other sixteenth-century Reformers all began their movements with a call for freedom from this ecclesiastical regime — freedom of the individual conscience from intrusive canon laws and clerical controls, freedom of political officials from ecclesiastical power and privileges, freedom of the local clergy from central papal rule and oppressive princely controls. "Freedom of the Christian" became the rallying cry of the early Reformation. It drove theologians and jurists, clergy and laity,

42. See sources and discussion in William Johnson Everett, "Human Rights in the Church," in *Religious Human Rights I,* 121.

43. See, e.g., Stackhouse, *Creeds, Society, and Human Rights;* Huber, *Menschenrechte;* Johan D. van der Vyver, *Seven Lectures on Human Rights* (Pretoria: Juta, 1977).

princes and peasants alike to denounce canon laws and ecclesiastical authorities with unprecedented alacrity, and to urge radical constitutional reforms.

The Protestant Reformation permanently broke the unity of law and religion in Western Christendom, and thereby introduced the foundations for the modern constitutional system of confessional pluralism. The Anglican Reformation nationalized the faith through the famous Supremacy Acts and the Act of Uniformity (1559) of the Church and Commonwealth of England. Citizens of the commonwealth were required to be communicants of the Church of England, subject to the final ecclesiastical and political authority of the monarch. The Toleration Act (1689) extended a modicum of rights to some Protestant dissenters. But it was not until the Jewish and Catholic Emancipation Acts of 1829 and 1833 that the national identity of the Church and Commonwealth of England was finally broken.[44]

The Lutheran Reformation territorialized the faith through the principle of *cuius regio, eius religio* (whosoever region, his religion) established by the Peace of Augsburg (1555). Under this principle, princes or city councils were authorized to prescribe the appropriate forms of Evangelical or Catholic doctrine, liturgy, and education for their polities — with religious dissenters granted the right to worship privately in their homes or to emigrate peaceably from the polity. After decades of bitter civil war, the Peace of Westphalia (1648) extended this privilege to Calvinists as well, rendering Germany and beyond a veritable honeycomb of religious plurality for the next two centuries.[45]

The Anabaptist Reformation communalized the faith by introducing what Menno Simmons called the *Scheidingsmaurer* — the wall of separation between the redeemed realm of religion and the fallen realm of the world. Anabaptist religious communities were ascetically withdrawn from the world into small, self-sufficient, intensely democratic communities, governed internally by biblical principles of discipleship, simplicity, charity, and Christian obedience. When such communities grew too large or too divided, they deliberately colonized themselves, eventually spreading the Anabap-

---

44. See sources in Carl Stephenson and Frederick G. Marcham, eds., *Sources of English Constitutional History*, rev. ed. (New York: Harper & Row, 1972).

45. See main legal sources in Ehler and Morrall, *Church and State through the Centuries*.

tist communities from Russia to Ireland and to the furthest frontiers of North America.[46]

The Calvinist Reformation congregationalized the faith by introducing rule by a democratically elected consistory of pastors, elders, and deacons. In John Calvin's day, the Geneva consistory was still appointed and held broad personal and subject-matter jurisdiction over all members of the city. By the seventeenth century, most Calvinist communities in Europe and North America had reduced the consistory to an elected, representative system of government within each church. These consistories featured separation among the offices of preaching, discipline, and charity, and a fluid, dialogical form of religious polity and policing centered around collective worship and the congregational meeting.[47]

The Protestant Reformation also broke the primacy of corporate Christianity and gave new emphasis to the role of the individual believer in the economy of salvation. This was true even in the more intensely communitarian traditions of Anglicanism and Anabaptism. The Anglican *Book of Common Prayer* was designed, in Thomas Cranmer's words, as a "textbook of liberty." The daily office of the lectionary, together with the vernacular Bible, encouraged the exercise of private devotion outside the church. The choices among liturgical rites and prayers within the prayer book encouraged the exercise of at least some clerical innovation within the church, with such opportunities for variation and innovation increasing with the 1662 and 1789 (Episcopalian) editions of the prayer book.

The Anabaptist doctrine of adult baptism gave new emphasis to a voluntarist understanding of religion, as opposed to conventional notions of a birthright or predestined faith. The adult individual was now called to make a conscientious choice to accept the faith — metaphorically, to scale the wall of separation between the fallen world and the realm of religion to come within the perfection of Christ. Later Free Church followers converted this cardinal image into a powerful platform of liberty of conscience, free exercise of re-

46. See sources and discussion in Walter Klaassen, ed., *Anabaptism in Outline: Selected Primary Sources* (Scottdale, Pa.: Herald Press, 1981); Robert Friedmann, *The Theology of Anabaptism* (Scottdale, Pa.: Herald Press, 1973); Guy Hershberger, ed., *The Recovery of the Anabaptist Vision* (Scottdale, Pa.: Herald Press, 1957); William C. McLoughlin, *New England Dissent, 1630–1833,* 2 vols. (Cambridge: Harvard University Press, 1971).

47. See sources and discussion in my "Moderate Religious Liberty in the Theology of John Calvin," *Calvin Theological Journal* 31 (1996): 359–403.

ligion, and separation of church and state—not only for Christians but eventually for all peaceable believers. Their views had a great influence on the formation of constitutional protections of religious liberty in eighteenth- and nineteenth-century North America and Western Europe.[48]

The Lutheran and Calvinist branches of the Reformation laid the anthropological basis for an even more expansive theory and law of rights. Classic Protestant theology teaches that a person is both saint and sinner. On the one hand, a person is created in the image of God and justified by faith in God. The person is called to a distinct vocation, which stands equal in dignity and sanctity to all others. The person is prophet, priest, and king and responsible to exhort, minister, and rule in the community. Every person, therefore, stands equal before God and before his or her neighbor. Every person is vested with a natural liberty to live, to believe, to serve God and neighbor. Every person is entitled to the vernacular scripture, to education, to work in a vocation. On the other hand, the person is sinful and prone to evil and egoism. He needs the restraint of the law to deter him from evil and to drive him to repentance. He needs the association of others to exhort, minister, and rule him with law and with love. Every person, therefore, is inherently a communal creature. Every person belongs to a family, a church, a political community.[49]

These social institutions of family, church, and state, Protestants believe, are divine in origin and human in organization. They are created by God and governed by godly ordinances. They stand equal before God and are called to discharge distinctive godly functions in the community. The family is called to rear and nurture children, to educate and discipline them, to exemplify love and cooperation. The church is called to preach the word, administer the sacraments, educate the young, aid the needy. The state is called to protect order, punish crime, promote community. Though divine in origin, these institutions are formed through human covenants. Such covenants confirm the divine functions, the created offices, of these institu-

48. See sources and discussion in Max L. Stackhouse and Deirdre King Hainsworth, "Deciding for God: The Right to Convert in Protestant Perspectives," 201–30, in *Sharing the Book: Religious Perspectives on the Rights and Wrongs of Mission,* ed. John Witte, Jr., and Richard C. Martin (Maryknoll, N.Y.: Orbis Books, 1999).

49. See sources and discussion in Witte, "Moderate Religious Liberty," and idem, *Law and Protestantism: The Legal Teachings of the Lutheran Reformation* (Cambridge: Cambridge University Press, forthcoming).

tions. Such covenants also organize these offices so that they are protected from the sinful excesses of officials who occupy them. Family, church, and state are thus organized as public institutions, accessible and accountable to each other and to their members. Particularly the church is to be organized as a democratic congregational polity, with a separation of ecclesiastical powers among pastors, elders, and deacons, election of officers to limited tenures of office, and ready participation of the congregation in the life and leadership of the church.[50]

Protestant groups in Europe and America cast these theological doctrines into democratic forms designed to protect human rights. Protestant doctrines of the person and society were cast into democratic social forms. Since all persons stand equal before God, they must stand equal before God's political agents in the state. Since God has vested all persons with natural liberties of life and belief, the state must ensure them of similar civil liberties. Since God has called all persons to be prophets, priests, and kings, the state must protect their freedoms to speak, to preach, and to rule in the community. Since God has created persons as social creatures, the state must promote and protect a plurality of social institutions, particularly the church and the family. Protestant doctrines of sin were cast into democratic political forms. The political office must be protected against the sinfulness of the political official. Political power, like ecclesiastical power, must be distributed among self-checking executive, legislative, and judicial branches. Officials must be elected to limited terms of office. Laws must be clearly codified, and discretion closely guarded. If officials abuse their office, they must be disobeyed; if they persist in their abuse, they must be removed, even by force.

These Protestant teachings helped to inspire many of the early modern revolutions fought in the name of human rights and democracy. They were the driving ideological forces behind the revolts of the French Huguenots, Dutch Pietists, and Scottish Presbyterians against their monarchical oppressors in the later sixteenth and seventeenth centuries. They were critical weapons in the arsenal of the revolutionaries in England, America, and France. They were important sources of the great age of democratic construction in later

50. See sources and discussion in Max L. Stackhouse, *Covenant and Commitments: Faith, Family, and Economic Life* (Louisville: Westminster/John Knox Press, 1996).

eighteenth- and nineteenth-century America and Western Europe. In the twentieth century, Protestant ideas of human rights and democracy helped to drive the constitutional reformation of Europe in the postwar period, and some of the human rights and democratic movements against colonial autocracy in Africa and against fascist revival in Latin America.[51]

These cardinal Protestant teachings and practices have much to offer to the regime of human rights in the twenty-first century. Protestant theology avoids the reductionist extremes of both libertarianism, which sacrifices the community for the individual, and totalitarianism, which sacrifices the individual for the community. It avoids the limitless expansion of human rights claims by grounding these norms in the creation order, divine callings, and covenant relationships. And it avoids uncritical adoption of human rights by judging their "civil, theological, and educational uses" in the lives of both individuals and communities. On this foundation, Protestant theology strikes unique balances between liberty and responsibility, dignity and depravity, individuality and community, politics and pluralism.

To translate these theological principles into human rights practices is the great challenge facing the Protestant churches in the immediate future. The Protestant tradition needs to have its own Vatican II, its own comprehensive and collective assessment of its future role in the human rights drama. Of course, Protestant congregationalism militates against such collective action, as do the many ancient animosities among Protestant sects. But this is no time for denominational snobbery or sniping. Protestants need to sow their own distinct seeds of human rights while the field is still open. Otherwise, there will be little time to harvest the fruits of what has been sown, and little room to plant in the twenty-first century.

Final Reflections

A number of distinguished commentators have recently encouraged the abandonment of the human rights paradigm altogether — as a tried and tired experiment that is no longer effective, even a fic-

51. See Michael Walzer, *The Revolution of the Saints: A Study in the Origins of Radical Politics* (Cambridge: Harvard University Press, 1965); Harold J. Berman, *Faith and Order: The Reconciliation of Law and Religion* (Atlanta: Scholars Press, 1993), 103–25.

tional faith whose folly has now been fully exposed.[52] Others have bolstered this claim with cultural critiques — that human rights are instruments of neocolonization which the West uses to impose its values on the rest, even toxic compounds that are exported abroad to breed cultural conflict, social instability, religious warfare, and thus dependence on the West.[53] Others have added philosophical critiques — that rights talk is the wrong talk for meaningful debate about deep questions of justice, peace, and the common good.[54] Still others have added theological critiques — that the secular beliefs in individualism, rationalism, and contractarianism inherent in the human rights paradigm cannot be squared with cardinal theological beliefs in creation, redemption, and covenant.[55]

Such criticisms properly soften the overly bright optimism of some human rights advocates. They properly curb the modern appetite for the limitless expansion and even monopolization of human rights in the quest for toleration, peace, and security. And they properly criticize the libertarian accents that still too often dominate our rights talk today. But such criticisms do not support the conclusion that we must abandon the human rights paradigm altogether — particularly when no viable alternative global forum is yet at hand. Instead, these criticisms support the proposition that the religious sources and dimensions of human rights need to be more robustly engaged and extended. Human rights norms are not a transient libertarian invention or an ornamental diplomatic convention. Human rights norms have grown out of millennium-long religious and cultural traditions. They have traditionally provided a forum and focus for sophisticated philosophical, theological, and political reflections on the common good and our common lives. And they have emerged today as part of the common law of the emerging world order. We should abandon these ancient principles

---

52. See samples and critical analysis of the views of Alasdair MacIntyre, Richard Rorty, Jean-François Lyotard, and others in Max L. Stackhouse and Stephen Healey, "Religion and Human Rights: A Theological Apologetic," in *Religious Human Rights I,* 485–516.

53. See critical discussion of this thesis, and its manifestations in recent debates about the cultural and moral relativity of human rights, in David Little, "Religion and Human Rights," *Journal of Religious Ethics* 27, no. 1 (1999), 151–77.

54. Mary Ann Glendon, *Rights Talk: The Impoverishment of Political Discourse* (New York: Maxwell MacMillan, 1991).

55. See esp. Joan Lockwood O'Donovan, "The Concept of Rights in Christian Moral Discourse," in Cromartie, *Preserving Grace,* 143–56; David Smolin, "Church, State, and International Human Rights," *Notre Dame Law Review* 73 (1998): 1515.

and practices only with trepidation, only with explanation, only with articulation of viable alternatives. To convert our tenured liberties into licenses to deconstruct human rights without posing real global alternatives is to insult the genius and the sacrifice of our forebears. For now, the human rights paradigm must stand, if nothing else, as the "null hypothesis." It must be constantly challenged to improve. But it should be discarded only on cogent proof of a better global norm and practice.

A number of other distinguished commentators have argued that religion can have no place in a modern regime of human rights. Religions might well have been the mothers of human rights in earlier eras, perhaps even the midwives of the modern human rights revolution. But religion has now outlived its utility. Indeed, the continued insistence on special roles and rights for religion is precisely what has introduced the Dickensian paradoxes which now befuddle us. Religion is, by its nature, too expansionistic and monopolistic, too patriarchal and hierarchical, too antithetical to the very ideals of pluralism, toleration, and equality inherent in a human rights regime. Purge religion entirely, this argument concludes, and the human rights paradigm will thrive.[56]

This argument states too much to be practicable. In the course of the twentieth century, religion defied the wistful assumptions of the Western academy that the spread of Enlightenment reason and science would slowly eclipse the sense of the sacred and the sensibility of the superstitious.[57] Religion has also defied the evil assumptions of Nazis, Fascists, and Communists alike that gulags and death camps, iconoclasm and book burnings, propaganda and mind controls would inevitably drive religion into extinction. Yet another great awakening of religion is upon us — now global in its sweep.

It is undeniable that religion has been, and still is, a formidable force for both political good and political evil, that it has fostered both benevolence and belligerence, peace and pathos of untold dimensions. But the proper response to religious belligerence and pathos cannot be to deny that religion exists or to dismiss it to the private sphere and sanctuary. The proper response is to castigate the vices and to cultivate the virtues of religion, to confirm those

---

56. For a critical analysis of this "standard secularist account" of human rights, see Max L. Stackhouse, "The Intellectual Crisis of a Good Idea," *Journal of Religious Ethics* 26, no. 2 (1998): 263.

57. See Roland Robertson, "Religion and the Global Field," *Social Compass* 41, no. 1 (1994): 121–35, at 127ff.

religious teachings and practices that are most conducive to human rights, democracy, and rule of law.

It has been said that "religions run wild must be tamed, for they cannot be long caged." Religion is an ineradicable condition of human lives and communities. Religion will invariably figure in the legal and political life of a community — however forcefully that community seeks to repress or deny its value or validity, however cogently the academy might logically bracket it from its political and legal calculus. Religion must be dealt with, because it exists — perennially, profoundly, pervasively, in every community.[58] Religion must be drawn into a constructive alliance with a regime of law, democracy, and human rights, or they will be pitted against each other.

58. See Martin E. Marty, "Religious Dimensions of Human Rights," in *Religious Human Rights I,* 1–16; Peter F. Beyer, "Privatization and the Public Influence of Religion in Global Society," in *Global Culture: Nationalism, Globalization, and Modernity,* ed. Mike Featherstone (London: Sage, 1990), 373–95.

– *Chapter 3* –

The Spirit of God and the Spirit of Medicine

The Church, Globalization, and a Mission of Health Care

Allen Verhey

"If we live by the Spirit, let us also be guided by the Spirit" (Gal. 5:25). So Paul advised Christians in Galatia in the middle of the first century. It is still good advice. It provides the text — or at least the pretext — for this effort to think about the mission of the church to care for the sick in a "globalized" world.

Our "globalized" world is a shrinking world. It is, to use Roland Robertson's phrase, a "compressed" world.[1] Communication and travel have made the world smaller, and the spread of both disease and information has become easier. Television and the Internet bring the remotest of strangers into our homes, where they intrude upon our consciousness as neighbors, as those who live next to us in this "global village." We do not always get along with our neighbors, of course, and whether the "global village" will be peaceable and hospitable to difference is not assured by the mere fact that the world is shrinking. Compression sometimes leads to an explosion, even to violence.

In a "compressed" world, cultures and traditions inevitably rub against each other, meeting and competing for human trust and loyalty. The healing traditions are no exception. Globalization has meant both the spread of Western (or "modern") medicine around

1. Roland Robertson, "Globalization and the Future of 'Traditional Religion,' " in *God and Globalization: Religion and the Powers of the Common Life*, ed. Max L. Stackhouse with Peter J. Paris (Harrisburg, Pa.: Trinity Press International, 2000), 53–68.

the world and the spread of other traditions of healing to the West. Alternative medicines grow more popular in the West, and native healing traditions continue where Western medicine has been imported. These facts provide a compelling example of Robertson's thesis that globalization does not lead inevitably to "McDonaldization," to the elimination of difference and variety by irresistible forces of homogenization.[2] The homogenizing forces of technical rationality are not irresistible. Even so, Western medicine continues to expand both its technological powers and its sphere of influence, asserting its hegemony among the traditions of healing.

While the world shrinks and medicine expands its powers, some things have not changed. People still die; death still threatens to alienate human beings from their own flesh, from their communities, and from God. To its credit, medicine resists death and those forerunners of death, sickness and suffering. Its resistance, however, is sometimes presumptuous, sometimes desperate, and finally powerless. Ironically, sometimes Western medicine and the technology it marshals against death prematurely alienate people from their flesh, from their communities, and from the Mystery who transcends both death and themselves.

Against the power of death the Christian church affirms with Paul that "we live by the Spirit." It has, by the gift of the same Spirit, whom Paul calls the "first fruits" of God's good future, a better sense of an ending. The last word is not death but life, not suffering but *shalom*. And it has, by the leading of the same Spirit, a mission. The Spirit sent — and sends — the church into all the world as a global community of peaceable difference, as a community of moral discourse and discernment, and as a community of healing.

The church does not control the Spirit or dispense it like so many aspirin tablets. In all the world it discovers that the Spirit of God is already present. From its beginnings the church has encountered other traditions and communities of healing. From its beginning it has had the task of discerning the spirits governing these traditions to see if they are of God and to judge whether they can be oriented toward God's good future. In memory and in hope the church throughout its history has had a complex relationship with medicine, ready to celebrate its service to the cause of God, but also ready to criticize and to reform it by setting medicine in the context of the work of the Spirit of God.

---

2. Ibid., 55.

In this shrinking world the church will encounter still other traditions and communities of healing, and it will encounter global inequities much less remotely. In the modernized world, where Western medicine asserts its hegemony among the healing traditions, the church led by the Spirit will continue to have a complex relationship with medicine. It may celebrate medicine's service to the cause of God, enlisting it in its mission, but it will also criticize and seek to reform Western medicine, challenging its confidence in technology and its distortion of compassion.

Such, at least, are the paths along which this essay moves. Whether they are the paths along which the Spirit moves is for the church to discern. This essay affirms with Paul that "we live by the Spirit" and encourages all who are called to do so to "be guided by the Spirit" as the Spirit continues to care for the sick while the world shrinks, even as Western medicine asserts hegemony over other traditions of healing, even as death continues to assert its doomed reign.

Medicine and the Power of Death

There can be no denial of the reality and power of death in this world. Against the power of death the church affirms that "we live by the Spirit," but it is against the very real power of death that the church dares to make such an affirmation. The churches' talk of the Spirit does not require—and will not permit—a denial of the reality of death. The "Spirit of Truth" does not make liars of us. It is the Spirit, after all, of the one who died a real death on a Roman cross. However many changes have taken place between the first century and the twenty-first, whatever differences mark human beings and cultures around the world, they are alike in this: people die.

Death, it seems, is our destiny. Our lives end in death. First we live and then we die. Death, not life, seems to have the last word. Pascal said it well, "The last act is tragic, however happy the rest of the play is; at the last a little earth is thrown upon our head, and that is the end forever."[3] Peter DeVries may have said it even better, "We're all like the cleaning woman. We come to dust."[4] They echo what scripture discloses: "You are dust, and to dust you shall return" (Gen. 3:19).

---

3. *Pascal's Pensées* (New York: E. P. Dutton, 1958), no. 210, p. 61.
4. *Slouching toward Kalamazoo* (New York: Penguin Books, 1984), 23.

Death is real — and it is a real evil. It is intimate with sickness and suffering, its forerunners and messengers.[5] The evil of death is not simply the termination of biological existence. It is rather that death — and sickness and suffering — threaten to alienate us from our own flesh, from our communities, and from God.[6] If death is our destiny, then so is alienation. To its great credit, medicine resists death — but if there is no other and better sense of destiny, then the resistance medicine offers grows presumptuous, sometimes desperate, and frequently ironically alienating.

Notice, first, that death threatens to alienate us from our own flesh. The threat is real and terrible, for we are embodied selves, not ghosts. Sickness reminds us that we *are* our bodies, that our "selves" depend on the integrity of the bodies we otherwise take for granted, that our health and our lives, our "selves," are radically contingent. This reminder, however, does not come gently; it is not like listening to some friendly preacher read from the Psalms. In sickness this *identification* with the body is experienced at the same time as *alienation* from the body. Death makes its power felt in serious illness and in severe pain, when the body is experienced not only as "me" but as "the enemy." It makes its power felt in the weakness that robs the sick of the capacity to exercise responsible control of themselves and of their world. It makes its power felt when the wonderful variety of God's creation is reduced to something barren and sterile or to something putrid and foul. It makes its power felt when the body no longer opens up into a larger and sharable world, when the body — and the world — of the sick shrinks to that place "a bandage hides."[7] It makes its power felt in the sense of betrayal of that fundamental trust we have in our bodies.

Medicine resists death — and its resistance is sometimes heroic. However, without some other and better sense of an ending, its resistance is sometimes presumptuous, pretending to rescue human beings from their mortality and their vulnerability to suffering, and frequently desperate, laboring under the tyranny of survival or ease. And sometimes — ironically and tragically — death makes its power

5. See Karl Barth, *Church Dogmatics* III/4, 363–73.

6. This point has been made elegantly by William F. May, "The Sacral Power of Death in Contemporary Experience," in *On Moral Medicine: Theological Perspectives in Medical Ethics,* ed. Stephen E. Lammers and Allen Verhey, 2d ed. (Grand Rapids, Mich.: Eerdmans, 1998), 197–208.

7. W. H. Auden, "Surgical Ward," in Lammers and Verhey, *On Moral Medicine,* 328.

felt in the sort of medicine which is technologically oriented to biological survival. When the sick, at once identified with their bodies and alienated from them, seek medical care, they sometimes find this simultaneous identification and alienation reinforced. Medicine sometimes reduces the self to body and treats the body as "the enemy," as that manipulable and untrustworthy "nature" which must — for the sake of the self — be overpowered, but which remains, willy-nilly, the self. Patients suffer then not only from the disease but also from the treatment of it — and death makes its power felt not only in sickness but also in medicine.

Notice, second, that death threatens to separate people from their communities. The threat is real and horrible, for we are communal beings, not isolated individuals. Our lives are lived with others, and death threatens separation and removal, exclusion and abandonment. Sickness comes, too, as the forerunner and messenger of this alienation. Death makes its power felt when the sick or dying are removed and separated from those with whom they share a common life. It makes its power felt when disease so monopolizes attention that there is no space for the tasks of reconciliation and forgiveness and community. It makes its power felt when the fear of abandonment is not met by the presence of others who care. The silence of death makes its power felt in lonely dumbness, when community and communication fail.

Sickness, with its pain and weakness, pushes people to the margins of public life, forces a withdrawal from the public activities of working and shopping, attending a concert or a ball game. And those of us who are "well" provide some of the leverage that moves the sick to the margins. We are autonomous, in charge of our lives, productive; "they" are not. We have been successful against the powerful threats of nature; they have not. They have been captured by the power of death, by the forces of chaos, by the nature that threatens us all, by the nature against which our best hope is technology, the power knowledge gives, the knowledge most of us do not have. They belong, therefore, in a hospital and under the care of a physician, not in public spaces reserved for strength and beauty, for efficiency and productivity, for life. They belong "elsewhere."[8]

Suffering, moreover, can rob the sick of their voice, as in W. H. Auden's wonderful and painful line, "Truth in their sense is how

8. Ibid.

much they can bear; / It is not like ours, but groans they smother." The point is not just that those who suffer are sometimes driven back to the sounds and cries human beings make before they learn a language. The point is rather that there are no words. The person in pain knows pain with a certainty that Descartes might envy, but the one suffering cannot make sense of it, cannot tell it, cannot communicate it or "share" it.

Medicine resists death and can sometimes identify the pain, can "objectify" it, make sense of it, and manage it by creating a language for it. But sometimes that medical language is not the language of the patient. Where that medical language is the "official" language, patients find themselves aliens, not knowing the language, "speechless," and with little hope for making their pain — or themselves — known.[9] Medicine resists death, but without another and better sense of an ending, sometimes — ironically and tragically — death makes its power felt, first, when a community abandons the sick to medicine, and then in a hospital when medicine neglects the community and the voice of the patient.

Third and finally, death threatens people in their relationship with God. The threat is real and terrible, for human beings are religious, in spite of the denials of secularism. Death threatens any sense that the one who bears down on us and sustains us is dependable and caring. It threatens abandonment by God and separation from God. It threatens human beings in their identity as cherished children of God. Death makes its power felt whenever the sick and dying — or those who would care for them — are not assured of the presence of a loving God who cares. Death makes its power felt not only in the sense of betrayal by our bodies, not only in the sense of betrayal by our communities, but also in the sense of betrayal by God.

Such at least was the experience of Stein, the character in Peter DeVries's *The Blood of the Lamb,* who describes his daughter's leukemia as a "sluggishly multiplying anarchy," "a souvenir from the primordial ooze. The original Chaos was without form and void. In de beginning was de void, and the void was vit God. Mustn't say

---

9. See the wonderful line that John Mbiti cites from an Indonesian Christian, "I could not die in a foreign language" ("'When the Bull Is in a Strange Country, It Does Not Bellow': Tribal Religions and Globalization," in *God and Globalization: Christ and the Civilizational Dominions,* ed. Max L. Stackhouse [Harrisburg, Pa.: Trinity Press International, forthcoming]).

de naughty void." Then medicine is just — as Stein says — "the art of prolonging disease [in] order to postpone grief."[10]

Medicine resists death, but with no other or better sense of human destiny its resistance is undertaken under the power of death, under the tyranny of survival, with the desperation of hopelessness. Medicine becomes a place where death makes its power felt by alienating patients from their bodies, from their communities, and from their God — before the end of their lives and for the sake of their survival.

The last word, it seems, belongs to death, and the horror of it is not simply the termination of existence, but the unraveling of meaning, the destruction of relationships, the lordship of chaos. It is the light that seems ephemeral; the darkness seems to surround and overcome the light and the life. Then we are right to be fearful of death, and to tremble before its messengers.

"We Live by the Spirit"

Christians claim, however, that the last word is not death. They believe, as they say, "in the Holy Spirit, the Lord and Giver of life" (Nicene Creed), and they list among the works of the Spirit "the resurrection of the body and the life everlasting" (Apostles' Creed). Christians have — and their creeds have — a different sense of an ending; they affirm with Paul that "we live by the Spirit." Christians do not deny the reality of death or the ways it threatens human beings in their relationships with their own bodies, with their communities, and with God. Nevertheless, Christians make the audacious (and finally hilarious) claim that the last word belongs to God and to the life-giving and gracious Spirit of God. The last word, then, is not death but life, not suffering but *shalom*. Two questions seem obvious. The first is whether there are any grounds for this confidence in a different and better destiny. Hope that has no basis is simply wishful thinking. The second question is whether such hope makes any difference. What difference does this hope make to human sickness and to human caring for the sick? Hope that has no consequence is simply sentimental optimism. The questions are related, of course, for in the grounds for hope we will also

---

10. Peter DeVries, *The Blood of the Lamb* (Boston: Little, Brown and Company, 1961), 181–83.

discover a direction. "If we live by the Spirit, let us also be guided by the Spirit."

Permit me, first, to consider — briefly and inadequately — the story of the Spirit as the grounds for a hope that is not illusion, evasion, or fantasy. Because this hope puts us to work, permit me then to suggest implications for the church's vocation in relation to medicine in a global village.

The story begins with the creation. In the beginning God made all things out of nothing and made all things good. The Spirit was there, of course, "in the beginning," the wind that swept across the waters of chaos to create a cosmos (Gen. 1:2), the breath of God that made of dust a living creature (Gen. 2:7). From that beginning it is clear that, if we live at all, we live by the Spirit. From that beginning it is clear that, without the Spirit of God, human weakness and mortality would make their inevitable way toward death, that, without the Spirit of God, human powers would demonstrate their weakness, their "flesh," by their inability to keep the cosmos from tilting back to chaos. The grounds for hope in the Christian tradition are not found in a "soul" that has its immortality independent of God and finds liberation in the death of the body. The grounds for hope are not located in a romantic account of the return of life in nature each spring. And the grounds of hope are not found in a Baconian account of technological mastery over nature, with human flourishing in its train. The grounds of hope are the powerful and creative word of God and the life-giving Spirit of God that can call a cosmos out of chaos, give light to the darkness, and life to the dust. The creation, of course, is not the whole story. The narrative continues with the story of human sin, which brought death and a curse in its wake.[11]

Sin left ugly marks of alienation on the world God made: the curse of patriarchy, the enmity and envy of brothers, the confusion of tongues at the Tower of Babel, and death. The power of death, as said, threatened to alienate human beings from their own bodies, from their communities, and from God.

The story might have ended there, the cosmos smashed back to chaos. But God did not abandon the world to sin or to death. The Spirit was still there, present in the chaos human beings had wrought, brooding on the waters of human tears, preserving, re-

---

11. It should be said that sin did not bring mortality in its wake, for human mortality was and is a simple sign that we do not have life the way God has life.

newing, pledging that death would not have the last word in the world God made. The Spirit came to Abraham and set him on a journey that had as its destiny a blessing on "all the nations." When Abraham's great-grandchildren found themselves reduced to slavery in Egypt, the Spirit was there in the pain, and made it God's own pain. When these slaves cried out to God, the Spirit was there to hear that cry and to answer their pain with promise. The Spirit was there in the promise then, and when the promise became reality, when Israel was delivered from Pharaoh's oppression. So the Spirit formed Israel's memory and Israel's hope. That memory and hope formed Israel's liturgy, its psalms and its prayers, and spilled over into all of its life. The Spirit was there when in remembrance the slaves and the poor and the weak were protected by law. The Spirit was there when in hope those who suffered cried out in lament. The Spirit was there when the prophets beat against injustice with their words and envisioned a different and better future, God's future. As the prophet Isaiah said, "The Spirit of the Lord God is upon me, because the Lord has anointed me to bring good news to the oppressed, to bind up the brokenhearted, ... [and] to comfort all who mourn" (Isa. 61:1–2).

Those words were repeated by Jesus of Nazareth and fulfilled in words of blessing and works of healing. The Spirit was "upon" him — at his birth, at his baptism, and in his ministry. He came announcing that the good future of God was "at hand," and he already made its power felt in his words and deeds. Many who are last shall be first, he said.[12]

In such words God's future made its power felt, and God's cause was disclosed. It was good news to those who did not count for much in Palestine, to women and their children, to the sick and the poor. And to those who did count, it was a call to repentance, a call to "be last of all and the servant of all" (Mark 9:35). By the power of the Spirit, this Jesus raised the dead and healed the sick, who were thought in the first century to be under the power of death. In such deeds the good future of God made its power felt, and God's cause was disclosed. God's cause is life, not death; God's cause is human flourishing, including the human flourishing we call health, not sickness. By the power of the Spirit this Jesus cast out demons; the "possessed" were restored to themselves (to self-control) and to their communities. In such deeds, however they

12. See Mark 10:31 and a number of parallel passages.

are to be understood, the good future of God made its power felt, and God's cause was disclosed. God's cause is human integrity and community.

It was not yet that good future, however, not even for Jesus. He "suffered under Pontius Pilate." He was put to death on a Roman cross. That cross was a threat to his embodiment, and he suffered it so, not as "mere" physical pain over which he exercised spiritual transcendence, not (like Socrates) as a release of an immortal soul from its prison of a body. That cross was a threat to his community, and he suffered it so, betrayed, denied, abandoned. And that cross threatened abandonment also by God; Jesus quoted the psalmist, "My God, my God, why . . . ?" (Mark 15:34; Ps. 22:1). Even so, he waited and watched for God's good future; Psalm 22 itself ends in confidence and hope (vv. 21–31), and Jesus surely knew the whole psalm. While he waited and watched for God's good future, he made the human cry of lament his own cry; his passion was com-passion. The Spirit was "upon" him in the readiness to "suffer with" another and not just in his readiness to heal. And in his suffering and death, the compassion and presence of God were revealed.

God raised this Jesus up, "the first fruits of those who have died" (1 Cor. 15:20). When the powers of death and doom had done their damnedest, God raised this Jesus up. God would not let death have the last word. The threat of alienation from our bodies, our communities, and our God received a reply. Jesus was raised in our world and in our history, and our world and our history have, happily, no escape. While death continues to assert its doomed reign, a different and a better destiny has been established. And lo, he said, "I am with you always" (Matt. 28:20).

Because Jesus was raised, the Spirit was poured out, the presence of Jesus in his absence, "the first fruits" (Rom. 8:23) and the "guarantee" (2 Cor. 1:22; 5:5; Eph. 1:13) of God's good future. Among the works of the Spirit is the church. When the Spirit was poured out, the church was created — itself a token, the "first fruits" of God's future and in the service of it. The Spirit points the church toward that future by reminding it of Jesus and by providing a foretaste of that future. So the Spirit forms the memory and hope of the church, and in that memory and hope the church discovers its mission of blessing to "all the nations."

I want to highlight three aspects of the Spirit's work in creating and sustaining the church as "first fruits" of God's good future — three aspects of the church's mission. The church is, in its beginnings and in its continuing mission by the power of the Spirit, a global community of peaceable difference, a community of moral discourse and discernment, and a community of healing.

The church was, and is called to be, a *global community of peaceable difference.* At its beginnings on a Pentecost Sunday, people from all over the world who had gathered in Jerusalem were suddenly and quite remarkably capable of understanding each other. The curse of Babel was lifted that day, and God's good future made its power felt. In the power of that same Spirit the church moved from Jerusalem to "the ends of the earth" (Acts 1:8). Communities of peaceable difference of Jews and Gentiles were formed across the world. In spite of traditional animosities and suspicions between Jews and Gentiles, the church was "one new humanity" of Jew and Gentile (Eph. 2:15), and God's good future made its power felt. The Spirit formed communities that included men and women as equals, communities in which the curse of patriarchy was being lifted. The Spirit created communities of peaceable difference that included both slaves and free as "brothers and sisters" and both patrons and clients as "friends," and God's good future made its power felt.

The Spirit formed such communities of peaceable difference neither by imposing an authoritarian hierarchy nor by nurturing moral indifference, but by forming *communities of moral discourse* in which moral discernment was set in the context of the community's memory and hope. There was moral discourse, conversation about what should be done and what left undone. That discourse prompted moral deliberation; they asked why they should do one thing rather than another or something rather than nothing. Personal responsibility was owned, but it was not regarded as private, as no one else's business. Personal responsibility was owned in the context of the community, with its diversity of members and its diversity of gifts. There was leadership, of course, but no leader whether by charismatic or institutional authority could simply say, "Do this because I say so." Reasons were given and heard. Not every reason counted as a good reason, of course. The deliberation required discernment. The reasons given and heard had to "fit" the story that they loved to tell and longed to live. They were a community of moral discourse, deliberation, and discernment finally by being a community of memory and hope. In the power of the Spirit the church was, and is called to be, a community of moral discourse and discernment.

The third aspect of the Spirit's work in creating the church is that the church was, and is called to be, a *community of healing*. In memory of Jesus and in the power of the Spirit it could hardly be otherwise. In memory and in hope the church continued the healing ministry of Jesus, and healing continued to be a sign of God's good future. The church remembered Jesus' instruction for mission: "heal the sick . . . and say to them, "The kingdom of God has come near to you" (Luke 10:9, cf. Matt. 10:7–8). Hard on the heels of Pentecost there is healing (Acts 3:1–10). Paul lists the gifts of healing among the gifts of the Spirit (e.g., 1 Cor. 12:9). The promise of the Spirit was always the promise of Christ: that the whole creation will be made new, that death shall be no more, that neither mourning nor crying nor pain shall be anymore (Rev. 21:4). The promise of the Spirit is not some Gnostic enlightenment; the promise of the Spirit is that "our bodies" will be redeemed (Rom. 8:23). The church entered the world, as Henry Sigerist said,[13] as a religion of healing. Healing was — and is — as much the vocation of faith as preaching. When, in the power of the Spirit, people were healed, there was a foretaste of God's good future.

Of course, that good future was not yet. The power of death continued to assert its doomed reign. The continuing power of death evidently prompted a crisis of hope in the Thessalonian church. People still die, the Thessalonians observed. Paul's reply (1 Thess. 4:13–18) reminded them that the basis for hope is not some power we have at our disposal but "that Jesus died and rose again" (1 Thess. 4:14). He assured them, in images drawn from the apocalyptic tradition, that even the dead have not been abandoned, that even death cannot separate them from the love and power of God (cf. Rom. 8:38). While death asserts its doomed reign, the church must wait and watch for God's good future, for that harvest of which the resurrection of Jesus and the gift of the Spirit are "first fruits." To "wait" for that harvest is not to do nothing. To wait is to delight in healings as tokens of God's future without supposing that the power to heal is simply at our disposal. To wait is to comfort the grieving (1 Thess. 4:18) and "help the weak" (1 Thess. 5:14). To wait under the sign of the cross is to share the suffering of those who hurt; to wait is compassion.

It is still, sadly, not yet God's good future. Even so, the Spirit has

---

13. Henry Sigerist, *Civilization and Disease* (Ithaca, N.Y.: Cornell University Press, 1943), 69.

been poured out upon the world. The church does not control the Spirit of God or offer the Spirit like a health food store. By the gift of the Spirit the church discerns that the Spirit is always present in the world—and that the power of death is, too.

Even now, the Spirit moves within globalization with a renewed sense of our interdependence and in the discovery that we are neighbors. The Spirit moves in the efforts to talk across our boundaries and in spite of the diversity of our languages—and in the understanding that sometimes results. The Spirit moves in every healing. The Spirit *is* present in the hurt and in the promise and wherever the promise has partial fulfillment. The Spirit *is* there when the suffering cry out in hope that someone will hear their cry, and when the whole creation groans in its pain (Rom. 8:22). The Spirit *is* there in the promise that the creation will be made new, that death shall be no more (Rev. 21:4), and that "our bodies" will be redeemed (Rom. 8:23). The Spirit *is* there wherever the fulfillment of that promise is given token, where the sick are healed, where the grieving are comforted, where the threat of death is met with confidence in God and with care for persons as embodied and communal selves.

The Spirit *is* there in the church. The Spirit *is* there in its worship, in the memory and hope that celebrates the resurrection. The Spirit *is* there in that global community of friends. The Spirit *is* there where, in memory and hope, the church talks together about the shape of a common life "according to the Spirit." The Spirit *is* present in that community when the good future of God makes its power felt in the practices of friendship and forgiveness—or, as the Creed says, "in the communion of the saints and the forgiveness of sins." The Spirit *is* there when, in memory and hope, the church cares for the sick.

Remembering the Mission of the Church

The Spirit sent the church into the world as a global and peaceable community, as a community of discourse, and as a community of healing. As the church developed, it found in the world a variety of healing practices. Its mission, both as a healing community and as a community of discourse and discernment, required that it think and talk about these alternative traditions, testing them by the memory and hope that the Spirit gives and orienting them toward God's good future. In the global village the continuing Church will again encounter a variety of healing traditions, and its mission continues to require that it discern the spirits.

The early church accepted miracle, of course, but it claimed that all healing comes from the God of creation and covenant, the God of Jesus and the Spirit. It was not by the power of Asclepius or Serapis that people were healed, but by the power of God.[14] The early church rejected magical healing practices as associated with "the deceitful rites of the demons" and as reliance on "incantations and charms" rather than on God, even when the name of Jesus was invoked.[15] It accommodated medicine without surrendering its conviction that all healing comes from God. Most Christians followed the sage advice of Jesus ben Sirach, who regarded physicians and their medicines as instruments of God (Ecclus. 38:1–14).

The church's acceptance of medicine as a form of healing did not mean, of course, that anything and everything "medical" was approved. When the church called Jesus "the great physician,"[16] it honored physicians, especially the "Hippocratic" physicians, commending their compassion and their commitment to the patient's good. But it also provided a model for medicine, setting it in the context of a story that reaches from creation to resurrection and God's good future.

Within that story the body and its health were regarded as great goods, but as part of a larger good, not as the *summum bonum.*[17] Sickness was regarded as part of a larger evil, as a feature of the

---

14. In his polemic against Christianity, Celsus also affirmed miracle, but he insisted that Asclepius was the agent of healing power and Jesus a mere magician (Origen, *Against Celsus* 3.22–24, 7.35).

15. Augustine, *City of God* 10.9. Consider also Peter's rejection of the offer of Simon Magus to pay for the power of Spirit (Acts 8:9–24). The magician recognized the divine presence and power, but he wanted to commodify it and then to manipulate it to serve the cause of the magician, to glorify Simon Magus, not God.

16. See O. Temkin, *Hippocrates in a World of Pagans and Christians* (Baltimore: Johns Hopkins University Press, 1991).

17. Some ancient philosophers insisted against some physicians that health is not the *summum bonum,* and that medicine itself is unable to determine how to rank health relative to other goods. See further Ludwig Edelstein, "The Relation of Ancient Philosophy to Medicine," in *Ancient Medicine: Selected Papers of Ludwig Edelstein,* ed. O. Temkin and C. L. Temkin (Baltimore: Johns Hopkins University Press, 1967), 349–66. The ancient church insisted on similar points. The contemporary church may need to reiterate them against the World Health Organization's definition of health as "a state of complete physical, mental, and social well-being," which runs the risk of making health the *summum bonum* and making it difficult to rank health relative to other goods. See Daniel Callahan's complaint in "The WHO Definition of 'Health,' " in Lammers and Verhey, *On Moral Medicine,* 253–61.

disorder introduced by human sin.[18] Although physical affliction is an evil, it might, by the grace of God, remind people of their finitude, their dependence, and indeed, of their sinfulness, of the disorder that infects the relations of persons to their bodies, to each other, and to God.

Christians did not consider the practices of physicians *de novo*. Among contending accounts of the appropriate conduct of physicians, the church adopted and adapted the medical ethic epitomized by the Hippocratic oath. The ascendancy of the oath itself in the Western tradition of medicine is probably a result of the rise of Christianity.[19] The church supported this tradition — but also modified it.

One result of this revisionary affirmation was a version of the oath "in so far as a Christian may swear it."[20] The Christian version began not by invoking Apollo, Asclepius, and the other pagan deities held to be pertinent to healing but with the doxology, "Blessed be the God and Father of our Lord Jesus Christ." It oriented the physician to the glory of God and set the Hippocratic tradition in the context of the story Christians told of Jesus and the Spirit.

Many of the provisions of the Christian version stood in obvious continuity with the Hippocratic oath. It reiterated the Hippocratic commitment of fidelity to the sick. Moreover, the prohibitions of euthanasia and abortion, which had stood in sharp contrast to the wide acceptance of abortion, infanticide, and euthanasia in Greece and Rome, were adopted as consistent with the church's condemnation of killing. The Christian version also accepted the prohibition of sexual relationships with patients or members of patients' households as consistent with the church's concerns about sexual fidelity. Finally, the Christian version affirmed the obligation of confidentiality; patients (like penitents) were required to reveal what they might prefer to keep secret, and the physician (like the priest) was forbidden to use such revelations for any other purpose than the professional end of helping the sick.

The Hippocratic tradition was adopted, but it was set within the

---

18. E.g., Augustine, *City of God* 14.3; 22.22.

19. Ludwig Edelstein, "The Hippocratic Oath," *Bulletin of the History of Medicine*, 1943, supp. 5, no. 1, 1–64.

20. See W. H. S. Jones, *The Doctor's Oath: An Essay in the History of Medicine* (Cambridge, 1924). The date of the Christian version of the Hippocratic oath is unknown; the oldest extant manuscript is from the tenth century.

context of response to God and to the cause of God made known in Christ, and a faithful response required modifications in that tradition. One such modification was described by Henry Sigerist as "the most revolutionary and decisive change" in Western medicine — ascribing the sick "a preferential position."[21]

Jesus was, after all, not just a healer, not just "the great physician"; he was also one who suffered and died. Remembering Jesus' suffering and death, Christians saw in the sick the very image of their Lord and discerned in their care for them (or in their abandoning them) an image of their care for Christ himself (or for their abandoning Christ himself). The classic passage, of course, is Matthew 25:31–45. The passage was explicitly cited, for example, in *The Rule of St. Benedict,* which prescribed care for the sick "as if it were Christ himself who was served" (chap. 36). The passage was surely reflected, for example, in the behavior of Christians during the outbreak of plague in the third century. To be guided by the Spirit in memory of Jesus has always meant that care for the sick be regarded as a duty of Christian community.

Because care for the sick was a duty, the church required competence and diligence of physicians. The medieval penitential literature, for example, required physicians to confess incompetence and negligence.[22] Care for the sick involved good medical care, but it could not be reduced to medical care. And although health and life were great goods, they were not the greatest goods, and neither physicians nor patients were permitted to seek them in ways that violated some greater or larger good.

Jesus was not only a healer, not only one who suffered, but also a preacher of good news to the poor (Luke 4:18); his words of blessing to the poor were no less a token and a promise of God's good future than his works of healing (e.g., Luke 6:20). The poor, along with the sick, were accorded a "preferential position" in memory of Jesus, and fidelity to God required that the needs of the sick poor not be forgotten, either by physicians or by their communities.

So clergy frequently took the lead in providing medical care for the sick and poor. The tradition of physician clergy stretched from the early Middle Ages into the modern period, with the practice

---

21. Sigerist, *Civilization and Disease,* 69–70.

22. See Darrel W. Amundsen, "Casuistry and Professional Obligations: The Regulation of Physicians by the Court of Conscience in the Late Middle Ages," in *Transactions and Studies of the College of Physicians of Philadelphia* 3 (1982): 22–39.

largely devoted to the care of the sick poor. There is, moreover, a tradition of medical texts written by clergy in service of the poor, books like *Thesaurus Pauperum,* a thirteenth-century list of simple herbal remedies available to the poor (authored by John XXI), and John Wesley's *Primitive Physick* (1747). Treatises exhorting physicians to care for rich and poor alike were commonplace.[23]

The hospital itself has its origin in the Christian concern for the poor.[24] In the fourth century, Christian communities began to establish *xenodocheia* (or hospices) to feed and shelter the poor. In 372, Basil the Great founded a vast *xenodocheion,* the Basileias, with buildings to care for the sick poor — and separate buildings for contagious and noncontagious diseases — and with a staff that included physicians. It was the prototype of many other such Christian and civil institutions.

In the missionary movement of the nineteenth century, the church retrieved its vocation as a global community, and in the development of a medical mission within that movement the church retrieved its vocation as a community of healing. The first medical missionaries were evidently sent to care for the "real" missionary and his family, but before long the memory of Jesus' suffering and healing was retrieved, prompting a richer vision of the medical mission of the churches. These are the words of a medical missionary in 1888:

> As [Christ's] ministry was a ministry of sympathy with suffering humanity, as He healed the sick, and went about continually doing good,... so His ambassadors must 'preach the Gospel', not by word alone, but likewise, by a compassionate Christ-like ministry, performed in Christ's name and for His sake.[25]

The medical mission in the nineteenth century frequently involved a clinic in an isolated context. Only curative medicine was practiced because there was not enough time for — and little understanding of — anything else. In the twentieth century, with the

23. See Martin Marty and Kenneth Vaux, eds., *Health/Medicine and the Faith Traditions* (Philadelphia: Fortress Press, 1982), 119–20.

24. Timothy S. Miller, *The Birth of the Hospital in the Byzantine Empire* (Baltimore: Johns Hopkins University Press, 1985).

25. John Lowe of the Edinburgh Medical Mission Society, in a report in James Johnson, ed., *Report of the Centenary Conference on the Protestant Missions of the World* (London, 1888), 2.104; cited in C. Peter Williams, "Healing and Evangelism: The Place of Medicine in Later Victorian Protestant Missionary Thinking," in *The Church and Healing,* ed. W. J. Sheils (Oxford: Basil Blackwell, 1982), 282.

expanding powers of medicine, the clinics grew into hospitals and into an educational mission to help train native physicians and nurses. Moreover, the focus on curative medicine has been supplemented with programs in rehabilitation and prevention, including sanitation, nutrition, and vaccination. The isolation has all but disappeared, as mass communication has shrunk the world.

Even when missionaries were isolated, they encountered other communities and traditions of healing. They consistently affirmed that all healing comes from God, and they consistently rejected magic, but there were a variety of responses to the local traditions of healing. Sometimes missionaries so identified Western medicine with the healing power of God that they rejected local traditions of healing, regarding them as primitive and pagan. Sometimes they found ways to accommodate local traditions, retrieving Christian traditions of miraculous and spiritual healing while qualifying and modifying native traditions.[26] Whatever expertise the medical missionaries sought to reserve for Western medicine, and whatever dynamic other missionaries discovered in local traditions, the warrant for healing within these missionary communities remained the command of Christ to preach and to heal. There were diverse responses to local healing traditions and diverse practices of healing within the missionary communities, but there was one Spirit guiding them in memory and in hope.

As the globalization of communication made the world smaller, it also spread Western medicine and the expectations that it prompts. In that context, medical missionaries frequently found themselves in competition not only with local healing traditions but also with medical programs run by governments. Eventually, however, most medical missions discovered ways to cooperate with civic health programs.

There is much in the history of medical missions to celebrate — and much in the tradition of medical missions to hold on to as medical capabilities continue to expand. There is also, however, much to rue, much of which to repent as the twenty-first century begins. The missionary movement was frequently infected with the impe-

---

26. See, for example, Terence Ranger, "Medical Science and Pentecost: the Dilemma of Anglicanism in Africa," in Sheils, *Church and Healing*, 333–66. Ranger gives an account not only of Anglican commitments to Western medicine as the "modern version of Christ's healing compassion," but also of Roman Catholic and Methodist retrievals of their respective traditions to accommodate and qualify local healing traditions.

rialistic attitudes of the nineteenth century. It sometimes created a global community of patrons and clients, rather than a global community of friends. It sometimes yielded to the temptation of the "conceit of philanthropy," dividing the world into needy and benighted beneficiaries and powerful and enlightened benefactors. It sometimes, therefore, was readier to speak than to listen, readier to teach than to learn. Medical missions were sometimes overtaken with triumphalist assumptions about the progress of European civilization. They sometimes identified and confused Western medicine with the good future of God. They sometimes transplanted inappropriate technologies and focused on rescue medicine rather than on the causes of sickness. But for all of these faults, one may discern in medical missions the memory and hope that the Spirit gives the church to be a global community of peaceable difference, moral discourse, and healing.

In the last half of the twentieth century, when hospitals became showcases for medical technology and patient care became increasingly "medicalized," theologians retrieved important elements of the tradition of the Christian community's encounter with medicine. The expanding powers of medicine had prompted a series of dramatic questions about experimentation and the protection of human subjects; about transplantation and the definition of death; about kidney dialysis and the allocation of scarce medical resources; about prenatal diagnosis and genetic counseling; and about reproductive technologies and the use of donated gametes. Such questions were not simply scientific questions; they were moral questions. Efforts to answer such questions always required judgments about the good to be sought and done, about the ends to seek with the powers medicine gives, about the appropriateness of certain means, and about how to use medical powers without violating the human material on which they work. Thus, new questions led — and lead — quickly to some very old questions, to fundamentally religious questions about the meaning of life and death, health and suffering, freedom and embodiment, love and justice. To these questions theologians brought the wisdom of their traditions. They helped to initiate moral discourse about medical ethics and played a major role in the emergence of the field.[27] Against idolatrous and extravagant expectations of either health or medicine,

27. Daniel Callahan, "Religion and the Secularization of Bioethics," *Hastings Center Report* (special supplement: "Theology, Religious Traditions, and Bioethics") 20 (July–August 1990): 2. See also Leroy Walters, "Religion and the Renaissance

they reminded their communities — and any who would listen — that God alone is God. Against the reduction of patients to their pathologies, they retrieved the professional commitment of fidelity to patients as *persons,* and underscored consent as a fundamental component of fidelity.[28] Against the subsequent reduction of persons to their capacities for agency, they insisted on embodiment.[29] The churches and their theologians in debates about access to health care have consistently reiterated the tradition's concern for the poor. Developments in technology continue to raise dramatic questions.[30] But as the church begins the twenty-first century it will be important to recognize a shrinking world as well as the expanding powers of medicine. It will be important for the church to be faithful to its mission, to be a global community of peaceable difference, moral discourse, and healing.

Globalization, Medicine, and the Future

As a community of healing in a global context, the church will continue to encounter other traditions and communities of healing. In this context the church must continue to affirm that all healing comes from God. It must, therefore, celebrate the contributions of various healing traditions to the human task of caring for the sick. As a community of discernment, it will test the spirits of these traditions, and it may sometimes be led to reject aspects which do not fit the story of the Spirit of God. It should continue to reject magic, for example, because magic attempts to manipulate the divine presence and power to serve the cause of the magician, not the cause of God. It will affirm embodiment and reject reduction of the self to either pure spirit or mere body, or a dualism that drives a wedge between body and spirit.[31]

of Medical Ethics," in *Theology and Bioethics: Exploring the Foundations and Frontiers,* ed. Earl E. Shelp (Dordrecht, Netherlands: D. Reidel, 1985), 3–16.

28. Paul Ramsey, *Patient as Person* (New Haven: Yale University Press, 1970).

29. Paul Ramsey, *Ethics at the Edges of Life* (New Haven: Yale University Press, 1978).

30. On the dramatic and important developments in genetics, see Ronald Cole-Turner's essay in this volume and Allen Verhey, " 'Playing God' and Invoking a Perspective," in Lammers and Verhey, *On Moral Medicine,* 287–308.

31. On embodiment and the Spirit of God, see Allen Verhey, "The Body and the Bible: Life in the Flesh according to the Spirit," in *Embodiment, Morality, and Medicine,* ed. L. Sowle Cahill and M. A. Farley (Dordrecht, Netherlands: Kluwer, 1995), 3–22. As the church tests other healing traditions, it is worth remembering that Christians have sometimes been guilty of treating prayer as a technology of last

As a community of healing in a global context, the church will encounter not only other traditions but also the claim of Western medicine to hegemony among those diverse traditions and communities. Since "globalization" includes not just the phenomenon of a shrinking world but also "modernization," or the spread of technical rationality, Western medicine can and will claim authority over diverse traditions and communities of healing. Even if the homogenization of health care is not inevitable, the assertion of hegemony by Western medicine is. How should the church respond?

Surely the church must celebrate the contributions of Western medicine to the human task of caring for the sick. It must acknowledge the scientific expertise of medicine and the (limited) power medicine gives to intervene in the sad stories of suffering and premature dying. So it must continue in its medical missions to cooperate in medical training programs. However, it must not allow itself as a community of healing simply to be identified with Western medicine. It must continue to affirm that all healing comes from God and to insist that the warrant for its vocation as a healing community is the command of Christ and the gift of the Spirit. The church envisions "the authorities" as subject to Christ. It recognizes the authority of expertise and the authority of power, but it sets both expertise and *dynamis* in the context of the authorization — the warrant — to heal given by Christ and the Spirit.[32] So it may not simply test the other traditions against Western medicine as the standard; it must test every tradition by the Spirit. It must be ready also to be critical of Western medicine, to continue its tradition of revisionary affirmation.

As we have seen, the health care mission of the churches for some time has been associated with the Western tradition of medicine. But, in a shrinking world, a readiness to be critical of Western medicine will be important to conversations with other communities and traditions of healing. Unless a capacity for self-critical reflection is preserved, the expectation of an honest and fruitful dialogue

---

resort, corrupting the practice of prayer into magic, and that both the church and Western medicine have been tempted by the dualism that drives a wedge between body and spirit.

32. See further Daniel P. Sulmasy, "*Exousia:* Healing with Authority in the Christian Tradition," in Lammers and Verhey, *On Moral Medicine,* 756–71, who distinguishes three senses of authority: authority as control, authority as expertise, and authority as warrant.

with others is diminished, and those who would teach have much to learn.

Moreover, because health is not primarily "medical," the church as a community of healing must not allow itself simply to be identified with Western medicine. The mission of the church as a healing community in a global context may not be purely or even primarily "medical." The primary causes of illness in the world are poverty, violence, pollution, and behavior. Many of the improvements in health in the United States during the nineteenth and twentieth centuries, for example, can be attributed to rising living standards, better nutrition, sanitation, and lower birth rates. A community of health in a global context has an agenda that cannot be purely or even primarily "medical." The mission of the church must include cooperation in sustainable economic development, agricultural development, nutritional programs, sanitation programs, and peacemaking.[33]

Here, too, however, it will be important for the church to preserve the capacity for self-critical reflection about the Western and triumphalist assumptions sometimes carried by the metaphor of "development." An image taken from the maturation of an organism, "development" may suggest that the most modern nations, like the United States, are the most "mature," the most civilized, and therefore models to imitate. Moreover, "development" has sometimes functioned as a powerful secular religion, as "the focus of redemptive hopes and expectations," to use the words of Peter Berger.[34] Development as a secular religion assumes that human fulfillment is to be found in activities that improve material living conditions. The church as a community of health may not neglect the material living conditions important to health, but it must and may nurture conversations that define the goals of development in qualitative terms as well as quantitative goods. It must remember in its own discourse and remind others that the "good life" may not be reduced to material goods or even to "health" as the *summum bonum,* that it includes goods such as truth, beauty, friendship, hu-

33. On the significance of death by violence and the importance of peacemaking to the mission of the church, see the essays by Donald W. Shriver, Jr., in vol. 1 ("The Taming of Mars: Can Humans of the Twenty-first Century Contain Their Propensity for Violence?" 140–83) and by John Mbiti in vol. 3 (forthcoming) of this series.

34. Peter Berger, *Pyramids of Sacrifice* (Garden City, N.Y.: Anchor Books, 1976), 17.

mility, and simplicity. Again, those who would teach have much to learn.

The church must not simply identify with Western medicine but continue its tradition of revisionary affirmation of medicine, because Western medicine has, as we have seen, sometimes been co-opted by the very power of death that it resists. The church as a healing community must articulate a different and a better destiny for caring for the sick, including the worthy practice of medicine. The church needs to preserve a prophetic distance from Western medicine even as it sometimes utilizes it in its priestly service. It needs still to test the spirit of Western medicine.

Western medicine has sat at the feet of Francis Bacon, and there it learned to regard knowledge as power over nature and to assume that such knowledge (or technology) leads inevitably toward human well-being.[35] In such an account, the fault that runs through our life and the world lies in nature, and our hope lies in technology. That is a creed ripe for doubt, but "the Baconian project" lives on in the spirit of medicine.[36] To be sure, Bacon had admitted that for knowledge to be beneficial humanity must "perfect and govern it in charity,"[37] but science, as Hans Jonas has observed, is "not self-sufficiently the source of that human quality that makes it beneficial."[38] For charity to "perfect and govern" human powers and for the wisdom to guide charity, humanity must call on something else. But on what? And how can humanity have "knowledge" of it? Such "speculative knowledge" had been dismissed by Bacon; it has no place in Bacon's theory. Bacon may have been guided and

---

35. Aquinas had made the traditional distinction between the "practical" and the "speculative" sciences. The practical sciences were for the sake of some work to be done, while the speculative (or theoretical) sciences were for their own sake (Aquinas, *Commentary on Aristotle's "On the Soul"* 1.3, cited by Hans Jonas, *The Phenomenon of Life: Toward a Philosophical Biology* [New York: Dell, 1966], 188). Bacon rejected the "speculative" sciences as the "boyhood of knowledge" and "barren of works" (Francis Bacon, *The New Organon and Related Writings,* ed. F. H. Anderson [1620; Indianapolis: Bobbs-Merrill, 1960], 8). The knowledge Bacon commended, and the knowledge celebrated in the modern world, was "no mere felicity of speculation" (ibid., 29). Bacon commended the practical sciences for their utility, "for the benefit and use of life" (15). He was confident that such knowledge would make humanity "capable of overcoming the difficulties and obscurities of nature" (19). "And so those twin objects, human knowledge and human power, do really meet in one" (29).

36. On "the Baconian project" see Gerald P. McKenny, "Bioethics, the Body, and the Legacy of Bacon," in Lammers and Verhey, *On Moral Medicine,* 308–23.

37. Bacon, *New Organon,* 15.

38. Jonas, *Phenomenon of Life,* 195.

sustained by theological convictions;[39] such convictions, however, were fully set aside by radical Enlightenment thinkers like Jeremy Bentham, for whom the moral project was to eliminate suffering and to maximize pleasure.

By its dismissal of "speculative" rationality in favor of technical rationality, the Baconian project insulates itself from the correction and guidance of other communities and traditions of healing, both religious and cultural. Absent such correction and guidance, (1) health becomes the *summum bonum* rather than a condition for living life virtuously; (2) medicine's confidence in technology finds itself unlimited by confidence in a greater power; and (3) medicine construes the sufferer as manipulable nature and trusts technology to eliminate death and suffering. Left to itself, medicine's resistance to death and suffering ends up alienating people from their bodies, from their communities, and from the Mystery.

The extraordinary new powers of Western medicine and the ordinary ancient task of caring for the sick inevitably raise moral questions. In a global context, of course, there will be diverse judgments, a variety of moral frameworks. The conversations will not be easy, but the church as a community of peaceable difference and moral discernment must sponsor and participate in such conversations. In the context of a globalized hegemony of technical rationality, the church must resist the silencing of "speculative" voices and judgments, whether by medicine or by "the standard forms of bioethics."[40]

The problem is not simply, however, that science and technology are "not self-sufficiently the source of that human quality that makes [them] beneficial."[41] Consider, furthermore, how this Baconian project, alive in the spirit of medicine, has distorted human compassion. Compassion is the ordinary human response to sickness and suffering, those forerunners and messengers of death. Compassion is a visceral response to the suffering of another; it

---

39. Indeed, Bacon recommended his "great instauration" as a form of obedience to God, as a restoration to humanity of the power over nature which was given at creation but lost through the Fall. He prays "that things human may not interfere with things divine," and that "there may arise in our minds no incredulity or darkness with regard to the divine mysteries" (Bacon, *New Organon,* 14–15).

40. McKenny, "Bioethics, the Body, and the Legacy of Bacon," 309, identifies the "standard forms of bioethics" as committed to the imperative "to eliminate suffering and to expand the realm of human choice." He accuses the "standard form," whether utilitarian or libertarian, of "complicity" in the Baconian project.

41. Hans Jonas, *The Phenomenon of Life: Toward a Philosophical Biology,* 195.

moves us to do *something,* but it does not tell us *what* to do.[42] For centuries, human beings had been almost helpless in the face of disease and death. Some were simply "overmastered by their diseases," to quote an ancient Hippocratic treatise. Then Francis Bacon made an innovative suggestion. He urged the rejection of that old category of one "overmastered" by disease, and he insisted that to call any disease "incurable" "gives a legal sanction as it were to neglect and inattention and exempts ignorance from discredit."[43] Compassion prompted the gradual development of a medical science and technology that no longer leave us quite so helpless in the face of human suffering and premature death.

Sometimes the sad stories have a happy ending. The heroes of such stories, of course, are the doctors and nurses—enlisted on the side of human life, battling against the evil empire of disease and death. Their courage is their refusal to call any disease "incurable"; their strength, weapons forged in study and research; their allies, the universities and their laboratories. But if we rely on this story in response to suffering, we will encounter not only successes but also failures and temptations.

The most obvious failure of compassion as trained by the Baconian project, with its pervasive expectation that suffering can be avoided or ended, is that technology does not provide an escape either from our mortality or from our suffering. Not every sad story of human suffering and premature dying has a happy ending; all of us, in spite of Bacon, are "overmastered by our diseases." This is obvious, I say, but we have not been disposed to acknowledge the obvious. Our enthusiasm for technology as a response to suffering has blinded us to the limits of technology.

"Compassion" as the visceral response to the suffering of another moves us to do *something,* but it does not tell us what to do. Given our Baconian confidence in technology and our expectation that compassion can simply put an end to suffering, it is not surprising that we choose to use the tools at hand. The Baconian project trains compassion simply (and blindly) to arm itself with superior technique—to rely not on wisdom, but on artifice, against suffering.

---

42. Oliver O'Donovan, *Begotten or Made?* (Oxford: Oxford University Press, 1984), 10–12.

43. Francis Bacon, *De augmentis scientarum,* in *The Philosophical Works of Francis Bacon,* trans. P. L. Ellis and J. Spedding; ed. J. M. Robertson (1905; reprint, Freeport, N.Y.: Books for Libraries, 1970), 487.

Given our confidence in technology and our high expectations, compassion moves us to assign the sufferer to the care of medicine, to those armed with artifice. So the community abandons the sufferer to medicine — and removes the suffering one. Then this modern compassion moves those skilled with such tools to give the story a happy ending. If and when they fail, it licenses their withdrawal, since they no longer can do the patient any "good" — as if the only "good" were the elimination of mortality and suffering. Meanwhile, such patients, abandoned by both friends and experts, and surrounded by technology rather than by a community that knows and shares their suffering, suffer alone and pointlessly.

It is not surprising, perhaps, that a compassion formed by Bacon then looks for a technological solution to end that suffering — a final solution, the elimination of suffering by eliminating the sufferer.

Guided by the Spirit, and remembering one who made the human cry of lament his own, the church must practice a more ancient compassion, which includes a readiness to "suffer with" another. It should nurture the readiness to be silently present while a sufferer begins to recover, and the readiness to be supportive while the sufferer begins to construct the next chapter of their own story, even if the last chapter.[44]

Both Western medicine and the Western Church need to equip compassion, not only with artifice, but with ancient wisdom about life in a mortal body and in community. There is much to relearn concerning compassion in the memory of Jesus, and much to learn from communities across the globe. The church in its liturgy has made too little place for lament. It has not attended to the suffering or made the human cry of lament its own. It has too often pretended to possess a perfection that denies the not-yet character of our medicine and of our lives. The result has sometimes been the alienation of sufferers who have difficulty lifting themselves to the heights of triumphant liturgy — precisely when they need their communities and religious traditions the most.

Even so, the church knows that to look to God is not to look away from suffering. It knows that, by the Spirit of God, death is not the last word. If guided by that Spirit, the church has much to teach. The church can teach by providing a moral framework

44. See Margaret Mohrmann, *Medicine as Ministry* (Cleveland: Pilgrim Press, 1995), 62–88.

for both a reformed compassion and medicine's wise use of technology, lest, in resistance to death, medicine prematurely alienate people from their bodies and communities. While Western medicine asserts hegemony in a globalized world of technical rationality, the church must test and criticize the spirit that lives in it. A continuing tradition of revisionist affirmation will be of no small service to the global village.

The revisionist affirmation will challenge modern medicine, but it will also affirm and make use of it. As said above, as a community of healing the church has an agenda that is not purely or even mainly medical. Even so, because medicine does make a real, if small, contribution to health, the church's vocation does include medicine in part. The prophetic voice of the church should protest the idolatry of technology, but it should not regard technology as demonic or make an idol of "Mother Nature." It should call for a renewal of the compassion distorted by Baconian assumptions, but when equipped with wisdom and piety, compassion should not reject all artifice.

The church must, in memory of Christ, and in token of God's good future, help medically in a global effort to protect and serve the health of children. It should, for example, contribute to the effort to immunize children against polio, measles, diphtheria, typhoid, and whooping cough. It should help to prevent, by rehydration therapy, for example, the diseases associated with diarrhea. It should contribute to the effort to eradicate diseases like polio and guinea worm.[45] It should cooperate with the initiatives of the World Health Organization entitled *Health for All by the Year 2000*.[46]

The church undertakes its mission, including its medical mission, not only as a community of healing but also as a global community of peaceable difference. The church is, by the gift and calling of the Spirit, a community of friends that reaches across geographical frontiers and national boundaries, across ethnic and tribal differences, across gender and class. The Spirit created one world and one family, and it creates "one new humanity." The Spirit moves within a shrinking world wherever there is interdependence, wherever there is compassion prepared to befriend a sick stranger. The church should celebrate a shrinking world as the work of the Spirit;

---

45. The Carter Center in Atlanta has been leading the way for the church as a community of health with a global mission.

46. World Health Organization, *Global Strategy for Health for All by the Year 2000* (Geneva: World Health Organization, 1981).

it is called to give a token of the *shalom* of the Spirit—a peace that is important to health. The fault in our world is not to be found in nature, but neither is it to be found in differences among people. The problem with our world is the human sin that left patriarchy, envy, violence, and the confusion of tongues in its wake.

This shrinking world is not yet God's good future. It is marked and marred by asymmetries of power and by other inequities. Those inequities of power and resources give rise in turn to moral ambiguities and complexities. And those ambiguities and complexity require moral discourse and discernment. The church should sponsor conversations in which all stakeholders have a voice. It will continue to find its own voice in the memory and hope that the Spirit gives.

The church finds its life—and its voice—in its memory of Jesus. The Spirit guides the church by way of remembrance, reminding it again of a Jesus who announced "good news to the poor." The Spirit reminds us of Jesus' story of a rich man and Lazarus (Luke 16:19–31); one who remembers cannot be content when the poor must scavenge and beg for crumbs from the richly supplied tables—or medicine chests—of the rich. The Spirit reminds us of the story of the shepherd separating sheep and goats (Matt. 25:31–46); one who remembers sees in the sick, poor, and powerless the image of the one called "Lord." This person sees that what is done to the sick is done to the Lord. The Spirit reminds us of the story told in response to the inquiry, "Who is my neighbor?" (Luke 10:25–37); one who remembers the story of the Good Samaritan will not be complacent when some lie hurting and half-dead on the road to the global village. Such stories give us eyes to see a neighbor in the remotest stranger and to see the neighbor as the image of the Lord. Such stories give us ears to hear the human cry of lament without being overwhelmed and enervated.

To own such stories as one's own — whether in health care or policy formation — will mean, for example, speaking up for the sick poor in a shrinking world. Consider more fully the story of the Good Samaritan in the context of global inequities.

The church has frequently told the story of the Good Samaritan as a model for health care, and it has struggled to live the story in medical mission and in the founding of hospitals. But the story, in the context of expanding medical powers and limited resources, seems odd. Compassion can lead to costly care. We have today an assortment of technologies to help and to heal that make the Samaritan's binding of wounds seem quaint. To these technologies are attached costs which make the Samaritan's two *denarii* seem laughable — even if two days' wages for an agricultural worker of the time. Can the church live this story in a global context? Or are there simply too many along the side of the road? Can we still be Good Samaritans, or Fair Samaritans, in the midst of scarce resources and great need?

The answer, I think, is that we can still be Good Samaritans — but not without attention to policy. To be good, a Samaritan who encountered stranger after stranger left "half-dead" would have to give attention to policy. The Samaritan's compassion perhaps would finally insist on increased police protection along the Jericho road, or health care policies to assure access to hospitality. The compassion that moved the Samaritan to care for *one* would motivate attention to policy to care for *many*.

Let me quickly mention two caveats. First, the story does not suggest a particular policy; details of policy are not magically provided by compassion. Second, the story may not be reduced to policy. The story should result not just in policy formation, but in the formation of health care ministries among the poor, in village clinics staffed by contemporary Good Samaritans. The story is lived not just through public programs but in doctors and nurses who learn to see their work, not only as a collection of skills, but as a form of discipleship to the sick.

The story not only motivates attention to policy; it also helps shape the church's voice in the discourse concerning global inequities. The story shapes, first, a prophetic voice. In memory and in hope the church will protest injustice. The church must attract public attention to health care availability by speaking prophetically, by raising its voice. The inequities of the shrinking world must not be forgotten. That the West has been a net exporter of disease and an importer of resources should not be overlooked. Actions from the past need repentance: the marketing of infant formula that discouraged breast-feeding, the continuing commerce in tobacco, the exporting of waste for disposal, and the emigration of health professionals to the West. Items for prevention include the commodification of body parts, research in developing countries on therapies for which the citizens receive no direct benefit,[47]

---

47. Consider, for example, the placebo-controlled trial of zidovudine (AZT) in Thailand to determine the safety and efficacy of a short course of AZT in preventing transmission of HIV from mothers to infants. See Leonard H. Glantz et al., "Research

and the dominance of marketplace values in the development of an international biotech industry.[48]

Prophetic indictments of unjust patterns are significant contributions to public deliberation in the global village, but prophets do not necessarily make good managers. Prophetic voices are appropriate and important, but they are insufficient for the formation of policy. The Spirit and the biblical story help form, not just a prophetic voice, but a sage voice. The sage is willing to test conviction by experience, urging virtues and a vision that policy by itself cannot supply but that are critically important to the formation of good policy, and on which the success of any policy may depend. The global Good Samaritan will need to nurture virtues besides compassion to be good and to form good policy. The first virtue is truthfulness, the readiness to acknowledge the truth about the world, medicine, the limits imposed by mortality, and the finitude of resources. The twin of truthfulness is humility, the readiness to acknowledge that we are not gods but creatures of God, mortal creatures in need, finally, of God's care, and watching for God's future. Joined to both is gratitude, the thankfulness for opportunities to care for those regarded among "the least of these." We have come again to compassion. The Samaritan will never be good without compassion, without love, for the neighbor.

Jesus was asked, "But who is my neighbor?" It is a question of great importance in a shrinking world. He replied with the story of the Good Samaritan and with his own question: "Who was a neighbor to the one left half-dead?" Notice two things: first, the Samaritan *was* a neighbor, not just a stranger or enemy. We are neighbors, even to those we do not know. The Spirit creates a global community of peaceable difference, a community of neighbors and friends. Second, the answer to the question "Who is my neighbor?" comes indirectly, not as much by theoretical analysis as by a readi-

in Developing Countries: Taking 'Benefit' Seriously," *Hastings Center Report* 28 (November–December 1998): 38–42.

48. Consider, for example, that the Geron Corporation expects profit from its human embryonic stem cell research. To its credit, the Geron Ethics Advisory Board included the following in its guidelines for stem cell research: "All such research must be done in a context of concern for global justice." See Geron Ethics Advisory Board, "Research with Human Embryonic Stem Cells: Ethical Considerations," *Hastings Center Report* 29 (March–April 1999): 31–36. A thoughtful commentary on this guideline may be found in Lisa Sowle Cahill, "The New Biotech World Order" (pp. 45–48), in the same issue of the *Hastings Center Report*.

ness to care. The global Good Samaritan will discover neighbors and friends in a shrinking world by caring for them.

The contemporary Samaritan will never be good with compassion alone; a *just* compassion is required. What justice requires is much disputed in the global village. In the power of the Spirit the church may nudge the analysis of justice toward the biblical story, such as accounts of exodus, liberation, and equality. Christians contribute to global policy sometimes by speaking prophetically, sometimes by speaking sagely, and sometimes by telling the biblical story. Let me repeat, however, that the story does not recommend particular policy. Policy is always developed within particular conditions. Policy making remains the art of the possible. The good and the right are always relevant, but relevant under constraints of the possible.[49] The conditions of a shrinking world include nation-states' limited influence over business and research conducted across national boundaries, beyond the scope of national laws. States now share power with international corporations, with multinational and nongovernmental organizations,[50] and the church must participate in policy discussions not only with and about the nation-state, but with and about these other organizations. The churches are themselves nongovernmental organizations; they need not see this shift as an opportunity to assert their own power, but as an opportunity to speak politically in their own voice.[51]

To the discourse about policy the church brings convictions learned at Pentecost. In memory and hope it looks for the curse of Babel to be lifted. It does not, like Enlightenment belief, assume that all must agree about universal and purely rational principles before we can understand each other. It does not, like the postmodernist, presume that there is no hope of communication across differences. Given asymmetries of power, the church must, in its own discourse and conversations, listen carefully to the stranger and especially to those who are least well off. Although globaliza-

49. See James M. Gustafson, "Moral Discourse about Medicine: A Variety of Forms," *Journal of Medicine and Philosophy* 15, no. 2 (1990): 125–42.

50. Jessica T. Mathews, "Power Shift," *Foreign Affairs* 76 (1997): 50–59.

51. On the contributions of NGOs to the Earth Summit in Rio de Janeiro in 1992, where they helped bridge differences between northern and southern hemispheres and mobilized public pressure to enact a treaty on greenhouse gases, resisted by governments, see ibid. On the contributions of NGOs, especially religious NGOs, to the UN International Conference on Population and Development in Cairo (1994), see Amy L. Girst and Larry L. Greenfield, "Population and Development: Conflict and Consensus at Cairo," *Second Opinion* 20 (April 1995): 51–61.

tion has been marked in part by the growth of communication, given moral differences and complexities, communication, even if possible technologically, is sometimes more difficult. The church as a community of discourse may be the "first fruits" of God's good future. But the church must demonstrate and teach that a congregation and a globe require a diversity of gifts—and a diversity of voices—if discourse is to be discerning. In memory and in hope Christians sometimes speak prophetically, sometimes sagely, sometimes analytically, sometimes politically, using policy analysis and compromise to accomplish good for those who hurt, or to avert harm toward which pride and greed still tilt the world.

The voice of the churches will only ring true if it enacts the word as well as speaks it, if it lives the story it loves to tell. "If we live by the Spirit, let us also be guided by the Spirit." The saying is still good advice for the church as it continues to care for the sick while the world shrinks, while Western medicine asserts hegemony over other traditions of healing, and while the power of death continues its doomed reign. To be guided by the Spirit means to remember, to hope, and to struggle against the evils that threaten our embodied lives and our common life in the global village.

– *Chapter 4* –

Science, Technology, and the Mission of Theology in a New Century

Ronald Cole-Turner

Science and technology constantly reinterpret and re-create our world. They are affected by the broad processes of globalization, but perhaps more than any other feature of globalization, they are themselves responsible for these processes. Whether we consider the global community of scientific research or the effects of mass communications technology, these forces and processes are intertwined. It is in this context that science reshapes our consciousness of ourselves, our cosmos, and our place in it. Technology fashions new realities and redefines old relationships. Of all the forces that shape our future, technology seems to be the most powerful.

But we must ask whether technology is a blind process beyond control, whether it transforms us in ways that we do not understand or cannot direct, and whether we have become mere playthings of a power we can no longer guide. How is technology itself shaped or guided, if it is at all? Can theology and the church comprehend the emerging insights of science or understand transformations that seem overwhelming? Dare we think that theology can shape technology?

This challenge involves a theological understanding of science but also a theological analysis of technology. This essay centers on the second of these challenges. However, because success in thinking theologically about technology depends first on understanding the relationship between theology and science, the first section offers a few suggestions about that relationship. Section two reviews recent developments in technology, particularly in computers and genetics, in an effort not simply to describe technology but to draw out the emerging cultural and religious questions. In section three, the religious assumptions about technology are described as a step toward section four, which offers modest proposals for undertaking an audacious task, namely, transforming technology.

Theology and Science

At the most concrete level, the challenge of science for theology is to the traditional doctrines of the church. At this level, that of *credo* or of the generalized beliefs on which a Christian life can be developed, rather than that of a merely academic theology, it is widely agreed by believers and unbelievers alike that science discredits belief. This challenge, therefore, is at once intellectual and pastoral, and we must say evangelical, because the inadequacy of theology's responses to the successes of science has convinced many that as science advances, theology must retreat. With each major advance of science, theology relinquishes its doctrines and its interest or claim to speak about portions of the creation.

This leads to a truncation of *credo* and finally to a complete crisis of faith, felt acutely today. In the seventeenth century, the geocentric universe was replaced; in the eighteenth, divine causality; in the nineteenth, special human creation; and in the twentieth, the human soul, whose final conquest by science was announced recently by Francis Crick, co-discoverer of the structure of DNA:

> Most religions hold that some kind of spirit exists that persists after one's bodily death and, to some degree, embodies the essence of that human being.... When a person dies his soul leaves the body, although what happens after that — whether the soul goes to heaven, hell, or purgatory or alternatively is reincarnated as a donkey or a mosquito — depends upon the particular religion.

Most people still believe in a soul, Crick says. "But then some four thousand years ago almost everyone believed the earth was flat. The main reason for this radical change of opinion is the spectacular advance of modern science."[1] As science continues to advance, Crick suggests, the soul will go the way of the flat earth. Recent studies in

---

1. Francis Crick, *The Astonishing Hypothesis: The Scientific Search for the Soul* (New York: Charles Scribner's Sons, 1994), 4.

the history of science now show Crick to be wrong, at least about modern science revealing the shape of the earth, and thus possibly about his inferences. But what can we say if he asks, Where is theological literature articulating a contemporary, scientifically literate view of what we once called the soul?[2]

Theology has often neglected the constructive task of ongoing doctrinal reinterpretation in light of emerging insight from the sciences. A deeper problem, however, is the sweeping confidence Crick and others attach to scientific reductionism. The success of explanatory reduction in science is widely presumed to support reductionism as a general worldview. Thus, whenever science succeeds in its legitimate exercise of reduction to simplest explanations, nonreductionist theological interpretations suddenly find themselves suspended at a higher but now disconnected explanatory level, no longer credible to many because they appear gratuitous, optional, and epiphenomenal. Soul becomes molecules and nothing more. Life becomes mutation and replication and little more.

Richard Dawkins is less charitable to theology than Crick. Compared to science and particularly to technology, Dawkins writes, theology is good for nothing:

> What has theology ever said that is of the smallest use to anybody? When has theology ever said anything that is demonstrably true and is not obvious? I have listened to theologians, read them, debated against them. I have never heard any of them ever say anything of the smallest use, anything that was not either platitudinously obvious or downright false. If all the achievements of scientists were wiped out tomorrow, there would be no doctors but witch doctors, no transport faster than horses, no computers, no printed books, no agriculture beyond subsistence peasant farming. If all the achievements of theologians were wiped out tomorrow, would anyone notice the slightest difference? Even the bad achievements of scientists, the bombs, and sonar-guided whaling vessels *work*. The achievements of theologians don't do anything, don't affect anything, don't mean anything.[3]

---

2. See the exception to this general gap: Warren S. Brown, Nancey Murphey, and H. Newton Malony, eds., *Whatever Became of the Soul?* (Minneapolis: Fortress Press, 1998).

3. Richard Dawkins, "The Emptiness of Theology," *Free Inquiry* (Spring 1998): 6.

Whether this is worthy of a reply — or whether Dawkins himself ever wonders how science can recognize bad science from good — is beside the point. Many people believe this, and it cannot pass unanswered.

And so we must ask: What good is theology? What of value does theology add to a scientific understanding of the world? Or, to expand the question, what constitutes good theology in an age of science? The answer to this question, although far beyond the scope of what can be offered here, is now being sought by a growing number of scholars, who are pursuing several strategies. For example, some ask what questions raised by science cannot be answered by science, but require normative and methodological answers, such as those offered by theology. Others consider how science illumines human religiosity by describing innate human openness to self-transcendence and morality. Still others inquire whether science (evolution in particular) either presupposes or supports confidence in our ability to know our environment in ways that can minimally be described as "successful adaptations" in the evolutionary pathway of our species. Others ask what science is, what its rules and methods are, and what counts as good science, all in relationship to similar but distinct tasks and methods in theology. Even more pursue the question of theological method and ask specifically about the sciences as sources of insight for theology, even claiming that, in science, theology finds a source of revelatory significance along the lines intimated by John Calvin: "If we regard the Spirit of God as the sole fountain of truth, we shall neither reject the truth itself, nor despise it wherever it shall appear, unless we wish to dishonor the Spirit of God."[4]

These strategies of theological research have been pursued with new rigor since the 1960s, resulting in a rich and growing literature. By themselves, however, such strategies are inadequate in that they neglect the distinctive features of technology. While science and technology are deeply intertwined, they are distinct in aim and context. Technology, which has already transformed the face of the planet, now stands poised to transform human nature. The Human Genome Project has produced a complete "rough draft" in 2000. We are rapidly gaining the power to modify that code

4. John Calvin, *Institutes of the Christian Religion,* ed. John T. McNeill, trans. Ford Lewis Battles, Library of Christian Classics 20 (Philadelphia: Westminster Press, 1960), 1.273–74 (II.2.15).

in our bodies and in our offspring. Digital communications link us as never before, and soon the computer chip will be cheap, ubiquitous, even disposable and implantable. Genetic and digital technology will merge, as they have done already with the "gene chip" and with computer/brain interfaces. While genetic science seeks to understand gene/protein relationships, genetic engineering creates new combinations of genes or generates new gene sequences. In engineering, creation precedes understanding. Indeed, it *revises valid understanding*, for when Ian Wilmut produced Dolly, he did not merely create a new lamb or a new technique; he changed biology by reversing a fundamental principle of cell differentiation. It is now possible for adult mammalian cells to de-differentiate. Human technique changes not just the way we see nature, not just what exists in nature, but nature's own rules.

It would be too easy to say that theology interprets science and that theological ethics should guide technology. That double pairing of theology/science and ethics/technology has become the standard approach and is valuable as far as it goes.[5] Yet if we are limited to these pairs, we miss the critical fact that technology creates new realities that call for theological interpretation. These technologies are not mere gadgets or toys. They are changes in our humanity that call for theological insight. How are we to understand these changes? What are we making of ourselves? Such technology changes not only the world, but also what theology once called the human soul. Will its changes be consistent with God's redemption and transformation of the creation? Or will technology's changes plunge us into deeper and ever more intractable structures of injustice, sin, and bondage? Will it contribute to the glorious liberty of the children of God or to their enslavement to the powers of the present age? We cannot *not* answer, for ignoring the questions will leave contemporary technological culture to its own devices.

In the world that will be, technology will transform persons, institutions, cultures, and souls. It is altogether too likely that the church will marginalize itself in the role of chaplain, picking up the pieces, caring for the bruised, mopping up the damage, but never engaging the engines of transformation themselves, steering, persuading, and transforming the transformers.

---

5. This is the organizational structure of Ian Barbour's two-volume Gifford Lectures, originally published as Ian Barbour, *Religion in an Age of Science*, vol. 1, and *Ethics in an Age of Technology*, vol. 2, The Gifford Lectures 1989–91 (San Francisco: Harper & Row, 1990, 1994).

Questions Raised by Contemporary Technologies

We have experienced two decades of rapid expansion and declining costs of computer technology, and recent fundamental breakthroughs suggest that the end is nowhere in sight. The Internet, a global system through which computers share data, is doubling in volume every hundred days. "Within the next five to ten years, the vast majority of Americans should be able to interact with the Internet from their television sets, watch television on the PCs, and make telephone calls from both devices. These combined services will be brought to homes by satellite, wireless, microwave, television cable and telephone lines, all interconnected in one overall system."[6]

But more important than explosive growth is the qualitative impact of computers and the Internet on persons, community, culture, pedagogy, and the mission of the church. The Internet is creating a vast new reality, invisible but anything but unreal. In that it parallels previously existing realities, it may be called virtual; for instance, an Internet educational activity might be called a virtual classroom. But the Internet is hardly virtual; it is as real as anything Columbus discovered, even if created in garages rather than discovered in boats.

We are only beginning to think about how the digital age is changing the human psyche. What does it do to us to spend hours in front of the screen, to converse with people we have never seen, to click from task to task, to rely on the machine for our memory?

> People can get lost in virtual worlds. Some are tempted to think of life in cyberspace as insignificant, as escape or meaningless diversion. It is not. Our experiences there are serious play. We belittle them at our risk. We must understand the dynamics of virtual experience both to foresee who might be in danger and to put these experiences to best use.[7]

How will the digital revolution transform human community, as face-to-face contact becomes supplemented more and more with technology? Face-to-face interaction becomes face-to-screen, even "face as screen" and "screen as face" as we look at others through

---

6. U.S. Department of Commerce, *The Emerging Digital Economy* (Washington, D.C., 1998), 10. Online: http://www.ecommerce.gov/emerging.htm

7. Sherry Turkle, *Life on the Screen: Identity in the Age of the Internet* (New York: Touchstone, 1995), 268–69.

digitized pictures. Human community will be defined by communication independent of geography. These new communities, mediated by digital technology and composed of people of common interest rather than common space, are often termed "virtual communities," first defined by Howard Rheingold as "social aggregations that emerge from the Net when enough people carry on... public discussions long enough, with sufficient human feeling, to form webs of personal relationships in cyberspace."[8] For many, "virtual communities" supplement traditional communities, making it possible to work in electronic contact with the world while living in spatial contact with the neighborhood or village. Indeed, this technology may reverse the trend toward urbanization by making highly diverse, high-skill jobs accessible to people anywhere.

The Internet will restructure institutions, including educational and ecclesiastical structures.

> The Information marketplace will also increase the prospects for forming *virtual alliances* across hierarchical lines within an organization, with its suppliers and customers, and between sister organizations. We might reflexively assume that organizations will therefore become flatter and that all this distributed intelligence will conquer even the most difficult organizational problems because of the informality of the medium and the richness with which it can connect human resources.[9]

Traditional gatekeepers will lose their function, and relationships will be formed horizontally across an organization and between organizations, stripping traditional authorities of the power to control. Kevin Kelly is one of many to interpret the Internet using organic metaphors. It is as if the Internet were a single organism or perhaps a hive of bees, communicating as one and therefore capable of collective action.

> When everything is connected to everything in a distributed network, everything happens at once. When everything happens at once, wide and fast-moving problems simply route around any central authority. Therefore overall governance

---

8. Howard Rheingold, *The Virtual Community: Homesteading on the Electronic Frontier* (Reading, Mass.: Addison-Wesley, 1993), 5.

9. Michael L. Dertouzos, *What Will Be: How the New World of Information Will Change Our Lives* (San Francisco: Harperbusiness, 1998), 204.

> must arise from the most human interdependent acts done locally in parallel, and not from a central command. A mob *can* steer itself, and in the territory of rapid, massive, and heterogeneous change, only a mob can steer. To get something from nothing, control must rest at the bottom within simplicity.[10]

If biological metaphors are employed to describe the Internet and the Web, then we should expect that Darwinian evolution can be invoked to explain how they came into existence. The Internet evolved, perhaps not strictly by Darwinian rules, but through a process roughly like emergent evolution, according to which higher levels of organization lead to emergent phenomena, such as when the evolved brain attains consciousness. "When Tim Berners-Lee invented the Web, he envisioned it as a growing superhuman 'brain' formed by linking together a lot of individuals' knowledge around the world."[11] It has been suggested that the emergence of the "superhuman brain" was anticipated by Teilhard de Chardin forty years earlier: "[T]hanks to the prodigious biological event represented by the discovery of electro-magnetic waves, each individual finds himself henceforth (actively and passively) simultaneously present, over land and sea, in every corner of the earth."[12] In a Whiteheadian theological reflection on the Internet and the Web, Jennifer Cobb declares them to be "classic examples of emergent entities. The Net meets the basis definition of emergence — its whole is greater than the sum of its parts."[13] In this respect, Cobb believes, the digital revolution *is* organic evolution, with emergent levels of complexity arising unpredictably from simpler antecedents.

How apt are such biological and evolutionary metaphors? There is a sense in which the Internet and the Web evolve unpredictably and without centralized control. Furthermore, these metaphors have the value of relativizing the often excessive distance between the biological (natural) and the technological (artificial). But the underlying process of emergence is surely not Darwinian, nor does the whole function as an organism. People intentionally contribute pieces of the technology and modify its applications. Teilhardian metaphors

---

10. Kevin Kelly, *Out of Control: The New Biology of Machines, Social Systems, and the Economic World* (Reading, Mass.: Addison-Wesley, 1994), 469.

11. Dertouzos, *What Will Be*, 41.

12. Pierre Teilhard de Chardin, *The Phenomenon of Man*, quoted in Jennifer Cobb, *Cybergrace: The Search for God in the Digital World* (New York: Crown, 1998), 86.

13. Cobb, *Cybergrace*, 49.

in particular suggest that the Internet was inevitable and must represent progress, for like human consciousness itself, it represents the triumph of mind over mere matter—the emergence of intelligence, spirit, or unlimited information where there was only silicon and electrons. But does the Internet work this way? Is it not more accurate, if more prosaic, to say that the Internet merely connects fingertips and eyeballs, that it is a preeminent flow-through technology but not a superbrain or a newly emergent phenomenon of evolution? Whitehead cautioned against paying metaphysical compliments to deity. We should be much more wary of an exaggerated metaphysics of technology.

Nevertheless, having recognized that danger, we must insist that the importance of digital technology and the Internet should not be underestimated or their theological significance ignored. This technology is capable of profound transformations by renegotiating the connections between human beings. Nowhere is this more true than in regard to globalization. Indeed, for many, the Internet is not merely the key symbol of globalization; it is its driving force. Surely there is much to be said for the global connections mediated by the Internet. But in trying to understand this process, we must recognize that the Internet links but does not homogenize or reduce cultures to a common global culture. The Internet is a global network of linked and searchable particularities. Precisely by linking particular traditions, identities, cultures, values, and locales, it brings the diversity of the world to consciousness.

In the future, it is likely that we will wear chips to connect us to our home, office, and the world. But not only will chips surround our bodies, engulfing us in visual and tactile experiences indistinguishable from those they imitate, they will be implanted in or plugged into our bodies so that the human brain itself becomes an input/output device. These technologies may assist those with handicaps, but therapy may blur into enhancement with the advent of "a supersensory human being."

> Equipped with eyeglass cameras that can see not only visual images but radar, infrared, and ultraviolet images, ears that can hear conversations and higher- and lower-pitched sounds beyond the normal range, an electronic nose ... that can detect all kinds of faint smells, and tactile interfaces that translate environmental stimuli like odorless gasses or changes in barometric pressure into pressures on our skin, we may be able

to sharpen our conventional senses well beyond their usual activity.[14]

In the late 1990s, the first experiments in computer brain implants were conducted.[15] Attempts to restore sight to the blind by feeding electrical impulses directly from video cameras into the visual cortex of the brain have met with some early success, as have similar efforts to restore hearing. Patients who were unable to use their limbs received, in the motor cortex of their brains, special implants designed to serve as an interface between the brain's electrochemical activity and a computer's digital electronics. The device contained microscopic electrodes seeded with neural growth factor, a natural chemical that induces brain growth. Living cells in the patients' brains grow toward these tiny electrodes so that the electrodes can detect the brain's activity and turn it into computer input data. As of 1999, one paralyzed patient was able to think of moving a part of his body, and by doing so to move a cursor on a computer screen. In this way he could give the computer simple instructions, without any form of communication except brain activity.

Where might this lead? Few are troubled by using technology to help people with injuries regain their normal functions. But should such devices be implanted in people without illness or injury, but who merely want a way of enhancing their powers? It will likely become possible to provide enhanced data perception, enabling such capabilities as infrared vision, perhaps for soldiers or police. Someday it might be possible to implant chips that carry enormous amounts of data — virtual libraries — whose contents could then be recalled in an instant, as if they were part of the natural memory. Surely this will pose troubling questions of the self, its identity, memories, and the integrity of its own experience, and someday people with implants may no longer recognize the boundaries of their "true" self, or even whether such a distinction can be drawn at all.

Even more troubling is the possibility that the wiring could be reversed: Instead of using the brain to control the computer, the computer could be used to control the brain. It would be profoundly troubling to contemplate a person with an implant whose experi-

14. Dertouzos, *What Will Be,* 70–71.

15. For a helpful discussion, see G. Q. Maguire, Jr., and Ellen M. McGee, "Implantable Brain Chips? Time for Debate," *Hastings Center Report* 29 (January–February 1999): 7–13.

ences or moods are under the control of another person. Such use of technology would be deeply abhorrent to most people, because it would violate commonly held principles like autonomy and consent. But it is not clear that requested enhancement technologies can be opposed on these principles, or that the principles of bioethics offer much guidance or restraint.

This issue emerges with greater clarity when we consider genetic and biomedical technologies, which have arrived at almost exactly the same time and in many ways have depended on advances in computing power. Automatic DNA-sequencing machines now decipher the human genetic code and download the results nightly to the Web. DNA-chip technology is already on the market, making individual DNA testing relatively easy, portable, and inexpensive. Other species besides *Homo sapiens* are also being studied extensively, and technical breakthroughs, such as cloning (somatic-cell nuclear transfer) have now been achieved in sheep and mice. In late 1998, major advances in the isolation of human stem cells were announced. Together, these technologies pave the way to greater genetic control of the human body, even to introducing genetic modifications in offspring in ways that are inheritable by later generations.

Already today, many human pregnancies are being tested for the presence of genetic disease. While it is desirable to improve the health of the unborn, and while there are strong financial incentives to do so, many people are troubled by the idea that pregnancies should be tested and, if found to have a genetic problem, aborted. In part to find an alternative to prenatal testing and abortion, scientists have developed the ability to test an embryo before it is implanted. In this procedure, a couple conceives about eight embryos in vitro. Before any is implanted, all are tested. The embryos are allowed to divide to an eight-cell stage. One cell is removed from each embryo and genetically tested. In this way, scientists can determine which embryos will develop disease and which will not. Some find this procedure morally superior to traditional conception, testing, and abortion. But it does raise concern for the discarded embryos.

Another approach for dealing with genetic disease is to try to treat it at the genetic level by changing the genes. This is usually called "somatic-cell gene therapy," and hundreds of experiments involving thousands of patients have been performed, with ambiguous results. The concept is clear and elegant: if a disease is caused by genes, change the genes, at least in the affected tissues. But this is proving to be quite difficult to do, at least with the level of success needed for human medicine. Several key problems have to be solved. First, the corrected genes need to be inserted into the cells of the affected tissues, usually billions of cells. Often a virus is used as the vector or delivery system, since viruses naturally infect cells with foreign DNA. Second, once the corrected DNA is in the cell, it needs to be taken up by the genome in such a way that it will be expressed or make its gene product. Third, the corrected gene needs to remain in the affected tissue, which may mean that it needs to be reinserted at frequent intervals as cells die and are replaced. So far, these technical challenges have kept scientists from claiming clear success in helping a patient through gene therapy. At the same time, the field is characterized by great optimism, intense activity, and substantial private funding. Most so-called genetic diseases affect too few people to warrant private funding, so the current focus of privately funded gene-therapy research lies in cancer or other widespread diseases with a genetic component.

Recent experiments with rats suggest that an artificial genetic molecule can be constructed and function something like a "search-and-replace" computer command, seeking the precise location of a genetic problem and forcing it to change to a healthy or normal version of the gene.[16] If this approach is developed, it might greatly improve the accuracy and the safety of genetic modifications.

Few object to gene therapy on moral or religious grounds, especially to treating life-threatening disease. But what if the genetic modification affected not just the cells of the body but the sex cells, and what if the change were inheritable and passed to future generations, affecting *all* the cells of their bodies? This prospect, often called germ-line modification, is far more problematic than somatic-cell therapy, at least for many people. Questions of human foreknowledge, responsibility to future generations, and the limits of human control over human procreation are key questions usually raised when this step is proposed. Sometimes the term "designer children" is applied to the products of germ-line modification.

Until the late 1990s, a sharp line between somatic-cell and germ-line modification was observed. But in January 1999, the National Institutes of Health convened a Gene Therapy Policy Conference to discuss a proposal for gene therapy in fetuses. Aside from the special

---

16. Betsy T. Kren, Paramita Bandyopadhyay, and Clifford J. Steer, "*In Vivo* Site-Directed Mutagenesis of the *Factor IX* Gene by Chimeric RNA/DNA Oligonucleotides," *Nature Medicine* 4 (March 1998): 285–90.

ethical issues raised by any prenatal therapy, this proposal raised the likelihood that the genetic therapy performed on these fetuses would affect their sex cells. If the therapy were successful in the fetuses and they lived to reproduce, it seemed possible that the therapy would affect their sex cells and thus their offspring. This would constitute germ-line modification, although in this experiment the germ-line effect would not be the primary intention.

Protesting against this proposal, the Council on Responsible Genetics warned:

> This is it. This is how it begins. Of all the issues arising from genetic engineering, the threat of germ line manipulation is perhaps the most ominous. The Council for Responsible Genetics (CRG) strongly opposes any attempt to change future generations through genetic engineering. As CRG board member and developmental biologist Stuart Newman has said, "We must not accept a mind-set that would subject human beings to manufacturing technologies and eventually lead to designer children." Do we want a future in which babies are produced according to genetic recipes?[17]

The possibility of inadvertent germ-line modification cannot currently be ruled out for any somatic-cell treatment, unless the patient is sterile or beyond reproductive age. It may turn out that opposition to germ-line modification is so strong that it forces a slowing of research in somatic-cell gene therapy until the germ-line question is resolved. More likely, however, is the prospect that support for somatic-cell gene therapy will force acceptance of the risk of inadvertent germ-line modification, and that this in turn will promote acceptance of intentional germ-line modification as a new strategy against disease.

When thinking about the full possibilities of these technologies, we need to bear in mind that current understanding of the role of genes is very small. But already we can see that genes play a role not only in physical traits but in personality and behavioral traits as well. Recent findings link specific genes with human behaviors or predispositions such as intelligence, violence and aggressiveness, anxiety, and various mental illnesses. Other studies, less precise in their findings, strongly suggest a genetic basis for sexual orientation.

---

17. The Council for Responsible Genetics, "Say No to Designer Children," statement, September 18, 1998.

These are traits related to what theology traditionally defined as the soul. Because we are now learning the genetic basis of these traits, it is becoming possible to alter the genes that affect the innate tendencies of our moral and religious qualities.[18] The relationship between any gene and something as complex as a behavioral trait is subtle and subject to the richly modulating effects of environment, so we should not expect that human personality would become manipulable in detail. Nevertheless, we will be able to affect the predispositions of our offspring with genetic technology. When we think about the full significance of these technologies, we have to recognize that they will offer some possibility for the selection and enhancement of some behavioral traits, and not just be limited to treating disease. For some, it is precisely this potential for behavioral control that is the most objectionable part of the technology.

How would people respond to power to influence even slightly the behavioral makeup of their offspring? Perhaps we can see how this power is used already with psychopharmacology and with the widespread use of drugs such as Ritalin or selective serotonin reuptake inhibitors, the best known being Prozac. Peter D. Kramer, in his modern classic *Listening to Prozac,* writes: "We are edging toward what might be called the '*medicalization of personality.*' Or perhaps... we are over the edge."[19] Prozac not only treats certain forms of mental illness, but also alters the personality of the one who is well, to make them, in Kramer's terms, "better than well."[20]

Many feel that our experience with psychopharmacology is a good predictor of future use of genetic modification of behavior and personality. If so, we should predict that people will seek to alter themselves and especially to enhance themselves if they feel the threat of competition from others who have been enhanced. When it comes to the possibility of human germ-line modification, we should expect that people will someday choose to modify their offspring, not just to avoid disease, but to enhance desirable traits. Undoubtedly they will be disappointed with the results, as parents often are, but they will no doubt try and they will partly succeed, at least in effecting some alteration.

The technology of cloning by somatic-cell nuclear transfer will

18. For a recent summary of behavior genetics, see Dean Hamer and Peter Copeland, *Living with Our Genes: Why They Matter More Than You Think* (New York: Doubleday, 1998).

19. P. D. Kramer, *Listening to Prozac* (New York: Penguin Books, 1997), 37.

20. Ibid., xv.

play a role. Using cloning as an alternative reproductive technology may be repulsive to some and acceptable to others; even so, it is not very audacious technologically. Compared to germ-line modification, cloning is conservative. But combined with the ability to modify genes, to add and delete them, cloning will confer enormous powers to future parents over their offspring. Lee Silver is correct when he writes that the current success levels of germ-line modification are too low to be acceptable for human use, "but with cloning, the entire equation changes. Now, multiple cells grown from a single embryo could be subjected to genetic engineering" and the successfully altered embryos implanted. Dolly's makers have already taken this next step with sheep, and "it is in the very same manner — when the techniques of cloning and genetic engineering are combined — that the human species will gain control over its own destiny."[21]

These technologies will affect not only the control we have over conception, but through them we will gain great control over aging and longevity. As Silver points out, researchers are intensely engaged in studying the problems of aging, and some seem to believe not only that diseases can be "conquered" one by one, but that the fundamental processes of aging, at the cellular and genetic level, can be arrested. In addition, it appears likely that we will soon be able to replace the cells of the body that are damaged by injury or disease, especially the cells of key organs or of the brain. In 1998, researchers announced success in isolating human embryonic stem cells, which replicate indefinitely in the laboratory. Soon researchers hope to learn how to coax these cells to develop into any cell of the human body, suitable for implanting in patients who have lost the function of cells or tissues. For instance, in Parkinson's disease, diseased neurons in the region of the brain that produces dopamine might be replaced by brain stem cells, which could take up the location and the function of the impaired cells. This technology might even be combined with somatic-cell nuclear transfer to make a culture of cells that is genetically identical to the patient. Or some form of genetic modification might be used on the stem cells to make them superior to the cells with which the patient was born.

In all these ways, human cells, tissues, genes, and embryos are accessible to technological modification. The results will affect not merely the physiological functions of the organism but its psycho-

21. Lee Silver, *Remaking Eden: How Genetic Engineering and Cloning Will Transform the American Family* (New York: Avon Books, 1998), 152.

logical functions, traits, and capacities as well. The engineer will become the engineered. How far might this go? Consider the projections of Lee Silver. Referring to a time about two centuries from now, Silver comments:

> It was a critical turning point in the evolution of life in the universe.... Throughout it all, there were those who said we couldn't go any further, that there were limits to mental capacity and technological advances. But those prophesied limits were swept aside, one after another, as intelligence, knowledge, and technological power continued to rise.[22]

Silver foresees that we will make our offspring more intelligent, and so they will be better engineers than we are, and able to improve their offspring even more. The ratcheting effect of evolution will be put into fast-forward by genetic engineering.

Silver continues, referring to a time more than a millennium away:

> A special point has now been reached in the distant future. And in this era, there exists a special group of mental beings. Although these beings can trace their ancestry back directly to *homo sapiens,* they are as different from humans as humans are from the primitive worms with tiny brains that first crawled along the earth's surface.[23]

Silver believes that we will deliberately engineer our own replacement, the *transhuman,* and with an engineered eschatology, cease to exist. Thus we will become an intermediate or merely transitional species before full realization of an evolutionary process that has taken control of itself.

Even if we put, as an emergent phenomenon, Silver's visions of the transhuman in the same category as the Internet — that of metaphysical excess and technological giddiness — a more sober and unavoidable question arises. On the one hand, these technologies offer attractive approaches to serious disease. Inheritable or germline modifications may someday be especially attractive because they may make it possible to confer to future offspring a capacity to resist many diseases, such as cancer. But these technologies, both somatic and inheritable, can be used to enhance human traits.

---

22. Ibid., 292.
23. Ibid., 292–93.

Even heightened resistance to disease must be seen as a kind of enhancement. Much more so, however, would be the improvement of traits having nothing to do with disease, such as mental or athletic ability. Any of these improvements, if successful, could expand the gap that already exists between those who could afford them and those who could not, or between wealthy and poor nations. Equally troublesome is the prospect of the alteration of traits such as skin color in ways that are complicitous with prejudice and injustice. It is increasingly recognized even by bioethicists that standard bioethics, with its principle of autonomy in matters such as reproductive choice, has little to offer in the way of restraint or guidance. If that is true, then additional values and perspectives will need to be invoked.

Religions of Technology

Richer values and perspectives do, in fact, surround technology and undergird technological culture. We might even say that technology has a religion, perhaps more than one. Consider this comment of a computer scientist, Ralph Abraham, speaking in reverential terms about the creation of the Web:

> The WWW is miraculous.... It is theological creativity in action. If you look at the Web, there are all these different pieces of software without which it couldn't run. These pieces were created by volunteers, people who were responding to a kind of divine guidance. They were being pushed together toward creative synthesis.[24]

Here is the core of one version of technology's religion, emphasizing purpose, the drive toward problem-solving as divine guidance.

But consider another version of technology's religion. In a recent essay in *Science*, Kevin Kelly speaks of the culture of technology as distinct from both the culture of the arts *and* the culture of science. Technology is a "third culture," which Kelly dubs "nerd culture."

> While nerd culture deeply honors the rigor of the scientific method, its thrust is not pursuing truth, but pursuing novelty. "New," "improved," "different" are key attributes for this technological culture.... Outlined in the same broad strokes,

24. R. Abraham, cited in Cobb, *Cybergrace,* 47.

> we can say that the purpose of nerdism, then, is to create novelties as a means to truth and experience. In the third culture, the way to settle the question of how the mind works is to build a working mind. Scientists would measure and test a mind; artists would contemplate and abstract it. Nerds would manufacture one. Creation, rather than creativity, is the preferred mode of action. One would expect to see frenzied, messianic attempts to make stuff, to have creation race ahead of understanding, and this we see already. In the emerging nerd culture a question is framed so that the answer will usually be a new technology.
>
> The third culture creates new tools faster than new theories, because tools lead to novel discoveries quicker than theories do.... The third culture will favor the irrational if it brings options and possibilities, because new experiences trump rational proof.[25]

This is the second version of religion that undergirds technology. The focus is on sheer human creativity, not problem solving. The overarching metaphor is evolution, and creativity functions through mutations, some of which are retained, most of which are not. There is no guidance but there is advance, no purpose but always more stuff.

Some will protest that *good* engineering is *not* a "messianic attempt to make stuff" but the disciplined application of human intelligence to solve human problems. But this protest is grounded in the first version of religion, according to which good engineering solves human problems instead of blindly making stuff. But we must ask: How do we define a human problem? And who defines the problems? The most widely accepted answer today is found in "the market." If people need or want something, and will pay for it, they must see it as a solution to a problem. But we know that needs can be created to consume technologies, and that (for instance) computers and computer skills are now "needed" to participate in the emerging global economy and culture. More disturbingly, we know that many people see "normalcy" itself as a problem and want to be enhanced above their peers and, indeed, above them*selves*. Particularly with genetic technology, with the impossibility of distinguishing therapy from enhancement, the market populated by

25. Kevin Kelly, "The Third Culture," *Science* (February 13, 1998).

autonomous subjects who contract out the genetic design of their offspring is a profoundly unsatisfactory solution. In this setting, it is impossible to define "normal" or to refuse to treat it as if it were somehow deficient. An engineer may want to solve a problem (e.g., treat a genetic disease) but ends up enhancing traits above their normal range. This is already true of pharmacology, especially the growing field of psychopharmacology,[26] and may prove to be true of digital technologies, too.

Nonetheless, we speak confidently about solving human problems, treating diseases, overcoming genetic "defects," with a Baconian clarity about what we mean. In the writings of Francis Bacon, which perhaps more than other writings articulated the rationale of the modern technological project, a literal garden of Eden is presupposed. Human beings have fallen from that state of health and oneness with nature, so Bacon urges technology as a means of regaining a physical paradise. The Baconian confidence believes that a perfect condition of nature is knowable, that nature has deviated from that perfection, and that technology's mandate is to restore it to its right order. But there is no empirical normative past, no garden-of-Eden benchmark for health or for the normal or correct version of genes or atmospheric gases or anything else; our vision of normal is imagined, vague, and infinitely elastic. There is no conceptual line within science and technology between normal and deficient, and thus no corresponding moral clarity between therapy and enhancement or legitimate and illegitimate applications of technology. There is only relentless striving for improvement in the name of normalcy. At least for Bacon, technology had ends, both a purpose and a terminus: to restore Eden.[27] Once finished, Eden could go no further, because there could be no improving on what God had done first. For us, technology has no end and thus no ending, no *telos* and thus no *finis*. According to David Noble, Bacon's vision, now largely secularized and with its explicit theology silenced, still inspires technological culture: "[T]he present enchantment with things technological—the very measure of modern enlightenment—is rooted in religious myths and ancient imaginings. Although today's technologists, in their sober pursuit of utility, power, and profit, seem to set society's standard for rational-

26. See Kramer, *Listening to Prozac.*

27. An echo of the Baconian framework is rather obvious in Silver, and implicit in his title, *Remaking Eden.*

ity, they are driven also by distant dreams, spiritual yearnings for supernatural redemption."[28]

But if this, the first version of technology's religion, is beset with difficulty, so is the second. In the second version, creativity is good, and moral argument is reduced to persuading those who don't like new things to get used them. Kevin Kelly's *Wired,* the magazine of technological creativity, did not publish a discussion of the ethics of cloning but a report of the birth of a human clone, a cover story featuring a sweet little girl to whom no one could say no. The story was not fiction but a report filed a few years ahead of its time, as if it had been done. Lest anyone miss the point, the report appeared under this boldfaced challenge: "We're becoming the objects of our own technology, and we better get used to it."[29]

"We better get used to it" is the ethics of nerd culture. Ethical assessment is structurally retrospective, a reflexive quiver, not at the possibility of evil but at the oddness of the new. To be sure, the new can be shocking, viscerally revolting; or, in the technical language of bioethics, according to Arthur Caplan, the new can evoke a response of "Yuk." In a paper by Oliver Morton, "Overcoming Yuk," *Wired* reassures us: "The Yuk factor feels instinctual, primal, a law of nature. Yet it can pass quite quickly.... As we live with the unnatural... we begin first to accommodate it, then to accept it, then to appreciate it."[30] Ethicists still ask: What's under Yuk? Is there moral wisdom lurking beneath disgust? And if we have several Yuks together, do we have true anxiety, true moral worry? As eloquently as anyone, Leon Kass, in testimony before the National Bioethics Advisory Commission on human cloning, notes that many find cloning "revolting." In a comment based on his NBAC testimony, Kass grants that

> Revulsion is not an argument; and some of yesterday's repugnances are today calmly accepted — though, one must add, not always for the better. In crucial cases, however, repugnance is the emotional expression of deep wisdom, beyond reason's power fully to articulate it. Can anyone really give

---

28. David F. Noble, *The Religion of Technology: The Divinity of Man and the Spirit of Invention* (New York: Knopf, 1998), 3.

29. A headline for a *Wired* interview on cloning read, "Cloning: Problem? No Problem" (September 1997).

30. Oliver Morton, "Overcoming Yuk," *Wired* 6.10 (January 1998) at www.wired.com/wired/archive/6.01/morton.html.

> an argument fully adequate to the horror which is father-daughter incest (even with consent), or having sex with animals, or mutilating a corpse, or eating human flesh, or raping or murdering another human being? Would anybody's failure to give full rational justification for his revulsion at those practices make that revulsion ethically suspect? Not at all. On the contrary, we are suspicious of those who think that they can rationalize away our horror, say, by trying to explain the enormity of incest with arguments only about the genetic risks of inbreeding.[31]

But how do we distinguish permanent taboo from fleeting shock? Is cloning outrageous or will we just "get used to it"? Is it evil or merely novel? Some "hold dear" the idea of racial superiority and regard miscegenation with revulsion. Others claim a "deep wisdom" that warns them against birth control. Depth may reveal truth but may also blind us to our lies. Certainly, claims of "deep wisdom" need excavating. Nevertheless, there is something disquieting about the idea that moral judgment inevitably softens with time. Apparently this notion has been around for some time. Michael Dertouzos comments: "*[H]ardly any major innovation was welcome when it first appeared. Yet after a while, as the philosopher Arthur Schopenhauer notes, everyone would agree that 'it was all along an obviously great idea.'* "[32] If so, why bother with moral argument? Let the ethicist simply procrastinate a few days while the rest of us grow accustomed to what we thought we did not like, as if we were children outgrowing dislike for the idea of caviar.

Novelty can dazzle as well as repulse. When we see the novelty produced by technological prowess, sometimes we respond not by "Yuk" but "Wow!" or "Yo!" "I'm still thrilled by the feeling that I'm squinting into the future and catching the first revealing hint of revolutionary possibilities. I first experienced that particular kind of euphoria as a teenager," writes Bill Gates.[33] A very helpful Website, sponsored by the American Association for the Advancement of Science and linked to press releases announcing scientific discoveries, has the address of www.eurekalert.org, perpetuating the ancient

31. Leon R. Kass, "The Wisdom of Repugnance," in Leon R. Kass and James Q. Wilson, *The Ethics of Human Cloning* (Washington, D.C.: American Enterprise Institute, 1998), 18–19.
32. Dertouzos, *What Will Be,* 35 (emphasis in the original).
33. Bill Gates with Nathan Myhrvold and Peter Rinearson, *The Road Ahead* (New York: Penguin Books, 1995, 1996), 11.

tradition of magical exuberance of discovery. Or consider Richard Seed, so excited about cloning that he regards it as "the first serious step in becoming one with God."[34]

Should we therefore conclude that technology is wholly out of control? The religious visions that accompany technology seem incapable of distinguishing therapy from enhancement or good creativity from bad. Especially when we consider that technology is deeply enmeshed with global economic forces and political systems by which corporations and nation-states fund technology to assure future competitiveness, we must wonder how such a vast, interlocking system of technological advance can be stopped or controlled. Precisely because technology is both global and globalizing, it seems immune to regional or national control. Yet it is impossible to think of stopping technology cold, even if anyone wanted to. A global human population now in excess of six billion depends on technologically advanced systems to feed and sustain itself.

But short of stopping technology, is it not possible to nudge it, to tweak it along certain lines of development? Consider the recent public outcry over genetically modified (GM) food. As widely reported in the press, consumer rejection of the use of genetically modified foods in Europe and especially in the United Kingdom has led to their removal from the market. On account of the global links of biotechnology and trade, consumers in Britain were able to claim a surprising level of control over the United States and transnational corporations in a way that directly affected U.S. farmers. American companies that had hoped to sell genetically modified food products in Britain found their market limited; this influenced American farmers not to buy or plant GM seeds, sometimes not even on separate plots for fear that the non-GM crops would appear to be genetically modified in tests. As this essay is being written, debates in Europe, the United States, and international regulatory agencies are under way, with consumer preferences influencing local farmers' decisions, farmers and consumers influencing national politics, and global issues shaping national, local, and consumer practices. Whether these debates will endure long enough to cause permanent changes in the development of this technology is hard to predict. But clearly this episode demonstrates the link between particular cultures and potentially global technologies, showing that technology is anything but unaccountable.

---

34. Quoted in Silver, *Remaking Eden*, 307.

It should be noted that the decisive issue in Britain, the issue that brought many moderates to oppose the agricultural biotechnology, was that labels were not provided so consumers could distinguish between GM and non-GM foods. In other words, the power of the consumer to choose or refuse a technology was threatened; thus, the technology was rejected, although consumers learned about the GM foods through other, high-tech channels of communication. Again we see that *consumer choice* regarding technology is extremely important, and may be the condition on which technology is accepted. If so, there is a structural tie between technological development and cultural opinion. Again, far from being a power out of control, technology is intricately tied to public opinion, which is itself today technology-dependent.

Market forces and their structural expression can hardly be said to offer much collective wisdom. Consumer feedback is not exactly moral discernment. But, again, the GM debate is instructive. The biotechnology companies missed noticing that deep cultural values are at stake for many people when nature is altered or "improved." It was not cost-benefit analysis or mere consumer fad that prompted the revolt against GM food. Religious or quasi-religious sensitivities — deeply held values about nature and food, about living things and their relationship to each other — boiled to the surface. In the United States, religious concern about the embryo has had a similar impact and has led to specific contours in U.S. federal policy regarding technologies, especially when federal grants are at stake. It is currently illegal to use federal funds to support embryo research. The ironic impact of that law is to drive such research into private sectors, where it is unregulated and out of public view. In this case the effect of religious conviction has not been to guide or prevent the development of the technology but to push it out of public view. But the more important point is that deeply held religious values count in determining the development of technology and in assessing its status.

Nevertheless, in the United States, technology assessment, once an office of the Congress, is now largely left to the market. Technology assessment has been reduced to market research and focus groups. What do people want? What will they pay for? But even when institutionalized, technology assessment could not ask the most important question, namely, *what is good for us?* Speaking of U.S. and Canadian efforts in technology assessment, William Stahl notes:

> Lacking a conception of the common good, they were caught in a contradiction. Without a workable definition of the common good they had no standard of evaluation. But their notion of values as individual choices blocked such a definition.... An individualistic understanding of values cannot go beyond self-interest, the summing of private goods. But no calculus has ever been able to discover the common good by adding up private benefits.[35]

So despite the vague feeling that values bear on technology and that they occasionally affect its direction, for the most part technology advances without assessment, often setting off consequences quickly and with a complexity and unpredictability that surprises even those engaged in research.

Technology and Mission

Per Anderson has written about the need in our pervasively pro-technology culture for an open and critical forum, a public space where technology is challenged and cross-examined. Where might this happen, if not in the church? Anderson challenges us

> to enable the religious communities to be counter-cultural spaces for forming critical consciousness and social responsibility about science and technology.... Do the established institutions of science and technology need some kind of "loyal opposition," a cool, critical gaze from a different viewpoint, a different understanding of what it means to "live well"? They do, and the religious communities bear powers and potentiality to undertake this role with care and sophistication.[36]

By creating an open space for discussion, education, and critical reflection, the church would bestow a gift of enormous value on a society that almost entirely lacks such space.[37]

---

35. William A. Stahl, *God and the Chip: Religion and the Culture of Technology* (Waterloo, Ontario: Wilfrid Laurier University Press, 1999), 157–58.

36. Per Anderson, "Cultivating the Cool, Critical Gaze: On Saying 'No' to 'Dolly' and the Future of the Faith-Science Dialogue," *Covalence: The Bulletin of the Ecumenical Roundtable on Science, Technology, and the Church* 1, nos. 3–4 (May–August 1998): 4–5.

37. Where might the church offer such space? The most compelling answer is at the local level. Models at the national level can be found in the Society, Religion,

For example, theology might lay out the ways in which technology replaces traditional practices, sometime with obvious advantages, but sometime depriving us of value found in traditional forms. Or theology might examine how technology redefines fundamental relationships, such as that between patient and physician or, perhaps most important, between parent and child, especially as the child becomes an object acquired through the use of technology rather than an outgrowth of the expression of love.

Such informed criticism, however, is only the first step. By itself, such criticism only serves to warn us of technology's pretensions and risks. It does not guide us in the right use of technology, much less offer a framework of meaning out of which the future course of technology can be anticipated and guided. So a theology of technology must include an assessment of the theological appropriateness of technology. What, in reference to God, is technology for? Any answer, of course, lies in broad generalities: to glorify and serve God, to serve those in need. The struggle lies in making this vividly concrete, so that it can offer tangible guidance in response to today's questions. How is God glorified, or not, through embryonic stem cell cultures or through human germ-line modification? How is God served, or not, through HTML code? Needed in the wide space between theological generality and technological detail is an intense, ongoing, multifaceted conversation. Only then can we begin to see if we have the theological imagination to surround technology with theological meaning. If we do not, we should expect technology to remain unbounded and uncontrolled.

Beyond the public space for cross-examination, what else does theology have to offer? Two suggestions should be considered. First, theology and church can engage in criticism and reconstruction of the religious context of technology, specifically by revisiting the proposals made by Francis Bacon and by clarifying what is meant by creativity, especially technological creativity. Second, theology and church can engage in criticism and reconstruction of the language of worship and prayer through which human beings, including technologists, are formed as moral and religious beings.

In pursuing the first of these tasks, theology can take up critically the suggestions offered by the religion that already undergirds

---

and Technology Project of the Church of Scotland, the Church and Society Unit of the European Council of Churches, or the Ecumenical Roundtable on Science, Technology, and the Church in the United States and Canada.

technology. According to one view, technology solves problems and closes the gap between nature as it is and nature as it is meant to be. This vision of technology is derived from a theological view of nature as creation, but that sees creation as having departed from the original intention of the Creator. Any contemporary version of this argument must not only take Genesis 1–11 as story rather than science; it must also take evolution fully on board in a theological reinterpretation of the status of creation. When this is done, the notion of a theologically normative condition of nature vanishes; thus, theology cannot move concretely to a prescriptive judgment about what technology should do with nature and what it should not do. The theme that persists from the Genesis 1–11 stories is that creation is good and yet not precisely what God intends, and thus there is a general warrant for technology. This warrant is established further by considering the role of Jesus, who acts on nature and alters it according to the purposes of God.[38] But it must be stressed that this view is only of limited value in making specific judgments in hard cases about what constitutes a theologically legitimate use of technology to heal or to improve the condition of human beings or of nature as a whole.

According to the other view discussed earlier, creativity itself is seen as a good. This theme is echoed by theologians who develop the notion that technology can be seen as co-creation, whereby human beings offer their technological innovations as expansions of God's creative activity. Philip Hefner qualifies the term in a way that precludes the idea that we are equal partners with God or that we stand outside this sphere of nature on which we act, and for this purpose Hefner has proposed the term "created co-creator."[39] While it certainly qualifies and limits the notion of creativity to suggest that our creation is set reverently and humbly alongside God's, the term is not sufficiently clear about how we distinguish in practical terms between theologically approved creativity and that which is theologically suspect. Much more theological work is needed.

It may be, however, that theological judgment about technology is not so much a matter of clear argument and definitive position but

38. For further development of this argument, see Ronald Cole-Turner, *The New Genesis: Theology and the Genetic Revolution* (Louisville: Westminster/John Knox Press, 1993).

39. For an extended treatment, see Philip Hefner, *The Human Factor* (Minneapolis: Fortress Press, 1993). For a critical assessment of "co-creation," see Cole-Turner, *New Genesis.*

of ongoing discernment. After all, technology advances so rapidly that providing a lasting framework of interpretation is daunting. For this reason, theology and church should emphasize the liturgical context by which discernment can be honed within the setting of corporate worship. New resources for worship will be helpful, but, more than that, worshipers should be invited to reflect in worship and in prayer about the significance of science for their understanding of nature as creation and about the place of technology for the living of their vocation. This applies of course to scientists and technologists but also to people in other areas of life who are pondering the use of technology. Shall prospective parents subject a pregnancy to a prenatal genetic test? Should preimplantation diagnosis be used to avoid a specific genetic problem? As technology moves forward, questions about its use can be encouraged within prayer, with encouragement that in corporate worship and prayer the church discerns the will of God. Scientists and engineers, in particular, can be encouraged to engage in similar questions, but at a more profound level: Should I work to develop a technology for a certain purpose? What is most important for me to work on? How can I use my knowledge and skills in a way that is most consistent with my beliefs? All this reflection is subject to the general theological judgments that theology and church are prepared to make about technology. But it is based on a recognition that these general judgments are themselves inadequate and that they can be bolstered somewhat by disciplines of spiritual and moral formation.

Whatever modest insight is discovered can then be taken back into that public space which the church creates, to be offered to others who may not participate in other ways in the life of the church. In this way, the church can in fact exert a small but important influence on the development of technology. The amount of influence may be small, but because technology itself is of such great consequence in determining the future of life on earth and perhaps even beyond, even a small transformation of technology is a mission worthy of devotion.

– *Chapter 5* –

The Destruction and Healing of the Earth

ECOLOGY AND THEOLOGY

Jürgen Moltmann

Well before industrial technologies and economic markets were globalized, humankind faced a globalized threat from the deadly self-destruction in the East-West conflict and from the global fall-out of regional ecological crises. The Chernobyl catastrophe in 1986 contaminated not only the surrounding regions of the Ukraine and Belorussia, but also the forests of Scandinavia and the wildlife of Bavaria. What is called the "greenhouse effect" results from conditions in industrialized regions, but it also has global consequences. We cannot solve ecological crises on a national level anymore. Paralyzed by the East-West confrontation, a divided humanity became potential victims of the regnant "mutual assured destruction" by weapons of "mass annihilation." Humans became passive objects of the global consequences of these as well as ecological terrors.

With the end of the East-West conflict in 1989, the chance emerged for humankind to become an active subject in overcoming the crises it heretofore had to suffer passively. It has, for some years, been possible to accuse perpetrators of crimes against humanity, such as those recently committed in the Balkans, in the international court in the Hague, and this is a step for universal human rights. It should also be possible to take a step toward the prosecution of crimes against the natural environment, to realize the rights of na-

An earlier version of this contribution appeared as "The Destruction and Liberation of the Earth: Ecological Theology," in *God for a Secular Society: The Public Relevance of Theology* (Minneapolis: Fortress Press, 1999), pt. 2, chap. 2. Much of that chapter is contained in this revised version, thanks to Professor Moltmann with the permission of Fortress Press. (Ed.)

ture. These possibilities can be actualized if we want a globalization of human responsibility, and not only an extension of the human power to dominate. At first glance, however, it seems that only the global domination of multi- and transnational corporations is involved in globalization. Through mergers and "hostile takeovers" fewer, but larger, "global players" come into being. In the process, not only are conditions in the developed countries globalized, the conditions shaping the future of those countries are not extensively improved. Thus, while globalization has overcome the East-West confrontation, it has not overcome the old confrontations between rich and poor, and it has created new confrontations between humans and nature.[1] So far, the global economy has not produced solutions for the problems it has helped to bring into the world. I take one key problem as the focus of this essay, the globalization of ecological crises and the search for ways out of these dangers.

The Destruction of the Earth

The destruction of the environment which we are causing through our present global economic system will undoubtedly seriously jeopardize the survival of humanity in the twenty-first century.[2] Modern industrial society has thrown out of balance the equilibrium of the earth's organism and is on the way to universal ecological death, unless we can change the way things are developing. Scientists have shown that carbon dioxide and methane emissions are destroying the ozone layer in the atmosphere, while the use of chemical fertilizers and a multitude of pesticides is making the soil infertile. Scientists have proved that the global climate is changing so that we are now experiencing an increasing number of "natural" catastrophes, such as droughts and floods—catastrophes which are not natural at all, but manmade. The ice in the Arctic and Antarctic is melting, and in the twenty-first century, scientists tell us, coastal cities such as Hamburg, and coastal regions such as Bangladesh and many South Sea islands, are going to be flooded. All in all, life on this earth is under threat. The human race can become extinct, like the dinosaurs millions of years ago. What makes this thought so disquieting is that we can no longer retrieve the poisons rising into

1. See the articles in this volume by Allen Verhey and Ronald Cole-Turner.

2. The annual reports of the World Watch Institute, Washington, D.C. (ed. Lester Brown), speak an unequivocal language.

the earth's ozone layer and those seeping into the ground. Consequently, we do not know whether the fate of humanity already has been determined. The ecological crisis of the twentieth century has become an ecological catastrophe, at least for weaker living things, which are the first to perish in this struggle. Year by year, hundreds of plant and animal species are becoming extinct, and we cannot call them back to life. It can be said in many places: "First of all the forests die; then the children."

This ecological crisis is in the first place a crisis brought about by Western scientific and technological civilization. If everyone were to drive as many cars as the Americans and the Germans, and were to pollute the atmosphere through as many toxic emissions, humanity would already have suffocated. The Western standard of living cannot be universalized. It can only be sustained at the expense of others: at the expense of people in the "Third World," at the expense of coming generations, and at the expense of the earth. Only a universal "equalization of burdens"[3] can lead to a common standard of living and to sustainable development.

At the same time, it is mistaken to think that environmental problems are problems for the industrial countries of the West alone.[4] On the contrary, the ecological catastrophes are intensifying the already existing economic and social problems of countries in the Third World. The Western industrialized countries can try by means of technology and statutory provisions to preserve a clean environment in their own territories; the poorer countries are unable to do so. The Western industrial countries can try to foist environmentally harmful industrial plants on the countries of the Third World, and to sell these countries dangerous toxic waste; the poor countries of the Third World have no defense. But apart from that, Indira Gandhi was right when she said that "poverty is the worst pollution." I would add that the worst environmental pollution is not poverty as such; it is corruption that causes poverty. It is a vicious circle leading to death: impoverishment leads everywhere to overpopulation, because children are the only security life has to offer. Overpopulation

---

3. An "equalization of burdens" of this kind (a so-called *Lastenausgleich*) was attempted in West Germany at the end of the Second World War for the benefit of refugees and displaced persons from the eastern parts of Germany, which had passed to the USSR, Poland, and Czechoslovakia.

4. R. Arce Valentin, "Die Schöpfung muss gerettet werden: Aber für wen? Die ökologische Krise aus der Perspective lateinamerikanischer Theologie," *Evangelische Theologie* 51 (1991): 565–77.

leads to the consumption not only of all the foodstuffs, but of the very foundations from which people live. That is why the deserts are growing most rapidly in poor countries. In addition, the global market is compelling poor countries to give up their subsistence economy, to plant monocultures for the world market, to cut down the rain forests, and to overgraze the pastureland. They have to sell not just the apples but the apple trees as well, and that means that they can survive only at the cost of their children. In this way these countries are being forced inexorably toward self-destruction. In countries with massive social injustice, ruthlessness is part of "the culture of violence." Violence against weaker people justifies violence against weaker creatures. Social lawlessness reproduces itself in lawless dealings with nature.

The first ecological law is that for every intervention in nature there must be a compensation. If you cut down a tree, you must plant a new one. If your city builds a power station, it must plant a forest which produces as much oxygen as the power plant uses.

Where the destruction of nature is concerned, both worlds, the First and the Third, are imprisoned in a vicious circle. The interdependencies of the depredations can easily be seen. The Western world destroys nature in the Third World and forces Third World countries to destroy their own natural environment. Conversely, the destruction of nature in the Third World — the cutting down of rain forests and the pollution of the seas — strikes back at the First World by way of climatic changes. The Third World dies first, and then the First World: first the poor die and then the rich; first the children and then the adults. Is it not cheaper in the long run, as well as more humane, to combat poverty in the Third World now, and to dispense with First World growth, rather than to combat natural catastrophes all over the world in the next few decades? Is it not more sensible to restrict driving now rather than to run around in gas masks in the future? Without social justice between the First and the Third Worlds, there will be no peace; and without peace in the world of human beings, there will be only the destruction of nature. In the long run this one earth cannot sustain a divided humanity. And this one earth will no longer endure a hostile humanity. It will free itself from men and women, either through counter-evolution, or through the slow suicide of the human race.

In the light of these somber vistas of the future we have to set new priorities, politically and economically. Up to now national security, safeguarded through armaments, has been in the forefront. In the future, environmental security, safeguarded through the common protection of the common foundations of life, will take first place. Instead of more weapons turned against each other, we need joint efforts turned against the threatening destruction of the living space we share. We need sustainable development in the Third World, and a policy of environmental security in the First. We need what Ernst von Weizsäcker calls a joint "earth policy" and a "global market" that is ecologically oriented — an "earth market."[5]

I believe that the ecological crisis of the earth is a crisis of modern scientific and technological civilization. The great project of the modern world is threatened with failure. It is not only a "moral crisis" either, as Pope John Paul II maintained; it is a more profound crisis — a religious crisis involving that in which people in the Western world put their trust. In the next section, I try to show how this is so. I then illustrate three perspectives, drawn from the religious traditions of the Western world, which can lead us from the destruction of the earth to harmony and consensus with it.

The Religious Crisis of the Modern World

The living relationship of a human society to its natural environment is determined by the techniques by which human beings acquire their foodstuffs from nature and give it back their waste. This "metabolism" with nature is as natural as breathing in the air and breathing out again. Since the beginning of the Industrial Revolution, however, it has been increasingly determined and governed solely by human beings, and not by nature. In our throwaway society, we think that what we throw away "is gone." But something never becomes nothing, so nothing we throw away has ever "gone." That is an error of nihilism. It is still somewhere or other in nature. Where? Everything returns in the cycles of the earth.

Human technologies are the modalities in which the sciences are invested. Technology is applied science, and all scientific knowledge will, some time or other, be technologically applied and used, since — as Francis Bacon declared — "knowledge is power." Natural science is knowledge about the power to dispose of things and to dominate them. Philosophy and theology, in contrast, have to do

5. See E. von Weizsäcker, *Earth Politics* (New Brunswick, N.J.: Zed Books, 1994).

with orientation, and are disciplines which address the meaning of reality.

Technologies and sciences are always developed under the pressure of particular human interests.[6] We never have them value-free. Interests precede them, direct them, and put them to work. These human interests, for their part, are guided by the fundamental values and convictions of a given society. These fundamental values and convictions are quite simply what everyone in a particular society takes for granted, because within the system of that society they are self-evident and plausible.

If a crisis arises in a life-system of this kind, which links a human society with the nature surrounding it, the logical result will be a crisis of the whole system, its attitude to life, its lifestyle, and not least its fundamental values and convictions. The dying of the forests outside us is matched by the spread of neuroses in the mind and spirit within. The pollution of the waters finds its parallel in the nihilistic feeling about life which prevails among many people in the megacities. So the crisis which we experience is not just an "ecological" crisis, nor can it be solved merely by technology. A conversion of convictions and fundamental values is just as necessary as a conversion in attitudes to life and in lifestyle.

What interests, concerns, and values rule our scientific and technological civilization? To put the answer simply, it is the boundless will toward domination which has driven and still drives modern men and women to seize power over nature. In the competitive struggle for existence, scientific discoveries and technological inventions serve the political will to acquire, secure, and extend power. Growth and progress are still gauged by the relative increase of economic, financial, and military power. When these stop, we talk of zero-growth, for growth simply has to be.

If we compare our civilization with pre-modern cultures, the difference between growth and equilibrium leaps to mind. Those pre-modern civilizations were anything but "primitive" or "underdeveloped." On the contrary, they were highly complicated systems of equilibrium which ordered the relation of people to nature and to the gods. It is only modern Western civilizations that for the first time are one-sided, programmed solely toward development,

---

6. See J. Habermas, *Knowledge and Human Interests,* trans. J. J. Shapiro, 2d rev. ed. (Boston: Beacon Press, 1971). He coined the phrase "knowledge-constitutive interests," 195.

growth, expansion, and conquest. The acquisition of power and the securing of power, to which may be added the American "pursuit of happiness," are the fundamental values which really count and regulate everything in our society. How did this come about?

The deepest reason can probably be found in the religion of modern men and women. The Judeo-Christian religion is often made responsible for the human seizure of power over nature, and for the unbridled thrust of the human will for power.[7] Even if ordinary modern men and women do not see themselves as particularly religious, they have at least done everything they could to obey the divine commandment of their own destiny: "Be fruitful and multiply, and fill the earth and subdue it." One might say that they have done more than enough. But this commandment and this image of the human being are more than three thousand years old, whereas the modern culture of conquest and expansion originated in Europe with the conquest of America, no more than four hundred years ago. So we have to look elsewhere for the reasons. In my view, they can be found in the picture of God which modern men and women have adopted.

Ever since the Renaissance, the understanding of God in Western Europe has been increasingly one-sided: God is "the Almighty." Omnipotence has been considered the preeminent attribute of God's divinity. God is the Lord, the world is God's property, and God can do with it what he likes. God is the absolute determining subject, and the world is the passive object of God's sovereignty. In the Western tradition, God moved more into the transcendent sphere, while the world was understood in a purely immanent and this-worldly sense. God was thought of without a world, so the world could be understood without a God. The world lost the divine mystery of its creation, the "world soul," the *anima mundi,* and could be stripped of its magic by science, to adopt Max Weber's apt description of this process.[8] The strict monotheism of modern Western Christianity is an essential reason for the secularization of the world and nature, as Arnold Gehlen had already pointed out in 1956.

---

7. Lynn White, Jr., "The Historical Roots of Our Ecological Crisis," in Francis A. Schaeffer, *Pollution and the Death of Man: The Christian View of Ecology* (Wheaton, Ill.: Tyndale House, 1970), 95–115. This pioneering work of Lynn White Jr. has been followed by a host of European and American scholars.

8. Max Weber, *The Protestant Ethic and the Spirit of Capitalism,* trans. T. Parsons (London: Allen & Unwin, 1930), 105.

> At the end of a long history of culture and intellect, the view of the world as an "*entente secrète*" has been destroyed—the metaphysics of the concurring and conflicting powers of life. It has been destroyed by monotheism on the one hand, and on the other by the scientific and technological mechanism for which monotheism, for its part, first cleared the way, by de-demonizing and de-divinizing nature.[9]

God and the machine have survived the archaic world and now confront one another, by themselves. This presents a terrifying picture, because not only has nature disappeared from this final confrontation between God and the machine; the human being has vanished, too.

As God's image on earth, human beings were bound to see themselves, in complete correspondence with God, as rulers — that is, as the determining subjects of knowledge and will, standing over against their world, which was their passive object, and subduing it. For it is only through lordship over this earth that the human being can correspond to God, who is the Lord of the world. God is the Lord and owner of the whole world, and human beings must therefore strive to become the lords and owners of the earth, in order to prove themselves God's image. Human beings come to resemble their God, not through goodness and truth, not through patience and love, but through power and sovereignty. It was in this sense that, at the beginning of modern times, Francis Bacon lauded the sciences of his time: "Knowledge is power"; it was through their power over nature that human beings were to be restored in their character as the image of God. In his "Treatise on Scientific Method," René Descartes declared that science and technology make human beings "masters and possessors of nature."[10]

If we compare Descartes's statement with the famous indictment made by Chief Seattle in 1855, the point is evident: "Every part of this earth is sacred to my people, every glittering pine-needle, every sandy beach, all the mists in the dark forests.... The rocky hills, the gentle meadows, the bodily warmth of ponies — and of people — they all belong to the same family."[11]

---

9. A. Gehlen, *Urmensch und Spätkultur* (Bonn: Athanaum, 1956), 295.

10. R. Descartes, "Discourse on the Method of Rightly Conducting the Reason," in *The Philosophical Works of Descartes,* trans. E. S. Haldane and G. R. T. Ross, rev. ed. (Cambridge: Cambridge University Press, 1931; reprint, 1979), 119.

11. A free translation of the original speech, made by the American writer William

These reflections bring us face to face with the decisive question: is nature our property, so we can do what we like with it? Or are we one part of the wider family of nature, which we have to respect? Do the rain forests belong to us, so that we can cut and burn them down, or do the rain forests belong to a multiplicity of animals, plants, and trees, that is, to the earth, to which we also belong? Is this earth "our environment" and "our planetary home," or are we merely guests who have arrived on earth very late, and has the earth until now been putting up with us?

If nature is nothing more than our property — unclaimed property, which belongs to whoever takes possession — then we will counter the ecological crisis solely by technological methods. We will try through genetic engineering to make plants resistant to climate and to create animals of increased utility. By the same means we will breed a new human race which does not need a natural environment at all — merely a technological one. We could in fact be in a position to create a world capable of sustaining our numbers and practices; but it would be an artificial world, a global laboratory.[12] Alternatively we could change our practices and numbers, restore nature, and let her live again. But how can we change the way we live? Is the destruction of nature not the result of our disrupted relationship to nature and to ourselves and to God?

At the Global Forum Conference in Moscow in January 1990, we heard the moving message of the North American Indians. These "indigenous children of the earth" talked about their thousand-year-old great goddess: "The earth is our mother, the moon is our grandmother, and we all participate in the sacred cycles of life."[13] The Indian ambassador V. T. Singh, the Mongolian high priest, the African rainmaker, and the Californian New Age adherent implored us to return to "the womb" of the earth, from which all life comes. It all sounded splendid. But can the religious symbols of pre-modern times, when human beings were still hunters and gatherers, help the urbanized masses of the postmodern world solve the ecological problems of industrial society — the people in New York, Mexico

---

Arrowsmith. See Chief Seattle, *Brother Eagle, Sister Sky: A Message from Chief Seattle* (New York: Dial Books, 1991).

12. Bill McKibben, *The End of Nature* (New York: Anchor Books, 1989).

13. See *Conference Report: The Global Forum on Environment and Development for Survival* (Moscow, USSR, 15–19 January 1990, New York 1990), 193–95: "We are all the children of the Earth.... Indigenous people are nature's representatives to the modern human community. That which destroys nature destroys indigenous life. We are the people of the Earth."

City, or São Paulo, where the sun often cannot be seen for smog? All the politicians and scientists at the Moscow conference assumed that human beings have caused the ecological problems of industrial society, so human beings have to solve them. The message of the earth's indigenous peoples and the modern "depth ecologists" aims to free human beings from the burden of this responsibility, to once more make them happy and infantile "children of the earth." But can we give up the liberty we have acquired, now that it has become dangerous? Will nature take over responsibility if it becomes too heavy for us? I do not believe it. Can we translate preindustrial ideas of harmony with the earth into postindustrial conceptions of an ecological culture?

Three Conversions Regarding the Earth

In connection with the new burst of interest in "cosmic spirituality," the first conversion begins with the picture of God. The way we think about God is the way we think about ourselves and about nature. "Tell me what you believe in, and I will tell you who you are." Belief in God, the almighty Lord in heaven, led to the secularization of the world, and robbed nature of its divine mystery. What we need theologically is to rediscover the triune God. I know that sounds dogmatic, orthodox, and old-fashioned, but it could still be true. Even when we simply hear the name, "the Father, the Son, and the Holy Spirit," we sense that the divine mystery is a marvelous community. The triune God is not a solitary, unloved ruler in heaven who subjugates everything as earthly despots do. This is a God in community, rich in relationships. After all, "God is love."[14]

Father, Son, and Holy Spirit live with one another, for one another, and in one another in the most supreme and most perfect community of love we can conceive: "I am in the Father and the Father is in me," says Jesus in the Gospel of John. If that is true, then we correspond to God not through domination and subjugation but through community and relationships which further life. It is not the solitary human subject who is God's image on earth; it is the true human community.[15] It is not separate, individual parts

14. This is central to my argument in *The Trinity and the Kingdom* (New York: Fortress Press, 1981).
15. This has been argued extensively in L. Boff, *Trinity and Society*, trans. P. Burns (Maryknoll, N.Y.: Orbis Books, 1988).

of creation that reflect God's wisdom and triune vitality; it is the community of creation as a whole.

In the high-priestly prayer in John 17:21, Jesus prays "that they may all be one; as thou, Father, art in me, and I in thee, that they also may be one in us" (KJV). This is the foundational theological saying for the ecumenical movement, and it can become the foundational theological saying for the ecological movement as well. Mutual indwelling is the innermost mystery of the triune God. Mutual indwelling is also the secret of the divine love: "He who abides in love abides in God and God abides in him" (1 John 4:16).[16]

According to Christian understanding, creation is a trinitarian process: God the Father creates through the Son in the power of the Holy Spirit. Seen from the other side, this means that all things are created by God, formed "through God," and exist in God. We may, as Basil explained,

> See in the creation of these beings the Father as the preceding cause, the Son as the creative cause, and the Spirit as the perfecting cause, so that the ministering spirits have their beginning in the will of the Father, are brought into being through the efficacy of the Son, and are perfected through the assistance of the Spirit.[17]

For a long time the church's Western tradition stressed only the first aspect, so as to distinguish God, the almighty Creator, from his creation, and to stress God's transcendence. By so doing it stripped nature of her divine mystery and surrendered her to desacralization through secularization. The important thing today is therefore to rediscover the Creator's immanence in creation, so as to include the whole of creation in our reverence for the Creator. Through whom, or through what, did God create the world? According to Proverbs 8:22–31, God created the world through Wisdom:

> The Lord already had me at the beginning of his ways, before he created anything I was there. From eternity I was set up, from the beginning, before the earth.... Then I was beside him as his master workman and was daily his delight, playing

16. The Greek and Latin terms for this mutual indwelling are treated in A. Deneffe, "Perichoresis, circumincessio...," *Zeitschrift für katholische Theologie* 47 (1923): 497–532.

17. Basil, *De Spiritu Sancto* 31d–31e. See also *The Book of St. Basil the Great on the Holy Spirit,* revised text with notes by C. F. H. Johnston (Oxford: Clarendon Press, 1892).

before him always, playing upon his earth, and delighting in the children of men.

This divine daughter Wisdom (*ḥokmah*) was translated by Philo as *Logos,* the Word. Whenever "the Logos," "the Word," is used in the New Testament, as in the prologue to the Gospel of John, we should think of Wisdom.[18] According to Wisdom literature, this creative Wisdom can also be called God's Word or God's Spirit. But it is the presence of God in all things which is invariably meant, a presence immanent in the world. If all things are created by God, then their protean variety is preceded by an immanent unity. It is through Wisdom that God forms the community of created beings, who exist with one another and for one another.

Christian theology has recognized in Christ not just personal salvation but also the cosmic Wisdom through which all things are, as the Epistle to the Colossians shows. Christ is the divine mystery of the world. The person who reverences Christ also reverences all created things in him, and him in everything created. Where was Jesus after the devilish temptations in the desert? "He was among the beasts, and the angels ministered to him" (Mark 1:13).

In the apocryphal *Gospel of Thomas,* Logion 77, Jesus says:

> I am the light that is over all,
> I am the universe: the universe has gone out of me,
> and the universe has returned to me again.
> Cleave the wood and I am there.
> Lift up the stone and there thou shalt find me.[19]

This means that what we do to the earth, we do to Christ. Where God's Word is, there God's Spirit is also. According to Genesis 1:2, creation through the Word is preceded by the vibrating energy of God's Spirit. God creates everything though God's naming, differentiating, and judging words. That is why all things are different, "each according to its kind." But God always speaks in the breath of God's Spirit, which gives life. Where the community of creation is concerned, Word and Spirit complement one another. The Word specifies and differentiates. The Spirit joins and forms the harmony. The words are different, just as they are when human beings speak;

---

18. G. Schimanowski, *Weisheit und Messias: Die jüdische Voraussetzungen der urchristlichen Präexistenzchristologie* (Tübingen: J. C. B. Mohr, 1985).

19. J. Jeremias quoted this logion in part in *Unknown Sayings of Jesus,* trans. R. H. Fuller (London: SPCK, 1957, 1995), taking it from the Oxyrynchus Papyrus I.

but they are communicated in the same breath. So in a transferred sense we can say that God speaks through the individual things God has created, and, as an English hymn has it, "God ... breathes through all creation."[20] The totality of creation which I here call "the community of creation" is sustained by the breath of God's Spirit: "Thou sendest forth thy breath and renewest the face of the ground"(Ps. 104:30).

Through Word and Spirit the Creator communicates himself to the creation and enters into it:

> Lord, thou art the lover of life,
> thy immortal Spirit is in all things.
> (Wisd. of Sol. 12:1)

That is the way Calvin saw it, too: "For it is the Spirit who, everywhere diffused, sustains all things, causes them to grow, and quickens them in heaven and on earth.... In transfusing into all things his energy, and breathing into them essence, life, and movement, he is indeed plainly divine."[21] So creation must not just be called, in detached objectivity, a "work of God's hands." Creation is the indirect, mediating presence of God as well. All things are created so that, as "the shared home" of all creation, they may be "the house of God" in which God can live beside those he has created, and where those he has created can eternally live beside him. This is expressed biblically through the image of God's cosmic temple: "The Most High does not dwell in houses made with human hands; as the prophet says, 'Heaven is my throne, and the earth is my footstool. What kind of house will you build for me, says the Lord, or what is the place of my rest?' " (Acts 7:48–49, following Isa. 66:1–2). *That place is the cosmos!*

This viewpoint — the Spirit of God in all things and the preparation of all things to become God's dwelling place — leads to a cosmic adoration of God and an adoration of God in all things. What believers do in the churches is representative of, related to, and on behalf of the whole cosmos. Solomon's temple was built according to the dimensions of the cosmos as the cosmos was then understood, so that the temple might be a microcosm to represent

---

20. Timothy Rees: "God who laid the earth's foundation, / God who spread the heavens above, / God who breathes through all creation: / God is love, eternal Love" ("Abbots Leigh" [Carol Stream, Ill.: Hope Publishing Co., 1978], 20).

21. J. Calvin, *The Institutes of the Christian Religion,* ed. J. T. McNeill, trans. F. L. Battles (Philadelphia: Westminster Press, 1960), I/13, 14.

and correspond to the macrocosm.[22] The presence of God's Word and Spirit in Christ's church is the advance radiance and beginning of the presence of God's Word and Spirit in the new creation of all things. The church is oriented toward the cosmos, by reason of its foundation and its essential nature.[23] It was a dangerous modern contraction that restricted the church to the human world alone. But if the church is oriented toward the cosmos, then the ecological crisis of earthly creation is the church's crisis, too, for through the destruction of the earth, which is "bone of its bones and flesh of its flesh," it too will be destroyed. When the weaker creatures die, the whole community of creation suffers. If the church sees itself as representing creation, then it will feel this suffering of creation's weaker creatures as conscious pain, and it will have to cry out in public protest.[24] It is not just "our human environment" that is suffering, but the creation destined to be "God's environment." Every intervention in nature that can never be rectified is a sacrilege. The outcome is the self-imposed excommunication of the perpetrators. The nihilistic destruction of nature is practiced atheism.

Astonishingly enough, it was Christian mysticism which taught us to be alive to the language of God in nature. A modern mystic, the Nicaraguan poet and revolutionary Ernesto Cardenal, writes in his book *Love:*

> The bird chorus in the early morning sings to God. Volcanoes, clouds and trees shout about God. All creation cries out with a loud voice that God is, is beautiful and loves. Music sings in our ears and beautiful countryside tells our eyes. . . . God's signature is on the whole of nature. All creatures are love letters from God to us. The whole of nature is bursting with love, set in it by God, who is love, to kindle the fire of love in us. . . .
>
> Nature is like God's shadow, reflecting his beauty and splendor. The quiet blue lake has the splendor of God. . . . The image of the Trinity is in every atom, the figure of God the three in one. . . . And my body was also made for the love of God. Every

22. G. Strachan, "The New Jerusalem — Temple of Creation," *Shadow* 1 (December 1984): 45–58.

23. P. Gregorios, *The Human Presence: An Orthodox View of Nature* (Geneva: World Council of Churches, 1977).

24. Since about 1972, almost all church synods and ecumenical global conferences have brought this cry of tormented creation to public notice. As a survey is impossible here, I refer to my article in *Theologische Realenzyklopädie* (Berlin, 1995), 25.36–46, and its extensive bibliography.

cell in my body is a hymn to my creator and a declaration of love.[25]

In case anyone thinks that this is a typically Catholic eulogy in celebration of "natural theology," we may listen to the Reformer John Calvin, for Calvin saw the presence of God in nature in the same way.

> The final goal of the blessed life . . . rests in the knowledge of God. Lest anyone, then, be excluded from access to happiness, he not only sowed in men's minds that seed of religion of which we have spoken, but revealed himself and daily discloses himself in the whole workmanship of the universe. As a consequence, men cannot open their eyes without being compelled to see him. Indeed, his essence is incomprehensible; hence his divineness far escapes all human perception. But upon his individual works he has engraved unmistakable marks of his glory, so clear and so prominent that even unlettered and stupid folk cannot plead the excuse of ignorance. . . . Wherever you cast your eyes, there is no spot in the universe wherein you cannot discern at least some sparks of his glory.
>
> But [laments Calvin], it is in vain that so many burning lamps shine for us in the workmanship of the universe to show forth the glory of its Author. Although they bathe us wholly in their radiance . . . we have not the eyes to see. . . .[26]

The New Earth Hypothesis: "Gaia"

For us "the earth" means two things. On the one hand it means the ground *on which* we stand; on the other, it is the planet Earth, with its biosphere and atmosphere, *in which* we live. Photographs of the earth taken from satellites or the moon show our planet with its thin atmospheric covering, within which all life exists. In this second meaning of the word, we live *in* the earth, not *on* it.

How are we to understand in its totality this earth "in" which we live? Modern astroscientists have shown the reciprocal influence of the lived and the unlived sectors of the planet. This observation suggested that the earth's biosphere, together with the atmosphere,

25. E. Cardenal, *Love*, trans. D. Livingstone (London: SPCK, 1974), 24.
26. Calvin, *Institutes*, I/1, 51f., 68.

the oceans, and the expanses of land, form a single complex system. Since this system has the capacity to preserve our planet as a place suited to life, it can also be seen as a unique "organism."[27]

Through the constant absorption of solar energy, life is developed and sustained. That is the generally accepted theory of the English scientist James E. Lovelock, which he put forward in his book *Gaia — A New Look at Life on Earth*. Lovelock proposed calling this earth system "a universal bio-cybernetic system with a trend towards homeostasis." But a neighbor, the novelist William Golding, offered him the old Greek name for the earth goddess, Gaia. Thus, the theory became known became known as "the Gaia hypothesis."[28] This thesis does not imply a re-mystification of the earth. It means understanding our planet as a system of interactions and feedbacks, which strives to create the best possible environmental conditions for life. We call the preservation of relatively constant conditions by way of interactive controls "homeostasis." Lovelock has shown that our earth system has this tendency, and that it also makes use of living things in the process, especially the microorganisms in the seas.

As Lovelock himself says, the Gaia hypothesis offers an alternative to the modern viewpoint, which sees nature only as the embodiment of a primitive power which has to be subjugated and dominated. The hypothesis also offers an alternative to the depressing notion that our planet Earth is a mindless spaceship which circles the sun without meaning or purpose, and will do so until the day when it burns out or grows cold. But, in fact, the Gaia hypothesis also offers an alternative, which can also be scientifically tested, to the anthropocentrism which is fundamental to modern civilization. This hypothesis compels us to think biocentrically or, better, to orient our thinking toward the earth.[29]

The earth system in which the human race has spread and developed its civilizations works like a superorganism. With its own kind of subjectivity, it fashions life-forms out of macromolecules,

---

27. See the thematic issue of *Evangelische Theologie* 53, no. 5 (1993), with contributions by E. Moltmann-Wendel, J. Moltmann, L. Boff, S. Bergmann, and C. Rehberger.

28. J. E. Lovelock, *Gaia* (London: Oxford University Press, 1979). See also E. Sahtouris, *Vergangenheit und Zukunft der Erde*, with a foreword by James Lovelock (Frankfurt: Willis Harman, 1993).

29. Rosemary Radford Ruether, *Gaia and God: An Ecofeminist Theology of Earth Healing* (San Francisco: HarperSanFrancisco, 1993). However, she makes no reference to J. Lovelock's Gaia hypothesis.

microorganisms, and cells, and is in a position to keep these forms alive. The Gaia language is the genetic code, a universal language used by all cells. There is also an inbuilt, elaborate security system which resists genetic combinations hostile to life. And since this "organism earth" has finally produced intelligent living things such as human beings, then inherent in the organism itself must be a higher intelligence and a memory which bears the imprint of millions of years. It can therefore be said that the earth itself is "alive." According to Genesis 1:24, God created it to "bring forth" living things. This is said of nothing else in creation. According to a rabbinic tradition, God creates human beings *together with* the earth (Gen. 1:26).[30]

The link between human beings and the earth's biosphere is the genetic code. Through this code the cells and organisms communicate. The human genetic code is only one variant of the codes of all living things, from the microorganisms to the whales, from the first protozoa to the dinosaurs. By way of the genetic code, all living things are related and in communication. What we call consciousness, understanding, and will are only small parts of the organism steered by our genetic code. Is it possible to be conscious of the genetic code? Our total constitution expresses the code, as we see in people suffering from Down's syndrome, for example. But does the code say anything to our consciousness? About that we know very little. Some people have supposed that the genetic code speaks to us through bodily gestalts and body rhythms, through "body wisdom" in the way that dreams also speak to us. Peoples that have cultivated closeness to nature have always had a dream culture of their own. Through scientific knowledge of the genetic code, it ought to be possible today to establish conscious concurrences between the genetic and the cultural code.

The importance of the Gaia hypothesis can hardly be overestimated:

1. It makes it possible to recognize the global functions of local and regional ecosystems, and prevents them from being isolated.

2. It reverses classical scientific methods. Knowledge is no longer split into more detailed specialties. Instead, scientific disciplines cooperate and are integrated into "earth sciences" for the investigation of wider connections in the earth system.

---

30. See S. Schreiner, "Partner in Gottes Schöpfungswerk — Zur rabbinischen Auslegung von Gen. 1: 26–27," *Judaica* 49, no. 3 (1993): 131–41.

3. Integrated knowledge is no less scientific than isolated knowledge. But it no longer serves the interests of domination, according to the method of "divide and rule." Instead, it is guided by the concern for shared life and survival, by way of cooperation and symbiosis.

4. The Gaia hypothesis forces us to end the anthropocentric self-understanding and behavior of men and women, and constrains them to fit democratically into the life of the earth as a whole.

5. Politically, the threatening nuclear catastrophe has compelled us to rethink national foreign policies, and to see them as part of a shared "global domestic policy." The threatening ecological catastrophe forces us to understand this shared global domestic policy as "earth politics," again to use E. von Weizsäcker's phrase.

Without democracy, "biocracy" is not viable. It is only when, as the species "human beings," we understand ourselves in relation to the earth and not as conflicting peoples, nations, or races that we can enter into relationship with other species. This has nothing to do with the return of the earth goddess; nor does the Gaia hypothesis ascribe divine power to the earth, as some conservative Christians fear. But it has everything to do with the survival of the human race. This survival will only be possible in symbiosis, coordination, and concurrence with the total organism of the earth.

Human Beings and Nature in Covenant with God

Christians believe that God loves the creation and wants to bring it to full development and flowering. In God's eyes nothing created is a matter of indifference. Every creature has its own dignity and its own rights, for they are all included in God's covenant. That is said in the story of Noah: "Behold," says God, "I establish my covenant *with you* and *your descendants after you,* and with *every living creature*" (Gen. 9:9–10). It is this covenant "with us" which provides the basis for fundamental human rights.[31] Out of this covenant "with us and our descendants after us" follow the rights of future generations. Out of this covenant follow the rights of nature.[32] Before God the Creator, we "and our descendants and

---

31. See J. M. Lochman and J. Moltmann, *Gottes Recht und Menschenrechte: Studien und Empfehlungen des Reformierten Weltbundes* (Neukirchen: Neukirchener, 1976), esp. 44ff.

32. L. Vischer, ed., *Rights of Future Generations — Rights of Nature: A Proposal for Enlarging the Universal Declaration of Human Rights,* Studies from the World

all living things" are partners in God's covenant and enjoy equal rights. Nature is not our property. But we are not just a part of nature, either. All living things are partners in God's covenant, each in its own way. All living things must be respected by human beings as partners and confederates in God's covenant: the earth brings forth; human beings are God's image on earth. Anyone who injures the earth injures God. Anyone who hurts the dignity of animals hurts God. Today, now that the Universal Declaration of Human Rights of 1948 has become generally accepted, it is time to draw up a Universal Declaration of the Rights of Nature. Insofar as nature—the air, water, land, plants, and animals—is at the mercy of acts of violence committed by human beings, it must be protected by human law. A first attempt to free nature from human despotism and caprice was the World Charter for Nature, proclaimed by the General Assembly of the United Nations on October 28, 1982. This charter does not concede to nature rights of its own, or recognize nature as the subject of its own rights. But hints in what is said indicate that the charter is reaching beyond the anthropocentric and egotistical viewpoint of the modern world, according to which nature is only there for human beings as "unclaimed property." "Mankind is a part of nature," says the preamble, and, "Every form of life is unique, warranting respect regardless of its worth to man."[33]

But this moral appeal, right in itself, must also be given a legal basis, so that nature does not depend on the goodwill of human beings but is recognized as an independent subject, with its own rights. It was not the goodwill of masters that finally brought about the abolition of slavery; it was the fight of slaves for their freedom and human rights, together with the efforts of abolitionists and gradual public recognition that slavery was inadmissible. It is only through the recognition of its rights that nature will be liberated from its oppression and recognized as a partner for human beings, and a confederate in God's covenant.

But how? The protection of nature from destruction by human beings is thought by some politicians to be part of the minimum guarantee of individual human rights. Just as every human being has a right to freedom from bodily harm—which means freedom from murder, rape, assault, and torture—so every human being

---

Alliance of Reformed Churches 19 (Geneva: World Alliance of Reformed Churches, 1990).

33. Ibid., 62ff.

should have a right to an intact, unscathed environment: clean air, pure water, and unspoiled earth. But that way of formulating the issue does not go far enough, for it sees the rights of nature only in terms of what is good for human beings. Nature is required only for a "human environment," but it is not recognized for its own sake.

Yet if this earth, together with all living things, is God's creation, then its dignity must be respected for God's sake, and its continued existence must be protected for its own sake. Because nature is being destroyed by the economic forces of the free market, it must be put under the special protection of the state. By virtue of its constitution, the state has to respect human rights as the rights of all its citizens; and in the same way it must also, by virtue of its constitution, *protect the rights of stricken nature.* Thus, I propose that the following sentences should be included in our constitutions: "The natural world is under the special protection of the government. Through the way in which it acts, the state shows respect for the natural environment and protects it from exploitation and destruction by human beings for its own sake." Every democratic government has two responsibilities: (1) to protect the people; (2) to protect the land.

The German Animal Protection Act of 1986 is the first German law which no longer views animals merely as human property, but sees them as "fellow creatures" of human beings and protects them in their dignity. "The purpose of this law is to protect the life and well-being of the animal out of human responsibility for it as a fellow creature. No one may inflict pain, suffering or harm on an animal without reasonable grounds."[34]

To call animals "fellow creatures" is to recognize the Creator, the creature, and the community of creation. The theological word "creation" is more appropriate than the philosophical term "Nature," for it shows respect for God's rights to creation and therefore restricts the rights of human beings: God has the right of ownership — human beings only have the right of use.

A proposal to protect the rights of nature, presented by a group of theologians and lawyers belonging to the universities of Bern and Tübingen, was made to the World Alliance of Reformed Churches

34. On animal rights, see C. Hartshorne, "Rechte — nicht nur für die Menschen," *Zeitschrift für Evangelische Ethik* 22 (1978): 3–14; A. Lorz, *Tierschutzgesetz: Kommentar und Gegenwart* (Neukirchen: Neukirchener, 1995); G. M. Teutsch, *Mensch und Tier: Lexikon der Tierschutzethik* (Göttingen: Vandenhoeck & Ruprecht, 1987).

in 1989, the Ecumenical Assembly in Seoul in 1990, and the UN Conference in Rio de Janeiro in 1992:

1. Nature — animate or inanimate — has a right to existence, that is, to preservation and development.
2. Nature has a right to the protection of its ecosystems, species, and populations in their interconnectedness.
3. Animate nature has a right to the preservation and development of its genetic inheritance.
4. Organisms have a right to a life fit for their species, including procreation within their appropriate ecosystems.
5. Disturbances of nature require a justification. They are only permissible
    - when the presuppositions of the disturbance are determined in a democratically legitimate process and with respect for the rights of nature,
    - when the interests of the disturbance outweigh the interests of a complete protection of the rights of nature, and
    - when the disturbance is not inordinate.
    - Damaged nature is to be restored whenever and wherever possible.
6. Rare ecosystems, and above all those with an abundance of species, are to be placed under absolute protection. The driving of species to extinction is forbidden.

   We appeal to the United Nations to expand its Universal Declaration of Human Rights and to formulate explicitly the rights mentioned above.

   Simultaneously, we appeal to the individual nations to incorporate these rights into their constitutions and legislation.[35]

The Sabbath of the Earth: The Divine Ecology

For a long time men and women viewed nature and their own bodies only under the dominating interest of work. This meant that

35. "Covenanting with God's Creation," in *Seoul: 22nd General Council of the World Alliance of Reformed Churches, Section II: Justice, Peace and the Integrity of Creation* (Geneva: World Alliance of Reformed Churches, 1989), 73–104.

they perceived only the utilitarian side of nature, and only the instrumental side of their bodies. But ancient Jewish wisdom teaches us to understand nature and ourselves once more as God's creation. We find this wisdom in the celebration of the sabbath, the day of rest on which human beings and animals find peace and leave nature in peace.[36]

According to the first of the creation stories, the Creator "finished" the creation of the world by celebrating the world's sabbath: "And God rested from all his work." Through his resting presence God blessed the creation. God was no longer active, but was wholly present as God.

The seventh day is rightly called the feast of creation. It is the crown of creation. Everything that exists was created for this feast. So as not to celebrate the feast alone, God created heaven and earth, the dancing stars and the surging seas, the meadows and the woods, the animals, the plants, and last of all human beings. They are all invited to this sabbath feast. All of them are God's fellow celebrants, each in its own way. That is why God had "pleasure" in all God's works, as the psalms say. That is why the heavens declare the glory of the Eternal One. Everything that is, is created for God to rejoice over, for everything that is comes from God's love.

This divine sabbath is "the crown of creation," not the human being. On the contrary, human beings, together with all other created beings, are crowned by the divine "Queen Sabbath."[37] Through his sabbath rest, the creative God arrives at his goal. People who celebrate the sabbath recognize nature as God's creation, and let it be God's beloved creation. The sabbath is wise environmental policy and an excellent therapy for our own restless souls and tense bodies.

But the sabbath has another significance as well: the significance of the sabbath year for the land and for the people who live from the land. According to Exodus 23:11, every seventh year Israel is not to plant or till the ground, but is to let it rest, so that "the poor of your people may eat." Further, according to Leviticus 25:1ff., every seventh year Israel is not to plant or till the ground, so that "the

---

36. A. Heschel, *The Sabbath: Its Meaning for Modern Man* (New York: Farrar, Straus & Young, 1951); J. Moltmann, *God in Creation: An Ecological Doctrine of Creation,* trans. M. Kohl (Minneapolis: Fortress Press, 1993), chap. 11; S. Bacchiocci, *Deine Zeit ist meine Zeit: Der biblische Ruhetag als Chance für den modernen Menschen* (Hamburg: NS Zeit, 1988).

37. On this point, see my critical argument with A. Auer, "Ist der Mensch die Krone der Schöpfung?" *Publik Forum* 31 (May 1985): vi–vii.

land may come to rest." Leviticus 25:4 says: "In the seventh year the land shall keep its great sabbath to the Lord." The social reason is complemented by the ecological reason. For the Book of Leviticus, this sabbath rest for the land is of paramount importance. All God's blessings are experienced by the obedient, but the disobedient will be punished.

How? Leviticus 26:33ff.: "And I will scatter you among the nations . . . and your land shall be a desolation, and your cities shall be a waste." Why? "Then the land shall enjoy its sabbaths as long as it lies desolate, while you are in your enemies' land; then the land shall celebrate and enjoy its sabbaths."

This is a remarkable interpretation of Israel's Babylonian exile. We might even call it an ecological interpretation. God wanted to save his land. That is the reason why God permits his people to be defeated and to be carried off into captivity. God's land is to remain unworked for seventy years! By the time the seventy years are over, it will have recovered, and God's people can return to the land promised to them. We might call the sabbath year for the land God's environmental policy for those he has created, and for his earth.

All ancient agrarian cultures were familiar with the wisdom of fallowing, as a way of preserving the soil's fertility. When I was young, every fifth year the arable land in North Germany was left unplanted, so that plants and animals could return and we children could play. It was only the great empires which exploited the fertile regions nonstop, in order to feed their armies and their capital cities, until the soil was exhausted and became a desert. That is what happened in Persia, Rome, Babylon, and perhaps also to the Mayas on the Yucatan Peninsula.

Today the fallowing principle has almost entirely disappeared from agriculture. Its industrialization means the introduction of more chemical fertilizers into the soil. Monocultures have replaced the old rotation of crops. The result is that artificial fertilizing has to be intensified, and the soil and the crops are increasingly polluted.

The end will resemble the end that ancient Israel experienced. The uninterrupted exploitation of the land will lead to the exile of the country population, and in the end to the disappearance of the human race. After the death of the human race, God's earth will then celebrate the great sabbath which modern humanity had hitherto denied. If we want our civilization and nature as we have known it to survive, we should let ourselves be warned, and permit the land "to celebrate its great sabbath." The celebration of the sabbath, and reverence for "the sabbath of the earth," can become our own salvation and the salvation of earth from which we live. Simply to restrict ourselves on the sabbath, and to refrain from intervening in creation — this extolling helps both the land and ourselves.[38]

During the first oil crisis in 1972, one Sunday was declared to be a "car-free" day in West Germany. It was one of the loveliest days I can remember. Children played football on the motorways, grown-ups sat at the crossroads, dogs jumped about on the streets. It is possible that at least 50 percent of our traffic is superfluous.

What would it imply if the whole church were to include an Earth Day in its festivals to celebrate the creation that we torment? An "earth day" of this kind is unofficially celebrated by many congregations and churches in the United States on April 22. How would it be if in Europe and Asia, in Africa and South America, in Australia and the Pacific Islands, we were to declare April 27, the day of the Chernobyl disaster, such a day?

On Earth Day we should bow before the earth and beg for forgiveness for the injustice we have inflicted, so that we may once more be accepted into community with it. On Earth Day we could seek to renew the covenant which God made with Noah and the earth.

According to the Bible, the sabbath laws are God's ecological strategy, designed to preserve the life which God has created. In its rest and its rhythmical interruption of time, the sabbath is also the strategy which can lead us out of the ecological crisis and, after the one-sided forms of progress made at the expense of nature, can show us the values of sustainable development and harmony with nature.

Globalization and Ecumenism

"Globalization" means, when we take the term literally, a quantification: what was particular shall become universal, what existed only regionally shall be present throughout the world. The term can therefore be used for many things — from economy to values, from Coca-Cola to religions.

---

38. On the new mysticism of the earth, see L. Boff, *Cry of the Earth, Cry of the Poor* (Maryknoll, N.Y.: Orbis Books, 1997).

Ecumene, in contrast to "globalization," is a term for that quality which applies to "the whole inhabited earth" and corresponds to the original meaning of the Greek *oikos,* the home or place of dwelling. If world Christianity today calls itself "ecumenical," it implies not only its common catholicity, but also its missionary, ethical, and political direction toward the whole globe. The *ecumene* presupposes that this earth is habitable for the human race and has, or is, a storehouse for human beings. At the same time, the *ecumene* implies that humankind wants to live within the sphere of the earth and must not stand against it, as an alien outside of it or in contrast to earth's nature. If the divine destiny is an indwelling, and not a domination or an occupation, and if that is also the goal of human civilization, we must bring the modern struggle against nature to an end; we must liberate ourselves from the modern God-complex in which humans become "lords and owners of nature."

The argument for this transformed perspective is so simple that it is almost always overlooked: The earth can survive without human beings, and has done so for millions of years; but we humans cannot survive without the earth. We depend on the earth system but must not occupy it. Whoever wants to become lord over and owner of nature, but is only a natural being himself, is destroying nature and himself. Only strangers exploit recklessly, cutting down forests until they are gone, overfishing the sea until it is empty, polluting the air until nothing can breathe. Whoever dwells in earth and wants to live there is surely interested in preserving the conditions for life, and for preserving the environment for habitation. Many ecological struggles today are between strangers and inhabitants.

The ecumenical interest of world Christianity is the habitable condition of the earth and the peacefulness of human civilization. This planet Earth shall, in its end — and this is the final Christian hope — become the house and home for the eternal, indwelling God, the locus where God's very Self will come to rest: "Behold, the tabernacle of God is with men, and he will dwell with them, and they shall be His people" (Rev. 21:3).

– Chapter 6 –

Moral Exemplars in Global Community

Peter J. Paris

The purpose of this essay is to demonstrate that a modified virtue theory can contribute significantly to the ethical dimension of contemporary discourse about globalization. That discourse both impresses and terrorizes countless numbers around the world. In fact, perspectives on the value of globalization sometimes appear to differ in accordance with regional contexts. Those in the developed regions of the northern hemisphere are likely to view the subject positively because of their high regard for the efficiency, speed, and global impact of transportation systems, electronic communications, and expanded markets. By contrast, those in the so-called underdeveloped regions of the southern hemisphere greatly fear that the power of globalized systems will overwhelm them with new forms of domination.

Is a Common Moral Discourse Possible?

In order to mediate between these two conflicting perspectives, I propose a discussion of moral virtue and selected moral exemplars in global context, in order to discern the extent to which a common moral discourse is possible among diverse peoples. I argue that such discourse is evident in the global recognition of men and women who have become moral exemplars in their efforts to effect just peacemaking in various parts of the world. I begin with a brief introduction to virtue theory, to which Western philosophy and theology has often turned when encountering ethical and religious traditions other than its own, and when seeking bases for the reorganization of the common life. We may again have to modify the

Western tradition under the current circumstances of a wider multicultural encounter. But the capacity to recognize virtue in others across social and cultural boundaries remains a source of authority in human affairs. It engenders the possibility of peace between those who are strangers or in conflict.

Contrary to mistaken notions, virtue theory neither implies an individualistic ethic isolated from societal context nor a parochial ethic limited to the moral values of small homogeneous communities. Nor is virtue theory a substitute for ethical rules, principles, laws, or rights. Rather, it provides a basic understanding of the four-dimensional unity of the moral life: appropriate appetite, free choice, wise judgment, and good habits.[1] Apart from such an understanding of the moral life, there could be no way of knowing the nature of moral excellence in particular actions, formed characters, or specific communities.

Moral virtue pertains to the exercise of the human capacity to act well in preserving, promoting, and enhancing the quality of our common humanity. Neither prescribed procedures nor societal structures can guarantee such an outcome. Yet appropriate conditions are necessary for nurturing both the development and proper exercise of those capacities. For example, codes of human rights are the best contemporary examples of the necessary societal conditions for the development of moral virtue. Apart from those conditions, certain activities would have no societal legitimacy and humanity would have no legitimate defense against the whims of those who exercise power, either by the authority given them by tradition or by some other controlling force. Since all such sources of power invariably protect and strive to extend the privileges of the powerful, the powerless are left with no means of appeal and, hence, cannot press their claims for justice in any legitimate way. Aside from

1. This fourfold dimensional unity is derived from Aristotle's understanding of the human soul which is the originative principle or essence of human life. According to Aristotle, the soul has two parts: one rational and the other subrational. In other words, humans are a composite of reason and appetites. The goals they seek are set in motion by their appetites (i.e., desires), and the means to those goals are determined by the rational practice of calculation, called deliberation, which is terminated by choice, which is the first principle of action. The choice of a morally good person is the same as that of a moral exemplar of practical wisdom. Good moral character is never a matter of doing good acts every now and then, but rather a series of habitual good acts. Habits culminate in a settled state of character or a disposition. Thus, *appropriate appetite, free choice, wise judgment,* and *good habits* constitute a multidimensional unity, namely, a person of moral virtue. All of this is distilled from Aristotle's *Nicomachean Ethics,* bks. I–IV.

open rebellion, they can only place themselves at the mercy of those who exercise power over them. Such adaptation never eradicates the oppression.

Aristotle, one of the progenitors of virtue theory, taught the world many things about the nature of the moral life. Two of those lessons that endure are (*a*) that human beings are a composite of appetite and reason; and (*b*) that human beings are *political* animals, which means they naturally strive for participation in community which, for Aristotle, meant the *polis*.

Both then and now such participation necessitates a certain measure of economic and social well-being. The lack of such necessary conditions severely hinders the process of human development that leads to moral maturity and, hopefully, full citizenship in a moral state. Only in the latter context do humans experience the fullness of their humanity, where the well-being of the whole community constitutes the goal of their public speech and actions. In other words, the moral fulfillment of individuals is found in the service rendered to the whole community. Only in such a community is freedom fully experienced. Within this sphere, no one rules or is ruled and, all energy is devoted to discerning, promoting, and enhancing the well-being of all. Clearly, by modern standards, Aristotle's *polis* was very small. Yet I contend that the principles by which it was constituted are realizable in contemporary contexts that are both larger and more diverse. Since humans are a composite of appetite and reason, moral excellence must involve the whole person as a willing actor. Thus, ethics must attend to both dimensions of the human person, namely, feeling and intellect. Attention to one alone would lead either to an emotivist or a rationalist understanding of action, neither of which pertains to the art of moral formation. Rather, moral formation depends on willful, thoughtful practice in which the whole person is fully engaged. That is, the appetitive element must express itself in a desire for a particular goal. The means to that goal are then deliberated until one is able to choose freely among options; that choice marks the beginning of action. Desiring a good goal, deliberating among alternative means for its realization, and making a good choice are skills learned by habitually following the thought and practice of good mentors who, inevitably, are recognized as moral exemplars of the basic values of the community in which they were nurtured and trained.

In recent decades, there has been much thought about cultural diversity and the ways in which it militates against notions of a common world. Alasdair MacIntyre, the most prominent contemporary representative of this position, has argued in his provocative masterpiece, *After Virtue: A Study in Moral Theory*, that the necessary context for a common morality no longer exists in the modern world. As a consequence, he argues that moral agreement is no longer possible in our society.[2] If its attainment is impossible in the Western world, it must also be true for the world at large.

Contrary to MacIntyre,[3] I contend that virtue theory, coupled with appropriate respect for human rights and civil law, and linked with dynamic movements toward social justice, can provide an adequate understanding of the moral life that both respects and transcends cultural boundaries, religious traditions, and political ideologies. This does not mean, however, that there can or should be only one theory of moral virtue. Rather, the multiplicity of cultures might well produce alternative arguments in support of similar moral states and various ways of specifying morally virtuous activity. In other words, similar expressions of good moral character may be understood differently from one context to another. Such diverse understandings may depend on many factors: differing starting points with respect to methods of knowing; sources of moral authority; societal understandings of the person-community relationship; types of rationality; and the relation of the emotions to reason. In any case, I contend that, despite their diverse understandings of moral virtue, human beings everywhere agree on the basic attributes of a morally good person. For example, all peoples would expect a morally good person to exhibit such habitual practices as the following: faithful devotion to their particular divinity; respect for parents; repulsion toward blasphemy; and strong warrants against murder, lying, theft, and adultery. In addition, they would expect the morally good person to be just in his or her dealings with others, obedient to the law, magnanimous in spirit, generous with his or her goods, and hospitable to all strangers who come in peace.

---

2. Alasdair MacIntyre. *After Virtue: A Study in Moral Theory* (Notre Dame, Ind.: University of Notre Dame Press, 1984), 6ff.

3. According to Gilbert Meilaender, however, MacIntyre's most recent book, *Dependent Rational Animals: Why Human Beings Need the Virtues* (Chicago: Open Court, 1999), argues that he has moved closer to a possible Aristotelian Thomism by grounding moral theory in human nature and by demonstrating the nature of a common good both for individuals and others. However, Meilaender disagrees with the Aristotelian nature of MacIntyre's ethics, and would prefer an ethic grounded in theology rather than the nature of the self. See Gilbert Meilaender, "Still Waiting for Benedict," *First Things* 96 (October 1999): 48–55.

In my endeavor to argue that moral virtues have similar meanings in various cultures, let us look more closely at a few such practices. Friendship is one of the most important moral virtues. Based on its purpose, Aristotle identified three types of friendship: those based on pleasure, utility, and character. The first two types are necessarily temporary because they last only as long as they fulfill their purpose of giving pleasure or being useful. Only friendships based on the love of each other's character are permanent, since character is relatively permanent. Most important, friendship implies justice, the doing of the other's good. Thus, Aristotle wrote: "If people are friends, they have no need of justice, but if they are just they need friendship in addition; and the justice that is most just seems to belong to friendship."[4] Similarly, he claimed that true friendship implies trust that each will seek the other's good. "It is among good men that trust and the feeling that 'he would never wrong me' and all the other things that are demanded in true friendship are found. In the other kinds of friendship, however, there is nothing to prevent these evils arising."[5] This is seen most vividly in the friendship that exists between nations whose actions are based primarily on the utilitarian principle of national self-interest. The latter invariably enables nations to alter the nature of their relationships very quickly whenever their self-interest changes or undergoes a threat. Aristotle discerned as much when he wrote, "Alliances between cities seem to aim at expediency."[6] Suffice it to say that friendships among nations are necessarily temporary. Only those deeply rooted in common traditions are capable of enduring for a longer time.

Nobel Peace Prize Laureates

In every culture, moral development depends heavily on moral exemplars whose thought and action are crucial sources of inspiration and guidance. The principal burden of this essay is to demonstrate that many such moral exemplars are embraced not only by their own peoples but by others far beyond their cultural boundaries. For example, during the twentieth century, a select number of moral exemplars have received world renown as recipients of

4. Aristotle, *Nicomachean Ethics* 1155a26.
5. Ibid., 1157a24.
6. Ibid., 1157a26.

the Nobel Peace Prize,[7] all of whom, along with numerous others similarly honored, manifest the many and varied ways by which the virtue of peacemaking can be undertaken. Each has followed his or her own path toward a common goal and, insofar as each has become honored as a peacemaker, he or she has exhibited that common virtue. As President Jimmy Carter once recognized in the foreword to selected acceptance speeches of Nobel Peace laureates, these heroes represent a diversity of vocations: heads of government like Theodore Roosevelt, Oscar Arias Sánchez, Menachem Begin, and Anwar Sadat, who have made significant contributions to peacemaking; humanitarians like Albert Schweitzer and Mother Teresa; practitioners of nonviolence like the American Friends Service Committee and the Friends Service Council of Great Britain, and the Peace People in Northern Ireland;[8] religious leaders like the Dalai Lama of Tibet and Archbishop Söderblom of Sweden; United Nations peacemakers like Ralph Bunche and Dag Hammarskjöld; champions of human rights like Chief Albert Luthuli, Archbishop Desmond Tutu, Nelson Mandela, Martin Luther King, Jr., Adolfo Pérez Esquivel, Andrei Sakharov, Lech Walesa, Elie Wiesel, and the leaders of Amnesty International.[9]

In addressing the need for many kinds of peacemakers and insisting on justice as a prerequisite for a lasting peace, President Carter drew upon the words of selected prize winners in speaking about the spirit of the peacemaker:

> I am convinced that for peace to endure, it must encompass justice, and I am confident that we can perceive today an inexorable trend toward the enhancement of human rights.

---

7. Nobel Peace Prize laureates include the following sample: Theodore Roosevelt (U.S.A., 1906); Archbishop Nathan Söderblom (Sweden, 1930); Albert Schweitzer (France, 1952); Chief Albert Luthuli (South Africa, 1960); Martin Luther King, Jr. (U.S.A., 1964); Eisaku Sato (Japan, 1974); Andrei Sakharov (U.S.S.R., 1975); Menachem Begin (Israel, 1978)/Anwar al-Sadat (Egypt, 1978); Mother Teresa (India, 1979); Adolfo Pérez Esquivel (Argentina, 1980); Archbishop Desmond Mpilo Tutu (South Africa, 1984); Elie Wiesel (U.S.A., 1986); Oscar Arias Sánchez (Costa Rica, 1987); Dalai Lama of Tibet (Tibet, 1989); Mikhail Gorbachev (U.S.S.R., 1990); Aung San Suu Kyi (Burma, 1991); Nelson Mandela /Frederik Willem de Klerk (South Africa, 1993); Yasir Arafat (Palestine Liberation Organization, 1994)/Shimon Peres (Israel, 1994)/Yitzhak Rabin (Israel, 1994).

8. The 1976 prize went to cofounders of the Peace People, Mairead Corrigan and Betty Williams.

9. See the foreword by President Jimmy Carter in *The Words of Peace: Selections from the Speeches of the Winners of the Nobel Peace Prize,* ed. Irwin Abrams (New York: Newmarket Press, 1995), ii–xi.

> We need many kinds of peacemakers. We need those who work to resolve civil wars and international conflicts. We also need those who can establish ways to control and reduce armaments. Preventing nuclear holocaust remains the highest priority.
>
> We must also work to establish social and political conditions in which all human beings can enjoy freedom and the fullest measure of happiness. I think of those who struggle nonviolently for human rights, those who fight disease and poverty and hunger, and those who work to improve and preserve our environment. But even those efforts to build sound foundations for peace are in themselves not enough. Nobel's "fraternity between nations," the spirit of human brotherhood, must undergird any political or social structure of peace if it is to last. Archbishop Söderblom refers to this in these pages as the "soul" of such a structure; Albert Schweitzer speaks of it here as "the ethical spirit."[10]

In reading the acceptance speeches, one is struck by the dominance of justice as a necessary condition for peace. Theodore Roosevelt expressed that viewpoint in 1906:

> We must ever bear in mind that the great end in view is righteousness, justice as between man and man, nation and nation, the chance to lead our lives on a somewhat higher level, with a broader spirit of brotherly goodwill one for another. Peace is generally good in itself, but it is never the highest good unless it comes as the handmaid of righteousness; and it becomes a very evil thing if it serves merely as a mask for cowardice and sloth, or as an instrument to further the ends of despotism or anarchy.[11]

In 1964, Martin Luther King, Jr., reminded the world of the relationship between peace and justice in his acceptance speech:

> All that I have said boils down to the point of affirming that mankind's survival is dependent upon man's ability to solve the problems of racial injustice, poverty, and war; the solution of these problems is in turn dependent upon man's squaring

---

10. Ibid., x–xi.
11. Marek Thee, ed., *Peace! By the Nobel Peace Prize Laureates* (Paris: UNESCO, 1995), 41.

> his moral progress with his scientific progress, and learning the practical art of living in harmony.[12]

In 1984, Archbishop Desmond Tutu expressed a similar understanding of the relation of justice and peace:

> There is no peace in South Africa. There is no peace because there is no justice. There can be no real peace and security until there be first justice enjoyed by all the inhabitants of that beautiful land. The Bible knows nothing about peace without justice, for that would be crying, "Peace, peace, where there is no peace." God's Shalom, peace, involves inevitably righteousness, justice, wholeness, fullness of life, participation in decision making, goodness, laughter, joy, compassion, sharing, and reconciliation.[13]

In 1987, the president of Costa Rica, Oscar Arias Sánchez, offered these words:

> We believe that justice and peace can only thrive together, never apart. A nation that mistreats its own citizens is more likely to mistreat its neighbors.... Peace can only be achieved through its own instruments: dialogue and understanding; tolerance and forgiveness; freedom and democracy.[14]

In 1992, Rigoberta Menchú Túm, campaigner for human rights for indigenous peoples in Guatemala, said:

> I consider this Prize, not as an award to me personally, but rather as one of the greatest conquests in the struggle for peace, for human rights and for the rights of the indigenous people who, for 500 years, have been split, fragmented, as well as the victims of genocide, repression and discrimination.[15]

It would be difficult and perhaps impossible to find someone who would admit opposition either to the principle of peace or the practices of peacemaking. The words of Javier Pérez de Cuéllar, accepting the prize in 1988 for UN peacekeeping forces, seem self-evident: "Peace — the word evokes the simplest and most cherished dream of humanity. Peace is, and has always been, the

12. Ibid., 46–47.
13. Ibid., 521.
14. Ibid., 50
15. Ibid., 436.

ultimate human aspiration."[16] Whenever people oppose so-called peace initiatives in the midst of conflict, we can be certain that they perceive a lack of justice in the proposal for peace. All who desire peace also want the necessary conditions that contribute to its realization: water, food, shelter, health care, political freedom, economic resources, and personal security. Thus, the agencies of the United Nations — the Food and Agricultural Organization (FAO), the World Health Organization (WHO), the Economic and Social Council (ESC), the UN Educational, Scientific, and Cultural Organization (UNESCO), the UN International Children's Emergency Fund (UNICEF), along with the General Assembly and the Security Council — are designed to attend much more carefully to the conditions of social justice than its predecessor, the League of Nations. Such an organizational structure made the reflections of Nobel Peace Prize laureate Mikhail Gorbachev persuasive, if somewhat romantic: "Preparing for my address I found in an old Russian encyclopaedia a definition of 'peace' as a 'commune' — the traditional cell of Russian peasant life. I saw in that definition the people's profound understanding of peace as harmony, concord, mutual help, and co-operation."[17]

When the leader of the democratic movement in Burma, Aung San Suu Kyi, was awarded the Nobel Peace Prize in 1991, she had been placed under house arrest by the totalitarian government she was bent on overthrowing. Consequently, she was not allowed to travel to Oslo to receive the prize. Accepting the award on behalf of his mother, Alexander Aris tried to express his mother's sentiments had she been present. He described the struggle that his mother and the people of Burma were waging, namely, the realization of human rights and the basic conditions for human dignity.

> Firstly, I know that she would begin by saying that she accepts the Nobel Prize for Peace not in her own name, but in the name of all the people of Burma. She would say that this prize belongs not to her but to all those men, women and children who, even as I speak, continue to sacrifice their well-being, their freedom and their lives in pursuit of a democratic Burma. Theirs is the prize and theirs will be the eventual victory in Burma's long struggle for peace, freedom and democracy....

---

16. Ibid., 41.
17. Ibid., 54.

> And no one must underestimate that plight. The plight of those in the countryside and towns, living in poverty and destitution, those in prison, battered and tortured; the plight of the young people, the hope of Burma, dying of malaria in the jungles to which they have fled; that of the Buddhist monks, beaten and dishonoured. Nor should we forget the many senior and highly respected leaders besides my mother who are all incarcerated....
>
> We must also remember that the lonely struggle taking place in a heavily guarded compound in Rangoon is part of the much larger struggle, world-wide, for the emancipation of the human spirit from political tyranny and psychological subjection.[18]

In spite of the many debates over the selection of virtually every Nobel Peace Prize winner, few have disputed the virtue of any of the laureates as genuine peacemakers. In fact, all of the winners have been highly praised by peoples beyond their own ethnic, racial, religious, regional, and national borders. Clearly, therefore, peacemaking is recognized across cultural boundaries as a moral virtue. Analogously, I contend that other moral virtues like justice, friendship, and freedom are similarly recognizable and praiseworthy.[19] Apart from such a basic presupposition, there could be no effective treaties between warring nations and no reconciliation between cross-cultural disputants.

Since moral virtues are observable through habitual practices of speech and deed, the virtues of peacemaking, justice, friendship, and freedom exhibit similar characteristics wherever they occur. The content of moral practices, however, will inevitably differ in accordance with their specific context. Yet their value is understandable across cultural borders and, more often than not, worthy of praise from diverse cultural traditions.

Some practices, however, considered moral in certain cultures, are often abhorrent to those in other cultures. Some obvious exam-

18. Ibid., 433–34.

19. This does not imply that these three virtues are the totality of moral virtue. Nothing could be further from the truth. Rather, I have selected these three to demonstrate their cross-cultural nature. Other virtues could have been selected, such as truthfulness, self-esteem, courage, generosity, temperance, liberality, and beneficence, to mention only a few.

ples of these are widow's rites (*sati*) in India; *trokosi*[20] in West Africa and elsewhere; clitoridectomy rituals in Kenya and elsewhere; female infanticide in China; and the subordination of women in many parts of the world. In all such cultural and moral conflicts, constructive resolutions necessitate careful analysis, sensitive reflection, and civil discussion. When these are disallowed, various measures may be entertained by multinational groups to effect an open forum either by moral suasion or nonviolent coercion. Whenever possible, disputants should call on the experience of an appropriate international structure, like one of the agencies of the United Nations, for example.

The Person-Community Relationship

A fundamental assumption underlying my understanding of moral virtue is the dialectical relationship between person and community. This moral-theory tradition claims that personhood is established in community, which constitutes both a limiting condition and a liberating potentiality for all thought and practice. Similarly, community is constituted when persons come together for the purpose of creating, preserving, and enhancing the necessary conditions for their common life. Those conditions must include guarantees of personal security, adequate material resources, and the freedom of public participation. As the philosophical theologian Paul Tillich argued, the person-community dialectical relationship is ontological in nature. That is, it is expressive of reality itself. Personhood is not possible apart from participation in community, and a good community exists for the well-being of its members. Radical separation of the person-community relationship destroys both. Admittedly, various cultures have tended to give primacy to one or the other of these dialectical elements. For example, American culture tends to give moral primacy to the individual, while African cultures bestow primacy on the community.[21] Both tendencies generate disharmony, sometimes even a life-and-death struggle, at the center of human life. Continuing imbalance between the two can destroy the possibility of human life. Consequently, different cultures have different

20. The traditional practice of giving young girls as slaves to priests to atone for the sin of a male relative.

21. See my book *The Spirituality of African Peoples: The Search for a Common Moral Discourse* (Minneapolis: Fortress Press, 1994) for a full treatment of an African and African American theory of moral virtue.

understandings of such ethical matters as freedom, liberty, responsibility, law, and social order. Yet despite different understandings of the conditions for the moral life, these cultures share many of the same moral virtues, and many of these divergent understandings are efforts to find the right balance of personhood and community under specific circumstances. In these contexts, morally good people are praised for similar moral virtues and blamed for similar moral deficiencies, including their efforts to redress or maintain imbalances when they exist.

Such moral-virtue theory is heavily dependent on Aristotle's insights and ethical analyses. When that theory is augmented with the many insights drawn from the modern tradition of human rights, pragmatism, and sensitivity to various spiritual traditions, it has much to contribute to the notion of a common moral world. So modified, the Aristotelian tradition can be reaffirmed in our day: moral-virtue theory and political theory are integrally united. The aim of the former is to help persons become morally good; the aim of the latter is to provide the structured environment to do the same. Thus, the study of the moral life of the community — what traditionally was called "political theory" but has also been called "ethology" or "moral ecology" — is the major ethical science, while the study of how individuals become good is the minor science. The former pertains to the authoritative function of law and policy in the formation of human community; the latter pertains to the function of socialization and moral development in communities of family, school, and religion that are either enabled or hindered by the law. Accordingly, morally good persons can be morally good citizens only in a morally good state.[22] Conversely, in a bad state, good persons cannot be good citizens.

The process of moral development pertains to the quality of the psyche. When fully developed into a specific type of character, the psyche is known by its disposition to act in certain ways. That disposition is not given by nature but shaped by the cultivation of good moral habits. In other words, a good moral disposition pertains to the regulation of the impulses, drives, desires, passions, and appetites, and its form appears in a set of moral virtues acquired only by moral example and habitual practice.

The practical habits from which moral virtues emerge are not acquired easily because they involve effort and often a considerable

22. See Aristotle, *Politics* 1278b1–5.

amount of discomfort. Yet, as learning to play a musical instrument or ride a bicycle is stressful in the beginning, practice eventually renders the activity easy because it has become a habit and can be performed without thinking. This does not imply, however, that practice is devoid of thought. Rather, thought is absorbed into habitual activity. Thus the habit of moral practice is expressive of moral character. Once established, moral habits cannot be easily broken. Neither a racist nor a misogynist can be easily changed. Thought and knowledge alone cannot and will not effect the necessary transformation. In fact, thought itself, including great ideas, changes nothing. Like all action, a change in character involves an act of the will. Will is the internal principle of motion at the center of the human being, capable of integrating the person's reasoning and appetitive functions.

Thus, the moral transformation of a racist or misogynist person necessitates strong desire on the part of that person to do nonracist or nonmisognynist activities regularly over a long period of time. Only then will the activity become habitual and, eventually, expressive of the person's character. Gradually, others will confirm the change and begin viewing the person as one who has assumed the disposition to act either in nonmisognynist or nonracist ways.

Obviously, people cannot train themselves to become morally good in isolation from their community. The process of moral development must take place in a community and with mentors who exemplify the community's values in their own practice. The morphology of moral development involves many things, among which are freedom, will, authority, feeling, and reason. The level of trust and mutual respect between the child and his or her parents, teachers, and other mentors determines the efficacy of the process of moral development or, in other words, the extent to which the child internalizes the process and claims it as his or her own.

In virtually every culture, the family is the primary locus for moral development because it has almost exclusive control over the child's formative period of growth and development. During the early years of the child's life, the family determines how, when, and to what extent the child will be exposed to cognate institutions such as day-care centers, schools, religious organizations, and the like. In contemporary societies, a moral travesty occurs whenever families become dysfunctional and/or discover that they cannot find the appropriate cognate institutions needed for the ongoing development of their children. This occurs as the various "principalities" and "authorities" become more complex and governed by values that are not in accord with what parents think best for the child and community. For example, if the values of the family are not in harmony with those of the school and the religious organization to which the child is exposed, the child will likely experience moral confusion and may fail to grow in a morally consistent way. Disciplinary problems in each context may evidence such confusion.

Such moral confusion long existed in the many and varied loci of the Christian missionary movement, especially when the latter formed educational boarding schools. Given the antagonism between the values of Christian missionaries and those of the so-called pagan families from which the children came, the latter were exposed to two different systems of moral training. As a result, considerable alienation often occurred between the native children and their families. As nascent converts to Christianity, the children in missionary schools learned to disrespect the religion of their parents and all the teachings derived from it. Their families, on the other hand, often taught them to embrace Christianity without rejecting their traditional religious practices. Thus, the one influence taught them how to be intolerant of other religions while the other taught them tolerance. Furthermore, insofar as traditional religious or cultural traditions were declared to be false, the possibilities for wider developments of Christian doctrine, and the refinement of cultural and social practices related to it under new conditions, were stunted. They could not grow by continued enrichment. Such limiting practices and contradictory teaching produced highly varied results.

For similar reason, moral confusion is widespread today in many parts of the world, perhaps especially in American society. The desegregation of schools in the United States, for example, has resulted in African American children living in predominantly black residential neighborhoods and attending predominantly white schools in either hostile or semihostile areas. While some benefits have come from this, compared to the old patterns of segregation, the experience undoubtedly has had a deleterious effect on the moral development of many African American children. They are taught to embrace the values of two opposing communities, the home and the school. Similarly, the children of first-generation immigrants to this or any country invariably experience conflict between the teaching received in the schools and that received in their homes.

Further, the ever-expanding mass media of television, radio, and the World Wide Web expose children to values that contradict those learned either at home or in school. The countless images of personal liberties exercised by seemingly autonomous people, uncontrolled consumerism, simulated violence against human beings, graphic pornography, and the glorification of drugs, guns, and indecent language militate against the moral teachings and practices that most people want their children to affirm. Yet it is doubtful that any of these influences changes our basic views of moral goodness. They simply represent the institutionalization of values that makes it difficult for a more holistic process of moral development to produce fairly predictable results. Unlike the situation in simpler times and places, there no longer exists in many cities a symbiotic relationship among the various social institutions to which children are exposed. It is unlikely that censure is the answer to this problem, even though that is the method being adopted by some societies around the world, as some seek to establish more authoritarian controls. In my judgment, all such endeavors are destined to fail, since the capacity of the communications revolution to reach all parts of the world seems irreversible. Both in antiquity and beyond many peoples have discerned that moral education is a long-term exercise in community training, so that the quality of the individual's life is brought into harmonious rhythm with that of the community. The philosopher Martha Nussbaum has expressed it well in her discussion of Protagoras's understanding of moral development as a preventive against moral sickness, which he likens to preventive medicine as an antidote for disease. "Social excellence is, then, to our psychological nature as health is to our bodily nature—an intrinsic (non-instrumental) good, which is deeply involved in all our other pursuits."[23] In other words, moral virtue expresses the health of the soul and vice its disease.

Contemporary Christian Exemplars of Virtue

As indicated above, virtue theory claims that individuals cannot become morally good apart from being reared in a morally good community. As the community becomes the moral guide for its members, it sometimes happens that individual members become moral guides for the community. This has always been the case

23. Martha C. Nussbaum, *The Fragility of Goodness: Luck and Ethics in Greek Tragedy and Philosophy* (Cambridge: Cambridge University Press, 1987), 103.

with religious prophets and social reformers who, invariably, have an astounding sensitivity to matters pertaining to social justice and who courageously condemn injustice and point the way to its correction. More often than not, they do this both by recalling more harmonious principles of justice from the past and by proposing a new vision of how justice can be integrated in the future in view of present imbalances. Most important, such people inevitably seek to embody the justice they propose. Often they emerge from the ranks of those who have been treated unjustly and, because of their suffering, they cry out for justice. That cry for justice has a reflexive effect. They themselves become just as a result of their habitual complaint and, being just people, they seek to realize their societal vision in just ways. That is to say, they never cease advocating means of reform that respect the personhood of their enemies. The two most prominent moral exemplars in our day have been Dr. Martin Luther King, Jr., and Archbishop Desmond Mpilo Tutu. They are among the few who have gained international praise for their strong advocacy of nonviolent resistance to injustice. King, the apostle of nonviolent resistance and a primary source of inspiration for Tutu, spoke in this way about nonviolence:

> The method of nonviolent resistance is effective in that it has a way of disarming the opponent, it exposes his moral defenses, it weakens his morale and at the same time it works on his conscience. . . .
>
> We will take direct action against injustice without waiting for other agencies to act. We will not obey unjust laws or submit to unjust practices. We will do this peacefully, openly, cheerfully because our aim is to persuade. We adopt the means of nonviolence because our end is a community at peace with itself. We will try to persuade with our words, but if our words fail, we will try to persuade with our acts. We will always be willing to talk and seek fair compromise, but we are ready to suffer when necessary and even risk our lives to become witnesses to the truth as we see it.[24]

The belief of both of these men in the equality of all peoples was rooted in their understanding of God as Creator of all, which they believed implied the kinship of all peoples. Accordingly, the equality

24. James M. Washington, ed., *A Testament of Hope: The Essential Writings of Martin Luther King, Jr.* (San Francisco: Harper & Row, 1986), 102–3.

of all peoples under God implies steady resistance to all forms of racism, classism, sexism, and militarism, and an unwavering commitment to the realization of a society wherein every citizen is equal before the law. Archbishop Tutu consistently maintained that societal vision throughout the antiapartheid struggle in South Africa. In his condemnation of apartheid as both immoral and anti-Christian, he wrote:

> So apartheid is a system which is not only unjust, but totally immoral and totally un-Christian. Its claim that God created us human beings for separation, for apartness, and for division contradicts the Bible and the whole tradition of undivided Christendom. God has created us for fellowship, for community, for friendship with God, and with one another, so that we can live in harmony with the rest of creation as well. For my part, the day will never come when apartheid will be acceptable. It is an evil system and it is at variance with the gospel of Jesus Christ. That is why I oppose it and can never compromise with it. . . .
>
> The same gospel of Jesus Christ, which compels us to reject apartheid as totally un-Christian, is the very gospel that constrains us to work for justice, for peace and reconciliation. God has given us a mandate to be ministers of His reconciliation.[25]

As contemporary social-change agents, both King and Tutu inspired the world at large to embrace their common vision for social justice: a vision captioned by King's oft-repeated words, "Injustice anywhere is a threat to justice everywhere."

Further, both men devoted enormous amounts of energy both in thought and practice to ensure the well-being of their enemies and taught the importance of never giving up on their enemies' moral transformation. Thus, King repeatedly said: "Our aim must never be to defeat or to humiliate the white man, but to win his friendship and understanding, and thereby create a society in which all men will be able to live together as brothers."[26] Consequently, King believed in the redemptive power of suffering, as evidenced in the affliction endured by nonviolent resisters in their efforts to transform

---

25. John Webster, *Bishop Desmond Tutu, Crying in the Wilderness: The Struggle for Justice in South Africa* (Grand Rapids, Mich.: Eerdmans, 1986), 54–55.

26. Washington, *Testament of Hope,* 200.

their persecutors as well as the society at large. In short, the suffering and death of all who struggle for righteousness is redemptive, because it is a virtuous means to a virtuous end.

> Suffering can be a most creative and powerful social force. Suffering has certain moral attributes involved, but it can be a powerful and creative social force. . . . The nonviolent say that suffering becomes a powerful social force when you willingly accept that violence on yourself, so that self-suffering stands at the center of the nonviolent movement and the individuals involved are able to suffer in a creative manner, feeling that unearned suffering is redemptive, and that suffering may serve to transform the social situation.[27]

King easily saw the relationship between racism in America and colonialism around the world. He also saw the relation of racism to the collective injustices of poverty and militarism. He was keenly aware of the way young people in America were inspired by the liberation movements in Africa, Asia, and elsewhere for freedom, justice, and peace. Time and again, he acknowledged his indebtedness and that of the movement in general to the extraordinary example of Mahatma Gandhi, who challenged the British Empire for the freedom of India and won "by using only the weapons of truth, noninjury, courage, and soul-force."[28] King was always aware of the motivational impact that the independence movements in Africa had on the African American struggle to dismantle the structures of racism in the United States. Accordingly, he wrote: "The liberation struggle in Africa has been the greatest single international influence on American Negro students. Frequently, I hear them say that if their African brothers can break the bonds of colonialism, surely the American Negro can break Jim Crow."[29]

Both King and Tutu, born and reared in very different sociopolitical contexts on two different continents, shared a common moral spirit as manifested by their separate, yet related, struggles for freedom, justice, and peace. Both believed in the moral virtues of nonviolent resistance, justice, friendship, and freedom; the political virtues of forgiveness, reconciliation, and community; and the religious virtues of love, faith, and hope.

---

27. Ibid., 47.
28. Ibid., 103.
29. Ibid., 162.

Both men praised the emergence of a new humanity among the blacks who struggled for justice in nonviolent ways. Both celebrated the end of an older era wherein blacks had lost their self-respect, wallowed in acts of self-deprivation, and seemed ashamed that God had created them black. Thus, Bishop Tutu's oration at Stephen Biko's funeral could have been spoken by Dr. King, since the two shared sentiments about the divine gift of blackness as the means of healing the nation.

> God called Steve Biko to be his servant in South Africa, to speak up on behalf of God, declaring what the will of this God must be in a situation such as ours, a situation of evil, injustice, oppression and exploitation. God called him to be the founder of the Black Consciousness Movement against which we have had tirades and fulminations. It is a movement by which God, through Steve, sought to awaken in the Black person a sense of his intrinsic value and worth as a child of God, not needing to apologize for his existential condition as a black person, calling on blacks to glorify and praise God that he had created them black. Steve, with his brilliant mind that always saw to the heart of things, realized that until blacks asserted their humanity and their personhood, there was not the remotest chance for reconciliation in South Africa. For true reconciliation is a deeply personal matter. It can happen only between persons who assert their own personhood, and who acknowledge and respect that of others.[30]

Both King and Tutu discerned the special capacity of oppressed peoples to be the principal agents of social justice. Being part of the oppressed in their respective countries, both knew that a people's constant longing for freedom and justice would eventually erupt in a mass expression of outrage against its contrary. During the latter half of the 1950s and from that point on, both men saw that force rise up against structures of injustice in Africa, Asia, Latin America, and North America. It was a watershed period in human history. In discussing the cause of the crisis underlying the student movement in the United States, King attributed it to students' newly emergent sense of dignity and self-worth that African Americans and all peoples had come to feel and affirm. It was a sentiment that would never again be passive and quiescent:

---

30. Webster, *Bishop Desmond Tutu*, 62.

> And all of these forces have developed into massive resistance. But we must also say that the crisis has been precipitated on the other hand by the determination of hundreds and thousands and millions of Negro people to achieve freedom and human dignity. If the Negro stayed in his place and accepted discrimination and segregation, there would be no crisis. But the Negro has a new sense of dignity, a new self-respect and new determination. He has reevaluated his own intrinsic worth. Now this new sense of dignity on the part of the Negro grows out of the same longing for freedom and human dignity on the part of the oppressed people all over the world; for we see it in Africa, we see it in Asia, and we see it all over the world. Now we must say that this struggle for freedom will not come to an automatic halt, for history reveals to us that once oppressed people rise up against that oppression, there is no stopping point short of full freedom.[31]

Both King and Tutu believed that the long periods of suffering had bequeathed oppressed peoples with a special capacity to pursue justice in a just way—to affirm the humanity of all peoples and to uphold their right to the conditions needed to preserve their humanity. Neither King nor Tutu had a narrow, parochial societal vision. Rather, both had an expansive view of humanity and believed that the extension of justice was not based on a zero-sum equation.

Both men saw the importance of the oppressed taking charge of their own freedom struggles while welcoming the participation of others in their liberation processes. In fact, the participation of persons of various religions, races, and ethnicities modeled the societal end they both desired. In accord with the person-community relation implied by the moral-virtue theory, King's Southern Christian Leadership Conference and Tutu's South African Council of Churches welcomed the participation of peoples of every race, religion, and class. In brief, each believed in the realization of true democracy, wherein every person would be an equal participant and the democratic principle would apply not only to the political realm but to the social and economic domains as well. Neither believed that democracy meant the rule of blacks over whites, but each believed in majority rule, wherein all the people participated and none was excluded.

---

31. Washington, *Testament of Hope,* 44.

Both King and Tutu spent their public lives reaching out to their oppressors, striving to persuade them to negotiate their differences in rational, peaceful ways, to the end of seeking reconciliation and a harmonious life among all peoples. Both believed that a just solution to their respective societal problems would constitute significant models of conflict resolution for the entire world. All of King's many mass demonstrations were aimed at persuading those in power to help design a new social order. Tutu's countless sermons and speeches aimed at a similar end. The triumph of the new South Africa is seen not merely in the form of a new constitution, or in the extension of the franchise to all South Africans, but in a novel process of healing the wounds of the past via the formal procedures and reconciliatory outcomes of the Truth and Reconciliation Commission, inspired and chaired by Archbishop Tutu himself.

Thus, the moral excellence that the world has witnessed in the public deeds of Martin Luther King, Jr., and Desmond M. Tutu is worthy of embodiment by peoples everywhere. Short of serious disagreement about this thesis, I contend that this wish carries little of the baggage sometimes associated with other universal claims. The argument of this essay does not exclude the reality of moral virtues other than those that either have been or could have been named. In fact, I expect the peoples of the world, because of their differing contexts, to discover particular moral virtues different from the ones they cherish. Nevertheless, some virtues are shared by many diverse cultures, and these are peace, peacemaking, justice, friendship, and freedom. Were these virtues to be realized around the world, they would constitute the moral fabric of a lasting world community.

As stated above, the moral good for individuals and for communities is the same. Peaceful, just, free, friendly, benevolent peoples are produced by peaceful, just, free, friendly, and benevolent communities. The preservation of those and similar virtues necessitates commensurate practices.

Contemporary Political Exemplars of Virtue

Neither Martin Luther King, Jr. nor Archbishop Desmond Tutu was or aspired to be a head of state. Both were Christian clerics deeply committed to a prophetic vocation of boldly condemning the hegemony of racism and faithfully proclaiming God's justice for their respective nations. Each was bent on redeeming the whole nation by liberating the oppressed from their bondage and delivering the oppressors from their evil ways. As a consequence, each dreamed of a transformed society of reconciled peoples mutually dedicated to the preservation of justice, freedom, and peace. But neither aspired to direct political office, what is acknowledged as the other "anointed" office in biblical and some Christian theological traditions — the "kingly" role.

Two major political figures of the twentieth century who have felt called to that role are Nelson Rolihlahla Mandela, former president of South Africa, and Daw Aung San Suu Kyi, leader of the National League for Democracy party in Burma (now also known as Myanmar). Both persons were born in so-called first families of their respective homelands. Mandela's father was the chief of the Tembe people in the Transkei; Suu Kyi's mother was a prominent diplomat and her father, General Aung San, was the founder of modern Burma and its first elected leader. He was assassinated in 1947, and the country has been under military rule ever since. Because of their respective lineage, both Mandela and Suu Kyi were reared in contexts that afforded them considerable status and privilege. In retrospect, it might seem that they were destined for public leadership. Though neither is a religious leader, each is religious nonetheless. Mandela, a Christian adherent, is deeply respectful of all religions. Suu Kyi is a Buddhist. Both Mandela and Suu Kyi are well-educated and both have suffered greatly for their respective causes, namely, political freedom and justice for their people.

Like King and Tutu, both have gained the praise and respect of millions around the world. The honors bestowed on them from many parts of the world have been legion. Needless to say, both have greatly inspired a whole generation of peoples. Both have long been devotees of nonviolent resistance. Unfortunately, Mandela was forced to join his party in opting for armed resistance only after it became abundantly clear that the apartheid government of South Africa was unrelenting in its violence toward all forms of nonviolent protest, including peaceful demonstrations, publications, assemblies, and speeches. All were banned. There was even a ban on mentioning the names of banned persons. Consequently, for the twenty-seven years of Nelson Mandela's imprisonment, it was illegal to publish any information about him. Upon his release from prison, the nation and the world saw images of the man for the first time in twenty-seven years. In response to President Botha's offer of conditional freedom in 1985, Mandela's notions of freedom and nonviolence were made vivid in the following address prepared by him and read by his daughter, Zindzi, to the people of Soweto, who were celebrating Bishop Tutu's Nobel Peace Prize:

> I am surprised at the conditions that the government wants to impose on me. I am not a violent man. My colleagues and I wrote in 1952 to [Daniel] Malan asking for a roundtable conference to find a solution to the problems of our country but that was ignored.
>
> When [Johannes] Strijdom was in power, we made the same offer. Again it was ignored.
>
> When [Hendrik] Verwoerd was in power we asked for a National Convention for all the people in South Africa to decide on their future. This, too, was in vain.
>
> It was only then when all other forms of resistance were no longer open to us that we turned to armed struggle.
>
> Let Botha show that he is different to Malan, Strijdom and Verwoerd. Let him renounce violence. Let him say that he will dismantle apartheid.
>
> I cherish my own freedom dearly but I care even more for your freedom. Too many have died since I went to prison. Too many have suffered for the love of freedom. I owe it to their widows, to their orphans, to their mothers and to their fathers who have grieved and wept for them. Not only I have suffered during these long lonely wasted years. I am not less life-loving than you are. But I cannot sell my birthright nor am I prepared to sell the birthright of the people to be free. I am in prison as the representative of the people of your organization, the African National Congress, which was banned....
>
> Only free men can negotiate.[32]

Similarly, Suu Kyi had been placed under house arrest by the Burmese military junta from 1989 to 1995. When she was awarded the Nobel Peace Prize in 1991, she was not allowed to leave the country to receive the award. Her son, Alexander Aris, living outside the country, accepted it on her behalf. While her husband, Michael Aris, was on his deathbed in England during the spring of 1999, she chose not to leave the country because she feared the government would not allow her to return. When the junta finally decided to guarantee such permission, she had no reason to

---

32. The address was given on February 10, 1985. See Mary Benson, *Nelson Mandela: The Man and the Movement* (New York: W. W. Norton, 1986), 236–37.

trust its words. Like Mandela, she has remarked often that her personal plight is insignificant compared to hundreds of other National League for Democracy (NLD) members languishing in state prisons.

Like Mandela, she has become her nation's personified symbol of resistance to political oppression and, as such, has inspired the larger world to lend its moral and political support to her cause. Accordingly, in 1997, she again inspired students in Burma and around the world to join her in a fast as a nonviolent means of freeing Burma. The government had disallowed rule by the NLD, after Suu Kyi's party received 82 percent of the popular vote in 1990.

> The Free Burma fast will help to focus attention on the essentially peaceful nature of the quest for democracy in Burma. It is reminiscent of the "satyagraha" truth-force campaign with which Mahatma Gandhi set the very foundations of the British Indian empire rocking. Your action could well release an international truth-force that will join the current of our struggle for democracy in Burma.[33]

Again, like Mandela, Aung San Suu Kyi has called on the governments and corporations of the world to shun the junta and to refuse to enter alliances with it. Thus, in a 1997 commencement address (read by her husband) at American University in Washington, D.C., where she received her first honorary degree from a U.S. institution, Suu Kyi called on all who love and enjoy liberty to help those denied liberty in Burma and elsewhere. More specifically, she asked the international community to bring pressure on multinational corporations that are willing to do business with the junta.

> Their justification for economic involvement in Burma is that their presence will actually assist the process of democratization. Investment that only goes to enrich an already wealthy elite bent on monopolising both economic and political power cannot contribute towards equality and justice, the foundation stones for a sound democracy.[34]

---

33. See Aung San Suu Kyi's speech in support of the October 7–9, 1996, Free Burma fast. See http://www.euroburma.com/asia/euro-burma/daask/279a=01oct96-5.html.

34. See Aung San Suu Kyi's 1997 commencement address at American University, where she received an honorary degree *in absentia*. Online: http://www.freeburmacoalition.org/suukyi/suukyiau.html

In a message to the fiftieth-anniversary celebration of the United Nation's Declaration of Human Rights in Edmonton, Alberta, Suu Kyi discussed peace, justice, and freedom:

> Peace, justice and freedom could be viewed as universal values which form the foundation of our demand for those basic human rights that should be recognized by the international community and guaranteed by every state in the world.
>
> Few rational human beings anywhere, regardless of their race, religion or culture, would deny the supreme value of peace, justice and freedom in their positive, vigorous aspects. It is now widely seen that peace should be more than the mere absence of war: it should be a positive force that counters violence as a means of resolving the problems of human society. Justice should not only aim at controlling the negative traits in human nature, it should work to promote a sense of fairness, compassion and universal brotherhood. Freedom should be more than a lack of shackles, it should mean an environment where the right to develop one's own potential, without curbing that of others, can be exercised without fear.[35]

This necessarily cursory glance at the public profiles of Nelson Mandela and Aung San Suu Kyi reveals many striking similarities. Both have given their lives in support of a cause aimed at the liberation of their peoples from political oppression, economic deprivation, and social degradation. In doing so, both have placed themselves under the discipline of their respective parties: Mandela under the African National Congress and Suu Kyi under the National League for Democracy. Both have refused personal deals with their respective tormentors but have viewed themselves always as faithful servants of their parties, the locus of all decision-making authority. Further, though both have suffered greatly in pursuit of their goals, they have always viewed their own suffering as insignificant compared with that of oppressed peoples. Further still, both Mandela and Suu Kyi have maintained hope that their cause would

---

35. See Aung San Suu Kyi, "A Blueprint for Peace, Justice, and Freedom: An International Conference to Celebrate the Fiftieth Anniversary of the Universal Declaration of Human Rights," November 26–28, 1998, Edmonton, Alberta.

be victorious and that the long-desired negotiations between the oppressed and their oppressors would be realized.

The Virtue of Just Peacemaking throughout the World

As in every new age, the crucial problem of the twenty-first century is how humanity can establish a lasting and just peace throughout the world.[36] Human beings continue to seek ways to live together in harmony. Their natural inclination toward community implies a natural capacity for justice, since the former depends on the latter.

I am convinced that all of the major conflicts between and among communities around the world are caused by the domination of one group by another. Dominant groups may be characterized by class, race, gender, ethnicity, religion, political ideology, or by the capacity to impose their view of the principalities, authorities, and regencies, as discussed in volumes 1 and 2 of this series. Rarely do dominant groups acknowledge the injustices they perpetrate. Rather, they inevitably claim righteousness for themselves and their deeds.[37] In keeping with Reinhold Niebuhr's thought on this matter, the only means for controlling the aggressive nature of human groups is to construct counterbalances of power. Although such balances can be achieved to a limited extent by nation-states, human beings have always needed a more transcendent authority than the nation-state. The most prominent example of such a force was institutionalized a half-century ago in the United Nations. Though imperfect in form, it is, nevertheless, the best means presently available for the maintenance of world peace. Since the major powers of the world are reluctant to submit their own purposes to the adjudication of this body's assembly, its Security Council was designed to accommodate that reality. Yet as recent events have demonstrated, that structure has not been totally successful

---

36. See Donald W. Shriver's treatment of the problem of "Mars" in *God and Globalization: Religion and the Powers of the Common Life,* ed. Max L. Stackhouse with Peter J. Paris (Harrisburg, Pa.: Trinity Press International, 2000), 140–83.

37. I am indebted to Reinhold Niebuhr for this generalization. Though he discussed this human (sinful) characteristic in many places, the following works comprise a good introduction: *The Nature and Destiny of Man: Human Destiny*, vol. 2 (New York: Charles Scribner's Sons, 1964), chap. 9; *Moral Man and Immoral Society* (New York: Charles Scribner's Sons, 1960), chaps. 4 and 5.

in preventing war and similar animosities. It remains the best structure available for international mediation, nonviolent pressure, and peacekeeping.

As mentioned above, peace is not the mere absence of war but, rather, the presence of justice. King's proposed "War on Poverty" demonstrated his awareness of this maxim; Tutu's recognition of its import is seen in his recent call for a Year of Jubilee in 2000 C.E., which asks the International Monetary Fund and the World Bank to forgive all the foreign indebtedness of African countries. Most important, the same teaching concerning justice and peace was foreseen in the organizational structure of the United Nations. Such a message should have a place of primacy in the lives of individuals and on the agenda of their communities. This is the pressing need of the twenty-first century, namely, how to persuade the entire world to condemn unequivocally the barbarism of all warfare and, especially, the sophisticated, high-tech wars of this present generation. The physical and psychological devastation wrought by war in our day is infinitely more horrific than that of ancient war. Enhanced technological efficiency in warfare can never negate its terrible costs in human life, communal infrastructures, and environmental resources. Nothing is more important in the foreseeable future than a concentrated worldwide effort to persuade humanity to eliminate the menace of war from global civilization. Such an effort would require a long-term, unfailing commitment by the leaders, members, and sponsors of religious institutions, scholarly communities, educational institutions, nongovernmental organizations, and all dimensions of the mass media. Such an outpouring of sentiment, reason, and power would have a major effect on the morality of all. All spheres of world society would soon feel its impact and benefit. The educational blitz called for in this proposal would alter the consciousness of all peoples (young and old) in ways similar to public education on environmental preservation and the ban on smoking in public places.

The most troubling part of this proposal is its implications for the maintenance of standing military forces and the enhancement of weaponry. How the world moves from the armies of nation-states to global arrangements will require the ingenuity and wisdom of the entire world community. Similarly, since the nations of the world have been conditioned to think solely in terms of their specific national self-interests, they will have enormous difficulties in developing sufficient trust even to think seriously about the possibility of a "world without war." Yet constructive thought and commensurable practice[38] are not only possible but also necessary for the moral progress of human civilization.

Concluding Observations

Virtue theory is grounded in the capacity of humans to govern their appetites in accordance with reason and the well-being of the society at large. Such a viewpoint is not new. Rather, it was conceptualized by such ancient philosophers as Plato and Aristotle. One of the most important aspects of moral-virtue theory is the integral relation between theory and practice, reason and emotion, thought and action. Closely connected to those relations is the practical art of moral development, which can only be achieved by habitual practice under the guidance of morally good mentors.

Further, virtue theory presupposes an integral relation between person and community. Thus, I have illustrated the contemporary relevance of moral-virtue theory by discussing such moral exemplars as Martin Luther King, Jr., Desmond Tutu, Nelson Mandela, and Daw Aung San Suu Kyi, each of whom has embodied the virtues they advocate for their respective nations, and who, in the process, have become internationally recognized as symbols of virtues that transcend their own contexts. Further, they have stimulated the formation of communities of action for justice and peace both at home and abroad. Their lives and teachings demonstrate that the moral virtues of the good person are the same as those of the good state, and in some sense of common humanity. In fact, the relation between the person and the state is circular. That is to say, morally good persons are developed in morally good communities, as well as in the quest for morally good communities. The purpose of morally good communities is to nurture the development of morally good persons. Thus, moral virtue pertains to both individuals and states. As moral exemplars par excellence, I have argued that the practical wisdom[39] of King, Tutu, Mandela, and Suu Kyi is a necessary con-

38. Many good practices relative to this proposal are contained in a recent collection of essays by a group of religious ethicists, edited by Glen Stassen and entitled, *Just Peacemaking: Ten Practices for Abolishing War* (Cleveland: Pilgrim Press, 1998).

39. See bk. VI of the *Nicomachean Ethics* for a comprehensive analysis of practical wisdom, which is the excellence of reason in determining the nature of good action for persons and states.

dition for the political and moral development of their respective nations.

Finally, all these moral exemplars represent regions and peoples usually viewed in the discourse about globalization as beneficiaries of globalization rather than as contributors. This essay demonstrates the moral contributions such peoples can and do make to the moral quality of our global world. Thus, globalization is not a mere material phenomenon. It is also moral and spiritual. In fact, apart from the primacy of moral and spiritual qualities, globalization may well be feared as a vicious monster bent on devouring the world for its own satisfaction.

Selected Bibliography

Abrams, Irwin, ed. *The Words of Peace: Selections from the Speeches of the Winners of the Nobel Peace Prize.* New York: Newmarket Press, 1995.

Adams, James Luther. "The Social Import of the Professions." In *Voluntary Associations.* Ed. R. Engel. Chicago: Exploration Press, 1986.

———. *The Prophethood of All Believers.* Ed. G. K. Beach. Boston: Beacon Press, 1986.

Albrow, M. "Globalization, Knowledge, and Society." In *Globalization, Knowledge, and Society.* Ed. M. Albrow and E. King. Thousand Oaks, Calif.: Sage, 1990.

Alford, C. F. *Think No Evil: Korean Values in the Age of Globalization.* Ithaca, N.Y.: Cornell University Press, 1999.

Allen, Joseph. *Love and Conflict: A Covenantal Model of Christian Ethics.* Nashville: Abingdon Press, 1984.

Allenby, Braden. *Industrial Ecology: Policy Framework and Implementation.* London: Prentice Hall, 1999.

Amundsen, Darrel W. "Casuistry and Professional Obligations: The Regulation of Physicians by the Court of Conscience in the Late Middle Ages." In *Transactions and Studies of the College of Physicians of Philadelphia* 3 (1982): 22–39.

Anderson, Per. "Cultivating the Cool, Critical Gaze: On Saying 'No' to 'Dolly' and the Future of the Faith-Science Dialogue. *Covalence: The Bulletin of the Ecumenical Roundtable on Science, Technology, and the Church* 1, nos. 3–4 (May–August 1998): 4–5.

An-Na'im, Abdullahi Ahmed, ed. *Proselytization and Communal Self-Determination in Africa.* Maryknoll, N.Y.: Orbis Books, 1999.

———. "Toward an Islamic Hermeneutics for Human Rights." In *Religion and Human Rights Values: An Uneasy Relationship.* Grand Rapids, Mich: Eerdmans, 1995.

———. *Toward an Islamic Reformation: Civil Liberties, Human Rights, and International Law.* Syracuse: Syracuse University Press, 1990.

Appadurai, Arjun. *Modernity at Large: Cultural Dimensions of Globalization.* Minneapolis: University of Minnesota Press, 1996.

Arendt, Hannah. *The Human Condition.* Chicago: University of Chicago Press, 1958.

Bacchiocci, S. *Deine Zeit ist Meine Zeit: Der biblische Ruhetag als Chance für den modern Menschen.* Hamburg: NS Zeit, 1988.

Bacon, Francis. *The New Organon and Related Writings.* Ed. F. H. Anderson. Indianapolis: Bobbs-Merrill, 1960.

Banks, James. "The Need for a Broad Definition of Multicultural Education." *Multicultural Leader* 4 (Winter–Spring 1991).

Barber, Benjamin. *Jihad vs. McWorld: How Globalism and Tribalism Are Reshaping the World.* New York: Ballantine Books, 1995.

Barbour, Ian. *Religion in an Age of Science,* vol. 1, and *Ethics in an Age of Technology,* vol. 2. San Francisco: Harper & Row, 1990–1994.

Barnet, Richard, and John Cavanagh. *Global Dreams: Imperial Corporations and the New World Order.* New York: Touchstone Books, 1994.

Basil, St. *The Book of St. Basil the Great on the Holy Spirit.* Revised text with notes by C. F. H. Johnston. Oxford: Clarendon Press, 1892.

Bauer, Joanne R., and Daniel A. Bell. *The East Asian Challenge for Human Rights.* Cambridge: Cambridge University Press, 1999.

Bell, Daniel. " 'American Exceptionalism' Revisited: The Role of Civil Society," *Public Interest* 95 (Spring 1989): 38–56.

Bellah, Robert. "How to Understand the Church in an Individualistic Society." In *Christianity and Civil Society Theological Education for Public Life.* Ed. R. Petersen. Maryknoll, N.Y.: Orbis Books, 1995.

Benhabib, Seyla. *Situating the Self: Gender, Community, and Postmodernism in Contemporary Ethics.* New York: Routledge, 1992.

Benhabib, Seyla, ed. *Democracy and Difference.* Princeton: Princeton University Press, 1997.

Benhabib, Seyla, and F. Dallmayr, eds. *The Communicative Ethics Controversy.* Cambridge, Mass.: MIT Press, 1991.

Benjamin, Gail. *Japanese Lessons.* New York: New York University Press, 1997.

Benson, Mary. *Nelson Mandela: The Man and the Movement.* New York: W. W. Norton, 1986.

Benz, Ernst. *Evolution and Christian Hope.* Garden City, N.Y.: Doubleday, 1975.

Berger, Peter. *Pyramids of Sacrifice.* Garden City, N.Y.: Anchor Books, 1976.

Berman, Harold J. *Faith and Order: The Reconciliation of Law and Religion.* Atlanta: Scholars Press, 1993.

———. *Law and Revolution: The Formation of the Western Legal Tradition.* Cambridge: Harvard University Press, 1983.

———. "World Law." *Fordham International Law Journal* 18 (1995): 1617.

Beyer, Peter. *Religion and Globalization.* Thousand Oaks, Calif.: Sage, 1994.

Bloom, Irene, J. Paul Martin, and Wayne L. Proudfoot, eds. *Religious Diversity and Human Rights.* New York: Columbia University Press, 1996.

Boff, Leonardo. *Cry of the Earth, Cry of the Poor*. Maryknoll, N.Y.: Orbis Books, 1997.

———. *Trinity and Society*. Trans. P. Burns. Maryknoll, N.Y.: Orbis Books, 1988.

Boyle, Kevin, and Juliet Sheen. *Freedom of Religion and Belief: A World Report*. London and New York: Routledge, 1997.

Brown, Warren S. Nancey Murphey, and H. Newton Malony, eds. *Whatever Became of the Soul?* Minneapolis: Fortress Press, 1998.

Browning, Don. *A Fundamental Practical Theology: Descriptive and Strategic Proposals*. Minneapolis: Fortress Press, 1991.

Browning, Don, and Francis Fiorenza, eds. *Habermas, Modernity, and Public Theology*. New York: Crossroad, 1992.

Burtchaell, James T. *The Dying of the Light*. Grand Rapids, Mich.: Eerdmans, 1998.

Callahan, Daniel. "Religion and the Secularization of Bioethics." *Hastings Center Report* (special supplement: "Theology, Religious Traditions, and Bioethics") 20 (July–August 1990): 2.

Calvin, John. *Institutes of the Christian Religion*. Ed. John T. McNeill. Trans. Ford Lewis Battles. Library of Christian Classics 20. Philadelphia: Westminster Press, 1960.

Cardenal, Ernesto. *Love*. Trans. D. Livingstone. London: SPCK, 1974.

Carter, Stephen *Civility, Manners, Morals, and the Etiquette of Democracy*. New York: Basic Books, 1998.

Casanova, Jose. *Public Religions in the Modern World*. Chicago: University of Chicago Press, 1994.

Chief Seattle, *Brother Eagle, Sister Sky: A Message from Chief Seattle*. New York: Dial Books, 1991.

Cobb, Jennifer. *Cybergrace: The Search for God in the Digital World*. New York: Crown, 1998.

Cohen, I. B., ed. *Puritanism and the Rise of Modern Science: The Merton Thesis*. New Brunswick, N.J.: Rutgers University Press, 1990.

Cohen, Jean, and Andrew Arato, *Civil Society and Political Theory*. Cambridge, Mass.: MIT Press, 1992.

Cole-Turner, Ronald. *The New Genesis: Theology and the Genetic Revolution*. Louisville: Westminster/John Knox Press, 1993.

Collingwood, R. G. *The Idea of History*. New York: Galaxy Books, 1946.

———. *The Idea of Nature*. New York: Oxford University Press, 1945.

Conference Report: The Global Forum on Environment and Development for Survival. Moscow, USSR, January 15–19, 1990, New York 1990, 193–95.

Cotler, Irwin. "Jewish NGOs and Religious Human Rights: A Case Study." In *Human Rights in Judaism: Cultural, Religious, and Political Perspectives*. Ed. Michael J. Broyde and John Witte, Jr. Northvale, N.J., and Jerusalem: Jason Aronson, 1998.

"Covenanting with God's Creation." In *Seoul: 22nd General Council of the World Alliance of Reformed Churches, Section II: Justice, Peace and the Integrity of Creation*. Geneva: World Alliance of Reformed Churches, 1989), 73–104.

Crick, Francis. *The Astonishing Hypothesis: The Scientific Search for the Soul*. New York: Charles Scribner's Sons, 1994.

Cromartie, Michael, ed. *A Preserving Grace: Protestants, Catholics, and Natural Law*. Washington, D.C.: Ethics and Public Policy Center, 1997.

Cunningham, David. *These Three Are One: The Practice of Trinitarian Theology*. Malden, Mass.: Basil Blackwell, 1998.

Dawkins, Richard. "The Emptiness of Theology." *Free Inquiry* (Spring 1998): 6.

De Bary, Wm. Theodore, and Tu Weiming, eds. *Confucianism and Human Rights*. New York: Columbia University Press, 1998.

Deneffe, A. "Perichoresis, circumincessio . . . " *Zeitschrift für katholische Theologie* 47 (1923): 497–532.

Dertouzos, I. *What Will Be: How the New World of Information Will Change Our Lives*. San Francisco: Harperbusiness, 1998.

Descartes, René. "Discourse on the Method of Rightly Conducting the Reason." In *The Philosophical Works of Descartes*. Trans. E. S. Haldane and G. R. T. Ross. Rev. ed. 1931. Reprint, Cambridge: Cambridge University Press, 1979.

DeVries, Peter. *The Blood of the Lamb*. Boston: Little, Brown and Company, 1961.

———. *Slouching toward Kalamazoo*. New York: Penguin Books, 1984.

Dohse, K., U. Jürgens, and T. Malsch. "From 'Fordism' to 'Toyotism"? The Social Organization of the Japanese Automobile Industry," *Politics and Society* 14, no. 2:115–46.

Dryzek, John. *Discursive Democracy*. Cambridge: Cambridge University Press, 1990.

Dunning, James. *Multinational Enterprises in a Global Economy*. Workingham, England: Addison-Wesley, 1993.

Edelstein, Ludwig. "The Hippocratic Oath." *Bulletin of the History of Medicine* 1943, supp. 5, no. 1, 1–64.

Ehler, Sidney Z., and John B. Morrall, eds. *Church and State through the Centuries*. Westminster, Md.: Newman, 1954.

Elazar, Daniel J. *Constitutionalizing Globalization*. New York: Rowman and Littlefield, 1999.

Ellul, Jacques. "Technique and the Opening Chapters of Genesis." In *Theology and Technology*, ed. C. Mitchum, et al. Lanham, Md.: University Press of America, 1984.

———. *The Technological Society*. New York: Knopf, 1964.

Elsbernd, Mary. "Papal Statements on Rights: A Historical-Contextual Study of Encyclical Teachings from Pius VI–Pius XI (1791–1939)." Ph.D. diss., Catholic University of Louvain, 1985.

Evans, Malcolm D. *Religious Liberty and International Law in Europe*. Cambridge: Cambridge University Press, 1997.

Featherstone, Mike, ed. *Global Culture: Nationalism, Globalization, and Modernity*. London: Sage, 1990.

Fee, Gordon. *God's Empowering Presence: The Holy Spirit in the Letters of Paul*. Peabody, Mass.: Hendrickson, 1994.

Forrester, Duncan B. *Christian Justice and Public Policy*. Cambridge: Cambridge University Press, 1997.

Foster, Richard. *Prayer: Finding the Heart's True Home*. San Francisco: Harper & Row, 1992.

Fowler, James. *Faithful Change: The Personal and Public Challenges of Postmodern Life*. Nashville: Abingdon Press, 1996.

———. *Stages of Faith: The Psychology of Human Development and the Quest for Meaning*. San Francisco: Harper & Row, 1981.

Friedman, Thomas. "WTO Protesters: Senseless in Seattle." New York Times, December 2, 1999.

Friedmann, Robert. *The Theology of Anabaptism*. Scottdale, Pa.: Herald Press, 1973.

Fukuyama, Francis. *The End of History and the Last Man*. New York: Basic Books, 1991.

———. *Trust: The Social Virtues and the Creation of Prosperity*. New York: Free Press, 1995.

Gardner, Howard. *Art, Mind, and Brain*. New York: Basic Books, 1982.

———. "Artistic Intelligences." In *Art Education* 36, no. 2: 47–49.

———. *Frames of Mind: The Theory of Multiple Intelligences*. New York: Basic Books, 1985.

Gardner, Howard, and David Perkins. "Art, Mind, and Education." *Journal of Aesthetic Education* 22, no. 1 (1982).

Gates, Bill, with Nathan Myhrvold and Peter Rinearson. *The Road Ahead*. New York: Penguin Books, 1995.

Gehlen, Arnold. *Urmensch und Spätkultur*. Bonn: Athanaum, 1956.

Geron Ethics Advisory Board "Research with Human Embryonic Stem Cells: Ethical Considerations." *Hastings Center Report* 29 (March–April 1999): 31–36.

Giddens, Anthony. Living in a Post-Traditional Society." In U. Beck, A. Giddens, and S. Lash, *Reflexive Modernization*. Stanford, Calif.: Stanford University Press, 1994.

———. *Modernity and Self-Identity: Self and Society in the Late Modern Age*. Stanford, Calif.: Stanford University Press, 1991.

Girst, Amy L., and Larry L. Greenfield. "Population and Development: Conflict and Consensus at Cairo." *Second Opinion* 20 (April 1995): 51–61.

Glantz, Leonard H., et al. "Research in Developing Countries: Taking 'Benefit' Seriously." *Hastings Center Report* 28 (November–December 1998): 38–42.

Glendon, Mary Ann. *Rights Talk: The Impoverishment of Political Discourse*. New York: Maxwell MacMillan, 1991.

Gordon, Joy. "The Concept of Human Rights: The History and Meaning of Its Politicization." *Brooklyn Journal of International Law* 23 (1998): 689.

Gregorios, P. *The Human Presence: An Orthodox View of Nature*. Geneva: World Council of Churches, 1977.

Gustafson, James M. "Moral Discourse about Medicine: A Variety of Forms." *Journal of Medicine and Philosophy* 15, no. 2 (1990): 125–42.

Habermas, Jürgen. *Knowledge and Human Interests*. Trans. J. J. Shapiro, 2d rev. ed. Boston: Beacon Press, 1971.

———. *Moral Consciousness and Communicative Action*. Trans. C. Lenhardt and S. Weber Nicholsen. Cambridge, Mass.: MIT Press, 1990.

Hamer, Dean, and Peter Copeland. *Living with Our Genes: Why They Matter More Than You Think*. New York: Doubleday, 1998.

Hartshorne, C. "Rechte — nicht nur für die Menschen." *Zeitschrift für Evangelische Ethik* 22 (1978): 3–14.

Harvey, David. *The Postmodern Condition*. Oxford: Basil Blackwell, 1989.

Hefner, Philip. *The Human Factor*. Minneapolis: Fortress Press, 1993.

Held, David. *Democracy and the Global Order: From the Modern State to Cosmopolitan Governance*. Stanford, Calif.: Stanford University Press, 1995.

Helmholz, R. H. *The Spirit of Classical Canon Law*. Athens: University of Georgia, 1996.

Hershberger, Guy, ed. *The Recovery of the Anabaptist Vision*. Scottdale, Pa.: Herald Press, 1957.

Heschel, Abraham. *The Sabbath: Its Meaning for Modern Man*. New York: Farrar, Straus & Young, 1951.

Holl, Karl. "Die Geschichte des Worts Beruf." In Aufsätze zur Kirchengeschichte, vol. 3. Tübingen, 1928.

Hollenbach, David. *Claims in Conflict: Retrieving and Renewing the Catholic Human Rights Tradition*. New York: Paulist Press, 1979.

Hooykaas, R. J. *Religion and the Rise of Modern Science*. Oxford: Clarendon, 1974.

Huber, Wolfgang. *Gerechtigkeit und Recht: Grundlinien christlicher Rechtsethik*. Gütersloh: Chr. Kaiser, 1996.

Huber, Wolfgang, and Hans-Richard Reuter. *Friedensethik*. Stuttgart: W. Kohlhammer, 1990.

Huff, Toby E. *The Rise of Early Modern Science: Islam, China, and the West*. New York: Cambridge University Press, 1993.

Huntington, Samuel. *The Clash of Civilizations and the Remaking of World Order*. New York: Simon & Schuster, 1996.

Jamieson, Kathleen Hall. *Dirty Politics: Deception, Distraction, and Democracy*. New York: Oxford University Press, 1992.

Janis, Mark W. "Jeremy Bentham and the Fashioning of 'International Law." *American Journal of International Law* 78 (1984): 405.

Jellinek, Georg. *Die Erklärung der Menschen- und Bürgerrechte: Ein Beitrag zur modernen Verfassungsgeschichte.* Leipzig, 1895.

Jeremias, Joachim. *Unknown Sayings of Jesus.* Trans. R. H. Fuller. London: SPCK, 1995.

Jessup, Philip C. *Transnational Law.* New Haven: Yale University Press, 1956.

Johnston, Douglas, and Cynthia Sampson, eds. *Religion: The Missing Dimension of Statecraft.* New York: Oxford University Press, 1994.

Jonas, Hans. *The Phenomenon of Life: Toward a Philosophical Biology.* New York: Dell, 1966.

Jones, L. Gregory. *Embodying Forgiveness: A Theological Analysis.* Grand Rapids, Mich.: Eerdmans, 1995.

Jones, W. H. S. *The Doctor's Oath: An Essay in the History of Medicine.* Cambridge, 1924.

Kaiser, Christopher. *Creation and the History of Science.* Grand Rapids, Mich.: Eerdmans, 1991.

Kass, Leon R. "The Wisdom of Repugnance." In Leon R. Kass and James Q. Wilson, *The Ethics of Human Cloning.* Washington, D.C.: American Enterprise Institute, 1998.

Kegan, Robert. *In Over Our Heads: The Mental Demands of Modern Life.* Cambridge: Harvard University Press, 1994.

Kelly, Kevin. *Out of Control: The New Biology of Machines, Social Systems, and the Economic World.* Reading, Mass.: Addison-Wesley, 1994.

———. "The Third Culture." *Science* (February 13, 1998).

Kennedy, Paul. *Preparing for the Twenty-first Century.* New York: Random House, 1993.

Kerr, C. et al. *Industrialism and Industrial Man.* Harmondsworth, England: Penguin Books, 1973.

Klaaren, Eugene. *The Religious Origins of Modern Science.* Grand Rapids, Mich.: Eerdmans, 1977.

Klaassen, Walter, ed. *Anabaptism in Outline: Selected Primary Sources.* Scottdale, Pa.: Herald Press, 1981.

Kline, Stephen Jay. *Conceptual Foundations for Multidisciplinary Thinking.* Stanford, Calif.: Stanford University Press, 1995.

Kramer, P. D. *Listening to Prozac.* New York: Penguin Books, 1997.

Kren, Betsy T., Paramita Bandyopadhyay, and Clifford J. Steer. "*In Vivo* Site-Directed Mutagenesis of the *Factor IX* Gene by Chimeric RNA/DNA Oligonucleotides." *Nature Medicine* 4 (March 1998): 285–90.

Krueger, Anne O., ed. *The WTO as an International Organization.* Chicago: University of Chicago Press, 1998.

Küng, Hans. *The Church.* New York: Sheed and Ward.

Lammers, Stephen E., and Allen Verhey, eds. *On Moral Medicine: Theological Perspectives in Medical Ethics.* 2d ed. Grand Rapids, Mich.: Eerdmans, 1998.

Lickona, Thomas. *Raising Good Children: Helping Your Child through the Stages of Moral Development.* (New York: Bantam Books, 1983.

Little, David. "Religion and Human Rights." *Journal of Religious Ethics* 27, no. 1 (1999), 151–77.

Lochman, J. M., and Jürgen Moltmann. *Gottes Recht und Menschenrechte: Studien und Empfehlungen des Reformierten Weltbundes.* Neukirchen: Neukirchener, 1976.

Lorz, A. *Tierschutzgesetz: Kommentar und Gegenwart.* Neukirchen: Neukirchener, 1995.

Lovelock, J. E. *Gaia.* London: Oxford University Press, 1979.

MacIntyre, Alasdair. *After Virtue: A Study in Moral Theory.* Notre Dame, Ind.: University of Notre Dame Press, 1984.

———. *Dependent Rational Animals: Why Human Beings Need the Virtues.* Chicago: Open Court, 1999.

Maguire, G. Q. Jr., and Ellen M. McGee, "Implantable Brain Chips? Time for Debate." *Hastings Center Report* 29 (January–February 1999): 7–13.

Maritain, Jacques. "Introduction." In *Human Rights: Comments and Interpretations.* UNESCO. New York: United Nations, 1949.

———. *Man and the State.* Chicago: University of Chicago Press, 1951.

Marty, Martin, and Kenneth Vaux, eds. *Health/Medicine and the Faith Traditions.* Philadelphia: Fortress Press, 1982.

Marty, Martin, and Scott Appleby, eds. *Fundamentalisms and Society: Reclaiming the Sciences, the Family, and Education.* Chicago: University of Chicago Press, 1995.

Mathews, T. "Power Shift." *Foreign Affairs* 76 (1997): 50–59.

McCarthy, Thomas. "Rationality and Relativism: Habermas's 'Overcoming' of Hermeneutics." In *Habermas: Critical Debates,* ed. J. Thompson and D. Held. Cambridge, Mass.: MIT Press, 1982.

McKibben, Bill. *The End of Nature.* New York: Anchor Books, 1989.

McLoughlin, William C. *New England Dissent, 1630–1833.* 2 vols. Cambridge: Harvard University Press, 1971.

McLuhan, Marshall, and Q. Fiore. *The Medium Is the Message.* London: Allen Lane, 1967.

McNeill, William. "Fundamentalism and the World of the 1990s." In *Fundamentalisms and Society: Reclaiming the Sciences, the Family, and Education,* ed. M. Marty and S. Appleby. Chicago: University of Chicago Press, 1995.

Meron, Theodor, ed. *Human Rights in International Law: Legal and Policy Issues* Oxford: Clarendon Press, 1984.

Merton, R. K. *Science, Technology, and Society in Seventeenth-Century England.* New York: Harper, 1970.

———. *Social Theory and Social Structure* New York: Free Press, 1957.

Miller, Timothy S. *The Birth of the Hospital in the Byzantine Empire.* Baltimore: Johns Hopkins University Press, 1985.

Mohrmann, Margaret. *Medicine as Ministry*. Cleveland: Pilgrim Press, 1995.

Moltmann, Jürgen. *God in Creation: An Ecological Doctrine of Creation*. Trans. M. Kohl. Minneapolis: Fortress Press, 1993.

———. "Ist der Mensch die Krone der Schöpfung?" *Publik Forum* 31 (May 1985): vi–vii.

———. *Theology of Hope: On the Ground and the Implications of a Christian Eschatology*. New York: Harper & Row, 1967.

———. *The Trinity and the Kingdom*. New York: Fortress Press, 1981.

Montesquieu, Baron de. *The Spirit of the Laws*. Trans. Thomas Nugent. New York: Hafner Press, 1949.

Morton, Oliver. "Overcoming Yuk." *Wired* 6.10 (January 1998) at www.wired.com/wired/archive/6.01/morton.html.

Mount, Eric Jr. *Professional Ethics in Context* Philadelphia: Westminster Press, 1990.

Murphy, Nancey, and George Ellis. *On the Moral Nature of the Universe: Theology, Cosmology, and Ethics*. Minneapolis: Fortress Press, 1996.

Niebuhr, H. R. *Radical Monotheism and Western Culture*. New York: Harper & Brothers, 1960.

———. *The Responsible Self*. New York: Harper & Row, 1963.

Niebuhr, Reinhold. *Moral Man and Immoral Society*. New York: Charles Scribner's Sons, 1960.

———. *The Nature and Destiny of Man*. 2 vols. New York: Charles Scribner's Sons, 1939–41.

Noble, David F. *The Religion of Technology: The Divinity of Man and the Spirit of Invention*. New York: Knopf, 1998.

Nord, Warren. *Religion in American Education*. Chapel Hill: University of North Carolina Press, 1995.

Novak, David. *Covenantal Rights*. Princeton: Princeton University Press, 2000.

Nussbaum, Martha C. *The Fragility of Goodness: Luck and Ethics in Greek Tragedy and Philosophy*. Cambridge: Cambridge University Press, 1987.

O'Donovan, Oliver. *Begotten or Made?* Oxford: Oxford University Press, 1984.

Osmer, Richard. "A New Clue for a New Millennium: Cross-Disciplinary Thinking in the Quest for Integrity and Intelligibility." In *Toward a New Religious Education*. Birmingham, Ala.: Religious Education Press, 2000.

———. *A Teachable Spirit: Recovering the Teaching Office in the Church*. Louisville: Westminster/John Knox Press, 1990.

Paris, Peter J. *The Spirituality of African Peoples: The Search for a Common Moral Discourse*. Minneapolis: Fortress Press, 1994.

Parks, Sharon. *The Critical Years: The Young Adult Search for a Faith to Live By*. San Francisco: Harper & Row, 1986.

Pascal, Blaise. *Pensées*. New York: E. P. Dutton, 1958.

Pearcey, N. R. "Technology, History, and Worldview." In *Genetic Ethics: Do the Ends Justify the Genes?*. Ed. John Kilner. Grand Rapids, Mich.: Eerdmans, 1997.

Pearcey. N. R., with Charles Thaxton. *Soul of Science*. Wheaton, Ill.: Crossway, 1994.

Ramsey, Paul. *Ethics at the Edge of Life*. New Haven: Yale University Press, 1978.

———. *Patient as Person*. New Haven: Yale University Press, 1970.

Reich, Charles. *The Work of Nations*. New York: Vintage Books, 1991.

Reid, Charles J. Jr. "Thirteenth-Century Canon Law and Rights: The Word *ius* and Its Range of Subjective Meanings." *Studia Canonica* 30 (1996): 295.

Rheingold, Howard. *The Virtual Community: Homesteading on the Electronic Frontier*. Reading, Mass.: Addison-Wesley, 1993.

Robertson, J. M., ed. *The Philosophical Works of Francis Bacon*. Trans. P. L. Ellis and J. Spedding. 1905.

Reprint, Freeport, N.Y.: Books for Libraries, 1970.

Robertson, Roland. *Globalization: Social Theory and Global Culture*. Thousand Oaks, Calif.: Sage, 1992.

———. "Religion and the Global Field." *Social Compass* 41, no. 1 (1994): 121–35.

Rudolph, Susanne Hoeber, and James Piscatori, eds. *Transnational Religion and Fading States*. Boulder, Colo.: Westview Press, 1997.

Ruether, Rosemary Radford. *Gaia and God: An Ecofeminist Theology of Earth Healing*. San Francisco: HarperSanFrancisco, 1993.

Sahtouris, E. *Vergangenheit und Zukunft der Erde*. Vergangenheit und Zukunft der Erde. Foreword by James Lovelock. Frankfurt: Willis Harman, 1993.

Saliers, Don. *Worship and Spirituality*. Philadelphia: Westminster Press, 1984.

Schimanowski, G. *Weisheit und Messias: Die jüdische Voraussetzungen der urchristlichen Präexistenzchristologie*. Tübingen: J. C. B. Mohr, 1985.

Schreiner, S. "Partner in Gottes Schöpfungswerk — Zur rabbinischen Auslegung von Gen. 1: 26–27." *Judaica* 49, no. 3 (1993): 131–41.

Seligman, Adam. *The Idea of Civil Society*. Princeton: Princeton University Press, 1992.

Sheils, W. J., ed. *The Church and Healing*. Oxford: Basil Blackwell, 1982.

Shestack, Jerome J. "Globalization of Human Rights Law." *Fordham International Law Journal* 21 (1997): 558.

Shils, Edward. "The Virtue of Civil Society." *Government and Opposition* 26, no. 1: 3–20.

Shriver, Donald W. "Religion and Violence Prevention." In *Cases and Strategies for Prevention Action*. Ed. Barnett R. Rubin. New York: Century Foundation Press, 1998.

Sigerist, Henry. *Civilization and Disease*. Ithaca, N.Y.: Cornell University Press, 1943.

Silver, Lee. *Remaking Eden: How Genetic Engineering and Cloning Will Transform the American Family*. New York: Avon Books, 1998.

Smolin, David. "Church, State, and International Human Rights." *Notre Dame Law Review* 73 (1998): 1515.

Stackhouse, Max L. *Covenant and Commitments: Faith, Family, and Economic Life*. Louisville: Westminster/John Knox Press, 1997.

———. *Creeds, Society, and Human Rights*. Grand Rapids, Mich: Eerdmans, 1984.

———. "If Globalization Is True, What Then Shall We Do?" *Theological Education* 35 (Spring 1999): 155–66.

———. "The Intellectual Crisis of a Good Idea." *Journal of Religious Ethics* 26, no. 2 (1998): 263.

Stackhouse, Max L., and Stephen Healey. "Religion and Human Rights: A Theological Apologetic." *Religious Human Rights* I, 485–516.

Stackhouse, Max L., ed. *Christ and the Civilizational Dominions*. Vol. 3 of *God and Globalization*. Harrisburg, Pa.: Trinity Press International, forthcoming.

Stackhouse, Max L., et al. *Christian Social Ethics in a Global Era*. Nashville: Abingdon Press, 1995.

Stackhouse, Max L., with Dennis McCann, Shirley Roels, et al., eds. *On Moral Business: Classical and Contemporary Resources on Ethics and Economic Life. Grand* Rapids, Mich.: Eerdmans, 1995.

Stackhouse, Max L., with Peter J. Paris, eds. *Religion and the Powers of the Common Life*. Vol. 1 of *God and Globalization*. Harrisburg, Pa.: Trinity Press International, 2000.

Stahl, William A. *God and the Chip: Religion and the Culture of Technology*. Waterloo, Ontario: Wilfrid Laurier University Press, 1999.

Stahnke, Tad, and J. Paul Martin, eds. *Religion and Human Rights: Basic Documents*. New York: Columbia Center for the Study of Human Rights, 1998.

Stassen, Glen, ed. *Just Peacemaking: Ten Practices for Abolishing War*. Cleveland: Pilgrim Press, 1998.

Staudenmaier, John. *Technology's Storytellers*. Cambridge, Mass.: MIT Press, 1985.

Steiner, Henry, Detlev F. Vagts, and Harold H. Koh. *Transnational Legal Problems*. 4th ed. Mineola, N.Y.: Foundation Press, 1994.

Stephenson, Carl, and Frederick G. Marcham, eds. *Sources of English Constitutional History*. Rev. ed. New York: Harper & Row, 1972.

Strachan, G. "The New Jerusalem — Temple of Creation." *Shadow* 1 (December 1984): 45–58.

Stronstad, Roger. *The Prophethood of All Believers: A Study in Luke's Charismatic Theology.* Sheffield, England: Academic Press, 1999.

Suu Kyi, Aung San. "A Blueprint for Peace, Justice, and Freedom: An International Conference to Celebrate the Fiftieth Anniversary of the Universal Declaration of Human Rights." November 26–28, 1998, Edmonton, Alberta.

Sztompke, P., ed. *On Social Structure and Science*. Chicago: University of Chicago Press, 1996.

Taylor, Charles. "Modes of Civil Society." *Public Culture* 3 (Fall 1990): 95–131.

Temkin, O. *Hippocrates in a World of Pagans and Christians*. Baltimore: Johns Hopkins University Press, 1991.

Temkin, O., and C. L. Temkin, eds. *Ancient Medicine: Selected Papers of Ludwig Edelstein*. Baltimore: Johns Hopkins University Press, 1967.

Teutsch, G. M. *Mensch und Tier: Lexikon der Tierschutzethik*. Göttingen: Vandenhoeck & Ruprecht, 1987.

Thee, Marek, ed. *Peace! By the Nobel Peace Prize Laureates*. Paris: UNESCO, 1995.

Thompson, Marjorie. *Soul Feast: An Invitation to the Christian Spiritual Life*. Louisville: Westminster/John Knox Press, 1995.

Tierney, Brian. *Rights, Law, and Infallibility in Medieval Thought*. Aldershot, England: Variorum, 1997.

———. *The Idea of Natural Rights: Studies on Natural Rights, Natural Law, and Church Law,* 1150–1625. Atlanta: Scholars Press, 1997.

Tinder, Glenn. *The Fabric of Hope: An Essay*. Atlanta: Scholars Press, 1999.

———. *The Political Meaning of Christianity: The Prophetic Stance*. San Francisco: HarperSanFrancisco, 1991.

Traer, Robert. *Faith in Human Rights*. Washington, D.C.: Ethics and Public Policy Center, 1991.

Troeltsch, Ernst. "Stoic-Christian Natural Law and Modern Secular Natural Law." In *Religion in History*. Trans. J. L. Adams and W. F. Bense. Minneapolis: Fortress Press, 1991.

Turkle, Sherry. *Life on the Screen: Identity in the Age of the Internet*. New York: Touchstone, 1995.

Turning Point Project. *Economic Globalization,* #5. New York Times, December 13, 1999.

Valentin, R. Arce. "Die Schöpfung muss gerettet werden: Aber für wen? Die Ökologische Krise aus der Perspective lateinamerikanischer Theologie." *Evangelische Theologie* 51 (1991): 565–77.

Van der Vyver, Johan D. *Seven Lectures on Human Rights*. Pretoria: Juta, 1977.

———. "Universality and Relativism of Human Rights: American Relativism." *Buffalo Human Rights Law Review* 4 (1998): 43–78.

Vasak, Karel. "A Thirty-Year Struggle." *UNESCO Courier* (November 1977): 31–32.

———. "Pour une troisème génération des droits de l'homme." In *Études et essais sur le droit international humanitaire et sur les principes de la Croix-Rouge en l'honneur de Jean Pictet*. Ed. Christophe Swinarksi. Geneva and the Hague: Martinus Nijhoff, 1984.

Verhey, Allen. "The Body and the Bible: Life in the Flesh according to the Spirit." In *Embodiment, Morality, and Medicine,* ed. L. Sowle Cahill and M. A. Farley. Dordrecht, Netherlands: Kluwer, 1995, 3–22.

Villa-Vicencio, Charles. *A Theology of Reconstruction: Nation Building and Human Rights.* Cambridge: Cambridge University Press, 1992.

Vincent, R. J. *Human Rights and International Relations.* Cambridge, Mass.: Harvard University Press, 1986.

Vischer, Lukas, ed. *Rights of Future Generations — Rights of Nature: A Proposal for Enlarging the Universal Declaration of Human Rights.* Studies from the World Alliance of Reformed Churches 19. Geneva: World Alliance of Reformed Churches, 1990.

Von Weizsäcker, E. *Earth Politics.* New Brunswick, N.J.: Zed Books, 1994.

Wallerstein, Immanuel. *The Modern World-System.* 2 vols. New York: Academic Press, 1974–80.

Walters, Leroy. "Religion and the Renaissance of Medical Ethics." In *Theology and Bioethics: Exploring the Foundations and Frontiers,* ed. Earl E. Shelp. Dordrecht, Netherlands: D. Reidel, 1985, 3–16.

Walzer, Michael. "The Idea of Civil Society." *Dissent* (Spring 1991): 293–304.

———. *The Revolution of the Saints: A Study in the Origins of Radical Politics.* Cambridge: Harvard University Press, 1965.

———. *Thick and Thin.* Notre Dame, Ind.: University of Notre Dame Press, 1994.

Washington, James M., ed. *A Testament of Hope: The Essential Writings of Martin Luther King, Jr.* San Francisco: Harper & Row, 1986.

Waters, Malcolm. *Globalization.* New York: Routledge, 1995.

Watson, J. L. *Golden Arches East.* Stanford, Calif.: Stanford University Press, 1999.

Weber, Max. *Economy and Society: An Outline of Interpretive Sociology.* Berkeley: University of California Press, 1978.

———. *From Max Weber: Essays in Sociology.* Ed. H. Gerth and C. W. Mills. New York: Oxford University Press, 1946.

———. *The Protestant Ethic and the Spirit of Capitalism.* Trans. T. Parsons. London: Allen & Unwin, 1930.

Webster, John. *Bishop Desmond Tutu, Crying in the Wilderness: The Struggle for Justice in South Africa.* Grand Rapids, Mich.: Eerdmans, 1986.

Weigel, George. *The Final Revolution: The Resistance Church and the Collapse of Communism* New York: Oxford University Press, 1992.

Weigel, George, and Robert Royal, eds. *A Century of Catholic Social Thought: Essays on "Rerum Novarum" and Nine Other Key Documents.* Washington, D.C.: Ethics and Public Policy Center, 1991.

Weston, Burns H. "Human Rights." *Human Rights Quarterly* 6 (1984): 257.

White, Lynn Jr. "Cultural Climates and Technological Advance in the Middle Ages." *Viator* 2 (1971).

———. "The Historical Roots of Our Ecological Crisis." In Francis A. Schaeffer, *Pollution and the Death of Man: The Christian View of Ecology*. Wheaton, Ill.: Tyndale House, 1970, 95–115.

———. *Medieval Technology and Social Change*. New York: Oxford University Press, 1962.

Whitney, Elspeth. *Paradise Restored: The Mechanical Arts from Antiquity through the Thirteenth Century*. Philadelphia: American Philosophical Society, 1990.

Witte, John Jr. "A Dickensian Era' of Religious Rights." In *The Sacred, the Sword, and Global Security*. Ed. Scott Appleby. Notre Dame, Ind.: University of Notre Dame Press, forthcoming.

———. *Law and Protestantism: The Legal Teachings of the Lutheran Reformation*. Cambridge: Cambridge University Press, forthcoming.

———. "Law, Religion, and Human Rights." *Columbia Human Rights Law Review* 28 (1996): 1–31.

———. "Moderate Religious Liberty in the Theology of John Calvin." *Calvin Theological Journal* 31 (1996): 359–403.

———. *Religion and the American Constitutional Experiment*. Boulder, Colo.: Westview Press, 2000.

Witte, John Jr., and Johan D. van der Vyver, eds. *Religious Human Rights in Global Perspective*. 2 vols. The Hague and Boston: Martinus Nijhoff, 1996.

Witte, John Jr., and Michael Bourdeaux, eds. *Proselytism and Orthodoxy in Russia: The New War for Souls*. Maryknoll, N.Y.: Orbis Books, 1999.

Witte, John Jr., and Richard C. Martin, eds. *Sharing the Book: Religious Perspectives on the Rights and Wrongs of Mission*. Maryknoll, N.Y.: Orbis Books, 1999.

Wolter, Udo. "Amt und Officium in mittelalterlichen Quellen von 13. bis 15. Jahrhunderts." *Zeitschrift der Savigny-Stiftung* (Kanonische Abteilung) 105 (1988): 246.

World Health Organization. *Global Strategy for Health for All by the Year 2000*. Geneva: World Health Organization, 1981.

Wuthnow, Robert. *Christianity and Civil Society: The Contemporary Debate*. Valley Forge, Pa.: Trinity Press International, 1996.

Index